Restorer's
MODEL A
SHOP MANUAL
COMPLETE & ILLUSTRATED

Jim Schild

MBI Publishing Company

First published in 1985 by MBI Publishing Company,
PO Box 1, 729 Prospect Avenue, Osceola, WI
54020-0001 USA

MBI Publishing Company books are also available at
discounts in bulk quantity for industrial or sales-
promotional use. For details write to Special Sales
Manager at Motorbooks International Wholesalers &
Distributors, 729 Prospect Avenue, PO Box 1,
Osceola, WI 54020-0001 USA.

Library of Congress Cataloging-in-Publication Data

Schild, Jim.
    Restorer's Model A shop manual.

    Bibliography: p. 219
    1. Automobiles—Conservation and restoration.
2. Ford Model A automobile. I. Title.
TL152.2.S35   1985   629.28'722   84-29612
ISBN 0-87938-194-9 (soft)

ABOUT THE AUTHOR

Jim Schild has been involved in a love affair with the "New Ford" since he found and bought his first one at the age of thirteen. That $25 1929 Tudor was the center of attention for every waking moment for the next four years. The information and parts sources available in 1960 were not as extensive as they became in the seventies and eighties, but Jim read every book that could be found on the Model A Ford, and worked on that car at every opportunity. Although that first car was never really finished, it started a fire that became brighter through the years.

The old car hobby was put aside for a few years to make room for active duty in the Army as a combat platoon leader with the Seventh Cavalry in Vietnam, but the interest was never lost. Even when Jim returned from the service in 1969 and became involved in drag racing with Super Stock Dodges, the interest in the Model A didn't stop, but continued to grow in intensity.

Jim's automotive interests in recent years have leaned more and more toward writing and researching automotive history. A member of the Society of Automotive Historians, Jim has written articles on St. Louis automotive history and on trucks and the trucking industry. He is also a member of the Model A Restorers Club, Missouri Valley Region; The Model A Ford Club of America; the American Truck Historical Society; the Horseless Carriage Club of Missouri; the Classic Car Club of America and the Cadillac-LaSalle Club. In 1983, Jim was selected by the governor of the state of Missouri to help promote Automotive Appreciation Week in the state by appearing on radio and television shows and extolling the importance of Missouri and St. Louis as second in the nation for automotive production.

In 1982, Jim published his first book, *Selling the New Ford,* a comprehensive study of the advertising and sales program used to introduce and promote the Model A from early 1927 to early 1932. While researching this book, Jim became interested in automotive history and has since accumulated an extensive collection of books and original literature on the Ford Motor Company and the development of the Model T and A. These books and magazines are a constant source of knowledge and will hopefully be a source of material for future articles and books on the automobile business and on the Ford Motor Company and its cars.

At the time of this writing, Jim and his wife, Myrna, have restored a 1928 Ford roadster and are in the process of restoring a 1931 Ford AA long-wheelbase truck. Intermingled among the Fords is a 1931 Cadillac that they restored in 1983 and a 1940 Packard 180 now used as part of a tour and limousine service in St. Louis.

When Jim isn't working on old cars, writing or driving his limousine, he serves as a Major in the United States Army Reserve.

PREFACE

The concept for this shop manual came about from the demands of the many Model A Ford enthusiasts around the world who are in need of a complete and reliable source of restoration information. Although many books on the Model A have been written over the years, most of them are either incomplete or inaccurate in their presentations. The national Model A clubs provide a good source of knowledge and help, but the new restorer would have to purchase about twenty years' worth of the club magazines to acquire the solid basis of restoration information presented in this manual.

The methods and techniques described here have been checked against all available Ford literature and service bulletins for accuracy and workability. The procedures, for the most part, are the result of many years of experience by numerous Model A enthusiasts and mechanics who have attempted to offer their expert guidance to you. The depth and scope of the information in this manual will be useful to both new and experienced restorers who always look for better ways to do things. Most of the text provides data that will be valuable not only to the new restorer, but to the owner and driver as well.

This manual is ideal for the first-time restorer because it is the first Model A book to provide a complete breakdown of all part groups and areas in the Model A. For the first time, each system is presented in a logical work order so that the restorer can find each section or part and very easily trace the step-by-step procedures from beginning to end. This method of presentation greatly differs from any previous Model A manual.

The manual is organized by part number groups according to the Ford Parts Price List. In other words, if a restorer wishes to find information on a particular system, he has only to find the part number group and the appropriate chapter will cover every aspect of restoration that is applicable to that group. In many areas, components of an assembly have been broken down and described by individual part number where that information might be helpful.

Every chapter is organized in a similar way whenever possible. The logical sequence of description of purpose and function, disassembly, restoration and adjustment, and reassembly is followed throughout most systems. Easy-to-follow and specific instructions will carry even the inexperienced restorer through the proper procedures.

This book was designed to present a discussion on all the areas that the average restorer might be able to do at home with a reasonably well equipped shop. Most of the chapters include information on maintenance and adjustment that may be needed for everyday driving situations.

What has not been included is information on the basic skills needed for any restoration job such as welding, painting, body work and upholstering. These subjects have been well covered in other books and will not be approached here. This manual has also tried not to repeat any information that has been presented in other books such as colors, upholstery and body styles. This type of information is available in the Judging Standards and in other books, some of which are recommended in Chapter Two. What this shop manual does offer is the help that is not available elsewhere; the hands-on guidance as to how to accomplish the immense task of making the Model A look and operate like it should.

To use this manual most profitably, it should be used in conjunction with the Ford Parts Price List and the MARC/MAFCA Judging Standards. This is not a replacement for these books, but a companion to them.

Jim Schild

ACKNOWLEDGEMENTS

A book of this kind could not be produced without the combined cooperation, knowledge and experience of many people. Although my own experience with the Model A Ford encompasses twenty years, the contributors to this shop manual have based their recommendations and suggestions on a cumulative total of about one hundred years of working on Model A Fords for fun and profit.

This project could not have been completed without the help of Terry Oberer, whose twenty-five years of working with every phase of Model A restoration and repair left an indelible mark on every part of this book. The transmission and engine chapters, plus the basic structure, are the direct results of Terry's contributions.

Willis Schwent brought his expertise with steering gears to bear on the front end and steering chapter, and many thanks must go to him for his hours of help.

The list of others who helped to make this book possible includes everyone who donated time, experience, parts and shop space. Most are members of the Missouri Valley Region of the Model A Restorers Club. These contributors include Travis Barks, Hunter Bingaman, Ervin Herbel and Rich Richardson.

My final but not least important thanks must go to my wife, Myrna, who put up with hearing and seeing nothing but Model A parts, books and conversation for over a year.

CONTENTS

Chapter 1

WHAT IT MEANS TO RESTORE A MODEL A

ACCORDING to Webster's dictionary, to restore means to bring something back to its former state. To bring back an old car that has been used, abused and neglected for over fifty years can be an awesome task, to say the least. Many would-be restorers jump into the old car hobby without really understanding what lies before them. Sometimes, the immenseness of the whole thing is too much to cope with and the car ends up sitting in the garage for ten or fifteen years unfinished and in pieces.

The problem makes itself most evident when the restorer realizes that the cost of the entire project will greatly exceed original expectations and the parts and labor requirements seem to never end. The financial aspect of restoring an old car, even a Model A, is something that must be clearly understood and dealt with long before the car is purchased. An important part of this understanding must involve the decision of whether to restore the car to show quality, or build it as a nice driver for family fun. The difference in cost and in work between a fun car and a competitive show car can be substantial.

Why is there such a difference? There are more model A Fords restored for each year of production than any other make of automobile, which indicates that the Model A is by far the most popular and the most plentiful of antique cars. This can be attributed, of course, to the fact that almost five million of them were made from late 1927 to early

1932. If there are more Model A's available, more Model A's restored and more reproduction parts offered, why does a competitive show car cost so much more to build and own?

One of the important reasons is that because the Model A is so prevalent, there are more details known about it than any other car ever made. The winning show car today must be almost perfect down to the smallest detail, and it must have almost all original or new old stock (NOS) parts. Many reproduction parts such as ammeters, ignition switches, door handles and many bolts are simply not being produced in the quality required for show judge scrutiny.

Although many of the reproduction parts will fit and work well, they do not have the appearance of the original parts. If the car is competing on the national level at MARC (Model A Restorers Club) or MAFCA (Model A Ford Club of America) shows, the reproduction parts will cost points every time. In some areas, such as spring hangers for instance, the Judging Standards specify that reproduction parts will not receive any points in that area.

What this means to the restorer is that the original and NOS parts are going to have huge asking prices, which means that the price of restoring a competitive show car will rise substantially. The price of the cars and of the parts to build them are related and one need only look at the increase in the prices of restored cars to see that this is no longer a hobby for everyone as it was in the fifties. A comparison of prices for restored Model A's from 1970 to 1984 shows an average increase across the board of over 500 percent.

The investment required to build a winning show car that cannot really be driven and enjoyed with the family has brought many restorers to the alternative, which is to build a car that has all the looks and most of the authenticity of the show car, but can be driven and enjoyed on trips and tours with the family and club friends. Although a show car can bring a great deal of enjoyment and satisfaction, many people believe that the Model A was meant to be driven and that is what they will do with it. One of the things that makes the Model A so popular is that

New old stock (NOS) replacement fenders
with original markings from the factory.

it may be driven anywhere comfortably and reliably in any weather.

Most local clubs and chapters are built around the many tours and activities provided for members throughout the season. These tours, from fifty to 1,500 miles and more, are the source of a great deal of enjoyment and fellowship for Model A enthusiasts. The pleasure of building and owning a dependable tour car adds much to the old car hobbyist's life.

Even if a car is built for touring, it doesn't mean that it will look any different from the show car to the casual observer. Many restorations of tour cars are every bit as thorough and complete as their show-winning cousins. Many fun-car owners take great pride in building their cars as authentic as possible. The difference usually lies in the use of good replacement and reproduction parts rather than the NOS and original parts that the show car must have to win.

The decision to build a car for show or for tours is totally a personal one. There is a lot of satisfaction to be had with each. The important point is that whether a car is built for show or go, a good restoration will involve similar steps.

For a thorough restoration, complete disassembly (or frame up as it is called) is mandatory. There have been beautiful cars built without removing the body from the frame and without renewing all mechanical components, but these are exceptions and many times these are the cars that turn up later with breakdowns and malfunctions. There are just too many defects possible after more than fifty years of use to consider using any parts without at least checking them for quality and condition. It doesn't matter how good a part appears, metal fatigue, rust and wear can take their toll. Do not let the fear of a seemingly impossible job

Dean Bittick of Missouri enjoys showing his 1931 Deluxe Roadster at local and regional shows.

sway the decision to tear the car down to the bare frame.

As stated earlier, the steps involved in restoration are much the same regardless of the type of car or the use it may be put to. Planning for and following a system for a restoration project will ensure that the job will be accomplished with quality and completeness. "Plan the work and work the plan" is a good adage to follow.

One of the most important steps before even thinking about doing a Model A project is to join the national and local Model A clubs as soon as possible. The information available from other members and club publications will be invaluable in all phases of the restoration project. Many times, an inexperienced collector will not know what to look for or how much to pay when looking for a restoration subject. The advice of others who have gone through the experience before may save money and grief in the future.

It is probably a good idea to take an experienced Model A builder along when looking at a car to buy. Unless the new hobbyist knows how to identify the various changes in parts over the production years and knows how to tell a proper piece from an improper replacement, he may buy a lot of expensive trouble.

There are many choices involved when buying a Model A. One of these choices is what body style to look for. A family person will probably want to find a sedan or a Tudor so everyone in the family can go on tours together. The person who likes an open car must remember that the open car will probably cost more to buy than a closed car of equal quality. Also, the open car may be limited in the times that it may be driven in bad weather.

Sometimes even NOS and good original parts have to be closely scrutinized. Notice the difference in these fenders. The one on the right is for an early 1928 Tudor or Phaeton.

Another thing that may be important is the future value of the restored car. The average price of an open car seems to be $2,000 to $4,000 more than an equivalent closed car. It will probably be easier to get the investment back on an open car than a sedan.

A choice that is becoming more popular is the AA truck. The truck is a good choice for someone who may enjoy the show circuit, but not want to spend the money and time necessary for a deluxe roadster or convertible sedan. The AA truck does not have any exterior chrome to be concerned with, the upholstery is much simpler and less expensive than other body types, and difficult parts to find such as original shock absorbers and NOS rear fenders are not a problem on a truck because it doesn't have any of these. There are not many AA trucks in national competition and the judges are usually not very familiar with them, so winning trophies may be much easier.

The disadvantages of the truck are that it takes up a lot of storage space, it does not carry more than two, and it does not go very fast. Another disadvantage may be that it is probably more difficult to re cover an investment with trucks because they are not in as much demand as the cars. These disadvantages have not stopped the many hobbyists who have found great enjoyment in restoring and driving the "big iron," as it has been called.

When the car is purchased and brought home, the next step should be to take lots of photographs from all angles and of all parts possible. This advice should also be followed during disassembly, which is the next step.

Disassembly should be systematic in that all components should be grouped according to part number groups and kept in boxes or cans with identifying labels. Sandwich bags are good to keep bolts, screws

A completed 1928 engine on an engine stand ready to be installed in the chassis.

and other small parts. When something is removed, keep all fasteners with the part for later identification. There has probably never been a novice restorer who has not removed a part, confidently thinking that he will remember where it goes, only to find six months later that he doesn't even know what it is. Remember, the Model A has over 5,000 parts and only an experienced restorer will be able to clearly identify and replace every one of them.

In addition to lots of photographs, keep a notebook of the entire project; list parts purchased and make drawings of assemblies that may be unclear later. Many restorers find that about three quarters of the way through the restoration, they don't want to even *see* the list of parts already bought. It may be best to not even know what it costs because it is often much more than estimated.

It doesn't matter which areas are done first. Some people would rather start with the engine, others would rather do the chassis. Personal preference is the only guide here. As each component is completed, it usually ends up in the house where it is kept clean and dry until ready for installation. (The engine for my roadster was completed in the living room during the winter when a heated garage was not available.)

All during the restoration, weekends are usually filled with trips to swap meets and sales to find the right parts. The key here is to be first in line when the meet opens, if the best parts are to be found. Bring along a copy of the Judging Standards and the Parts Price List to be sure that the parts are correct for the car being restored. Many garages have

As the transmission is being attached to this 1931 engine, the car is beginning to look like a finished automobile. Notice the accessory oil breather tube.

been filled with the parts purchased at swap meets which turned out to be wrong. Careful shopping can be very important.

It is quite a feeling of accomplishment when the engine is finally completed. This task will probably be one of the most expensive parts of the project. The bearings will most likely have to be sent out for pouring and fitting. The crankshaft will have been turned by a machine shop, and the assembly may or may not be done by the restorer himself.

An eager excitement begins to build as the car nears completion. The chassis is finished and adjusted, the engine is together, the transmission is done, and the running gear is ready to be assembled. For the first time, the car begins to look like an automobile. It is a good idea at this time to assemble the running chassis for a test drive. It is helpful to test drive the chassis before the body is installed because if anything needs to be repaired or replaced, it is easier to do without the body in the way.

As the car nears completion, the task seems to get bigger and longer every day. The details are seemingly endless but somehow, the car is finally done. The pride of showing or driving a freshly restored Model A has to be experienced to be appreciated fully. The beautiful sound of the four cylinders clicking off slowly, that wonderful exhaust noise, the sensitive feel of the wheel as the road slips by at forty-five miles per hour leaving behind all the pain, work, frustration and time. All that is left now is the pleasure of owning one of the best cars ever made, the enjoyment of years of friendship and fun with the most popular collector car in the world.

A running chassis ready for the first test drive. This was a most exciting moment in the restoration of my 1928 roadster.

Chapter 2

BASIC REQUIREMENTS

BEFORE beginning a restoration project, the novice restorer should be aware of some of the things required to accomplish the project. Like any job, the proper tools are necessary to successfully complete the task, and restoration of a Model A Ford is no exception. There are three areas that are important for consideration during preparation for a complete rebuilding of an old car. These areas are tools, facilities and resources.

Most of the tools needed for restoration are usually the same ones found in any good home garage. There are few tools needed that are unusual or difficult to find for the average amateur mechanic. The place to start, of course, is a good set of 1/2 and 3/8 inch drive sockets, including a ratchet, extensions and breaker bar. The quality of these tools can make a lot of difference when it comes to properly fitting bolt and nut heads.

A good socket wrench set should include a torque wrench. This will be used for engine installation, rear end adjustment and assembly, and anywhere that even tightening of fasteners is required.

There are many good-quality tools on the market, but the names that are most familiar are SK, Snap-on and Craftsman. Quality tools cost a lot more, but they will last longer and do less damage to fasteners than cheap ones. Most good wrenches are guaranteed against breakage.

The next thing to consider is box- and open-end wrenches. Many mechanics like to use combination wrenches instead of the straight-open or box kind. It is purely a matter of personal preference. Again, good quality is important. Cheap wrenches will spread at the jaws and slip off the fasteners, damaging the corners of the nut or bolt head, not to mention the restorer's hands and arms.

A good addition to a restoration tool set would be the new adjustable-box wrenches being sold at discount outlets around the country. These are very useful for removing worn or damaged bolt heads that a conventional wrench will not fit. They will grip even a rounded surface tightly. These are usually very inexpensive tools.

A set of flat-nose screwdrivers of varying sizes will be valuable during all phases of restoration and maintenance. Phillips-head screwdrivers will not be needed as these screws were not used on cars of that period.

Adjustable pliers such as a Vise Grip will be useful for many parts of the job, as will some medium and large slip-joint pliers. Remember that many of the parts of an unrestored car will be worn, rusted and damaged to the point that removal will be very difficult.

A set of chisels will be important when it comes time to remove stubborn rusted parts. The frame rivets for the running-board brackets and fender braces are usually candidates for the chisel. A few punches of varying sizes will also be needed. Small punches are used for the steering gear and control rods; larger ones are used to remove frame rivets and align sheet metal panels.

A large, forty-ounce and a medium ball-peen hammer will be necessary for many jobs. Do not use a claw hammer as it is not made of the same material as the ball-peen and may chip and cause injury. Some body hammers will be required if the restorer is to do the body work. Good body hammers are expensive, but they will pay for themselves with the work they can do. Generally, a pick hammer with one flat end and a good dolly will take care of most body work for the amateur.

For facing machined surfaces and refinishing metal, a set of files will be indispensable. At least one large, broad, flat file will be needed for much transmission and engine work. Smaller ones will be used to work small parts back into shape.

Power tools are essential to any restoration project. The purchase of a good 3/8 or 1/2 inch drill will be appreciated many times over. Do not buy a cheap drill as the bearings will usually not hold up to the assorted uses a restoration will subject them to. If the frame must be drilled for side mounts or for changing the tail pipe mountings, a powerful motor will be required as frame steel is very tough on a Model A Ford.

A good right-angle grinder or sander-polisher will be very useful for cleaning body metal, frame members and springs. It can also be used to polish the paint when the job is done. A sander with a seven-inch disc is usually the best choice. These are not necessary, but they do save a lot of hand work.

A bench grinder is one tool that may be considered a necessity in a restorer's shop. For cleaning with the wire brush and for grinding rusted and worn parts, the bench grinder is really indispensable. Be sure to get one of at least one-third horsepower or it will not be powerful enough for the work needed. If any metal polishing will be done, it will take much more power than that, but it is usually best to leave that work to professionals rather than buy an expensive grinder just for that purpose.

For work like removing the secondary well in the carburetor, and removing the pins on the brake levers, a drill press is very helpful. If this work has to be done by hand, it can be very tedious and inaccurate. Very good drill presses may be found in discount stores now for very reasonable prices.

One of the most useful tools for any automotive shop is an oxyacetylene torch outfit. This will be useful not just for welding body panels and small parts, but for cutting and for heating and removing rusted and damaged parts. Acetylene welding is not difficult to learn at home, but the equipment will be a bit expensive for some hobbyists as the tanks must be leased rather than bought and they must be periodically replaced with filled ones. A torch outfit is a good choice for anyone but the most casual old car hobbyists. Of course, if someone else has one that can be used or he or she can do the work, that will save the expense of purchasing a welding outfit.

A necessary addition to any shop is a good bench vise. Be sure to get one large enough to handle shock absorber bodies and front end components. Along with the vise, a quality hacksaw will be one of the most used pieces of equipment in the shop.

With safety being a most important consideration, strong jackstands are a necessity for any shop work. A car should never be raised without having good jackstands or at least concrete blocks to support the weight. Jackstands are inexpensive and the cheapest form of insurance available.

If any electrical work is to be done, a good soldering gun would be a recommended purchase. It is indispensable for making wire harnesses, attaching wire ends and securing better grounds on light sockets and mountings. A gun of about 250 watts or more is usually needed for automotive work.

It is obvious that tools can be a substantial expense for the beginning restorer who may only do a single car. The answer to this problem is to join a local car club. One of the benefits of the club is that many of the members will have the tools needed and will either lend them or help do the work. Some clubs even have a pool of special tools and equipment for members' use, so buying these tools is not the only way out. Tool rental outlets should also be investigated if the restorer does not want to buy his own tools and equipment.

The second area for concern should probably be the first in the restorer's mind. The facilities needed to accomplish a restoration project include the space to store a car and disassemble it for rebuilding. A normal two-car garage is usually sufficient for most projects. The space will be cramped, but with proper planning it will be possible to do a good job in a home garage. Generally, most restorers place the frame on one side of the work area, and the body on the other after the disassembly is completed. If a basement is available, that is a good place for the engine and transmission assembly.

If space is very limited, a good idea for many restorers is to hang the frame from the rafters or ceiling with hooks and chains. This will keep it out of the way of the rest of the work until assembly time arrives. The area above the rafters in the garage is perfect for securing the fenders and doors as they are removed and restored.

A collection of coffee cans, oatmeal boxes or other small containers will be handy for storing small parts and separating the components after disassembly. Mark the boxes with the contents and keep fasteners with the parts they came with for easy identification later. Keep all original fasteners, as they should be compared with any reproduction parts to check the size and appearance.

There have been restorations completed outdoors without any garage space, but the odds are against a quality job being accomplished. The weather will take its toll on bare metal and wood, and if the job is not completed soon enough, the car may end up in worse shape than it was when the job was begun. One thing that should never be done is to store a primed body outside for more than a day or two. The primer will absorb the moisture and the metal will begin to rust very quickly. If primer is left in the weather for more than about two days, it will have to be sanded down and reprimed before painting or the moisture will come through later and destroy the finish. Within a few months, bubbles and rust will break through the paint and that area will need to be completely refinished. Try to find a garage to rent or use before trying to restore a car outside.

Although a separate painting booth is desirable, it is not necessary to do the actual painting inside. Many fine paint jobs have been done in the driveway or the backyard. If you select a day that is not too humid or windy, a very nice finish may be applied by the patient restorer. Good preparation and equipment are the most important things here.

The last area of discussion is resources. What are resources? They are the parts suppliers, the information and the assistance needed to accomplish the job well. Before any restoration project is started, all the resources should be available and ready.

The most important resource is a good, sound knowledge of just what kind of work lies ahead. That is one of the reasons for this book. The better a restorer or potential restorer is prepared for the project ahead, the better job he can do and the better he will feel about the whole thing.

As was mentioned earlier, the best place to start is to join a local Model A club, even before purchasing the car if possible. The wealth of information available through other members is the most valuable help around.

The next step is to get a good, basic background of Model A information by acquiring all the available books on the subject and becoming familiar with them. Besides this manual, there are four books that should be considered as absolutely necessary to the Model A restorer: *The Ford Model A As Henry Built It* by DeAngelis, Francis and Henry; *Model A Ford Service Bulletins; Model A Judging Standards* from the MARC/MAFCA; and the *Ford Parts Price List* for the Model A. These four books will describe in great detail how a Model A should look and how it was made. This manual will tell how to do the job.

An important recommendation is to join one of the national Model A restorers clubs, as the magazines they publish are a wealth of information for even the most experienced restorer. In the back of this book is a list of parts sources and the addresses of the national Model A clubs. A roster from either of the national clubs will provide a listing of any nearby members.

The last requirement is the desire to work hard and long to complete a seemingly never-ending project. This requirement must include the interest of your family. A good way to help them become interested is to take them on tours with a local club and let them ride in the Model A's. When the family discovers how much fun these activities involve and how great the people are, it should be much easier to get them interested in the restoration and in the old car hobby.

The Model A Ford and the old car hobby can become an addiction, but a good one. The fun and the fellowship of this great hobby will make all the work and frustration worthwhile in the end. The restorer will find himself looking for the next car as soon as the first one is completed.

Chapter 3

WHEELS, HUBS AND BRAKES

THERE is probably no part of an automobile that is more critical to safety than the brakes and wheels. It does not matter how well a car runs and looks if it will not stop well in an emergency situation or the wheels are not straight and solid.

The greatest of care should be given to the braking system of any car, but this care becomes more important on an antique automobile because even the best of them do not have braking systems that are comparable to newer cars. The traffic of today is heavier and faster than the traffic of the thirties and brakes must be required to do more work than they were designed to do. This increased stress on the wheels and brakes means that the system must be restored to the very best possible operating condition.

The brakes on the Model A were a big sales point when the car was introduced and the concept of four-wheel brakes on any car, much less a low-priced car, was a relatively new idea. The Model T had two-wheel brakes for nineteen years and when the New Ford came out, the quality of the brakes was lauded in advertising as one of its greatest assets.

Whenever the enthusiast tells someone he drives a Model A today, the first comment is usually about the brakes. "The brakes are no good." "Do you have hydraulic brakes?" "How do you stop it?" "I used to have one and the brakes were terrible."

The real hard-core Model A enthusiast knows that most of these people have only experienced driving old Model A's, not new ones. They know that the primary reason most Model A Ford brakes are not very good is that the operating parts are worn out and the brakes have not been adjusted properly. If the brake system is rebuilt, maintained and adjusted correctly, the Model A is perfectly comfortable to drive under any conditions. The brakes are not up to the level of power discs, of course, but they can be safe and reliable if put together properly.

Ford wheels were considered state-of-the-art in 1928, when the Ford was popular. The spokes were electrically welded to the rims making the wheels lightweight and extremely strong. It was shown that the five Ford wheels weighed thirty-six pounds less than four wooden wheels and a spare rim. The advantage of the welded spoke design was that the weight of the car was not carried on any of the spokes as it would be with conventional wire wheels. This gave a great advantage of strength to the Ford wheels.

Restoration of the wheels

The first step in wheel restoration is to inspect the wheels to see if they are in good enough condition to use. Model A wheels have probably taken as much or more abuse than any other part of the car. Many of them will be found with dents, bent rims and spokes, and cracks in the hub. This is a good time to mention that the restorer should be aware of the difference in the AR- and B-type twenty-one-inch wheels as shown on page 328 of the March 1929 Ford Service Bulletins. These wheels cannot be used interchangeably and must be matched to whichever brake system is present.

Look at the wheel closely to see if it appears straight to the eye from all directions. Roll the wheel on a smooth surface to see that it is round and then lay it on the ground to see if it rocks or wobbles. Look closely at any wheel that has bent spokes as the rest of the wheel may be bent as well. If a wheel has more than a couple of bent spokes or has bad wrinkles in the rim, it is best to find a better one if possible.

Examine the wheel for cracks in the hub or spokes and for any sign that it may have been welded. Do not mistake the normal weld in the rim for a repair. It is best not to use a cracked wheel if another one can be found. Make sure that heavy coats of paint do not cover a badly pitted wheel. Wheels are especially difficult to work on and a poor-quality wheel would require a lot of time and labor to look like new.

Check all spokes by tapping them with a screwdriver or punch. If a spoke has a dull sound rather than a ring, it is cracked or broken loose and should be repaired, or the wheel should not be used.

The last thing to inspect for is the condition of the mounting holes in the hub. See that the edges are round and free of cracks and chips. Check each hole by placing a new lug nut in it and checking to see if it comes through too far in the back to allow the wheel to be tightened. Spacers can be purchased to help correct this situation, but a good wheel is a better choice.

Once a good set of wheels has been found, the first step is to straighten the bad spokes that may be present using a hammer, pry bar, slide hammer or whatever else is required. A brass or lead hammer and brass rod are sometimes used to drive the bent spokes back into place. Make sure to check the spokes from all directions to be sure that they are straight.

It is probably a good idea to have the wheels stripped of paint and rust before the final inspection is made to be sure that any defects are not hidden. Although many restorers use sandblasting, an acid or Redi-strip dip is recommended for wheels to be sure that all spoke surfaces are reached and that a smooth surface is left for finishing. This is especially important for the twenty-one-inch wheel as the rim is hollow and the liquid solutions are the only way to get rust out of the inside of the rim. It may help to drill a small hole on the inside of the rim to assist in drainage of the stripper on the 1928 and 1929 wheels.

When the wheels are thoroughly cleaned they are ready for paint preparation. The painting of the wheels will be made easier if a turntable or spindle of some sort is constructed to mount the wheel. It will be much easier to turn the wheel when spraying than to walk around it dozens of times and risk dragging the hose across the fresh paint or stirring up dust. A mount may be made from scrap wood or an old hub and spindle.

Before priming, fill all pits and scratches with a good spot putty or body filler. Spread it in as smoothly as possible because sanding spoke wheels is difficult and the less sanding that is required the better. When the filling and sanding has been completed, spray on the primer-surfacer as soon as possible to prevent the formation of rust. Even if the wheels are to be painted with enamel, which is recommended, a lacquer

Model A front spindle may be used to construct a versatile wheel painting stand.

primer-surfacer should be used as it is easier to apply and dries faster than enamel.

It is recommended that the outer rim surface be painted first in the spraying sequence. Next spray the spokes, making sure that the gun sprays down through the spokes rather than toward the rim or hub. Move the gun back and forth at angles to the spokes to make sure that they are well covered, but be careful of applying too much paint or runs will appear easily. Spray the hub next, then the inner rim surface. Some painters like to get the upper and lower surfaces from the turntable, but others find that it works well to paint the backside of the wheel first and then turn it over and do the front.

If the wheel is turned on its front side, be sure to put something such as an old hubcap in the opening to prevent damage to the paint. It is a good idea to plug the holes for the lug nuts after the first couple of coats of paint to prevent too much paint build-up which will result in chipping later. Some old lug nuts with bolts or studs screwed to them will work very well for this purpose.

The primer-surfacer coats should be allowed to dry for a week or so before sanding to allow the primer to shrink into the pits and imperfections. After the final coat has been applied and sanded, a good enamel should be applied. Enamel is used rather than lacquer because it has a tougher finish and will resist chipping better than lacquer. Follow the manufacturer's directions for applying the paint. Ask about a hardener for acrylic enamel to speed up the drying time and make for a harder finish.

It is a good idea to bring the freshly enameled wheels into a dry, warm room to prevent damage from bugs and dust while the paint dries. This will cause a lot of odor from the acrylic enamel, but it is the best

This 19 inch wheel is ready to be fastened to the special wheel painting stand for finishing.

way to ensure a slick finish. Let the wheels harden for at least a week before trying to mount them.

Mounting tires on the rims

The tire mounting method recommended by Ford in the original owners manual works very well for many restorers, but an alternate method that leaves the wheel off the car is favored by some.

Mount the tires from the backside of the rim to prevent marring the paint and whitewalls. To begin, apply the rim liners and align the tube stem hole in the liner with the hole in the rim. Check the tire casing for any foreign matter which may chafe the tube causing a slow leak.

Lay the rim face down on a carpet to protect the paint. Lay the tire casing on the rim front side down with the name centered on the valve stem. This ensures that the name can be read when the tire is mounted on the rear tire carrier with the stem on top. On blackwall tires, the serial number is on the back of the tire.

Push the front bead down over at least half of the rim. Work it all the way down into the drop center and then walk the remaining front bead over the rest of the rim using the heels. At the same time, keep working the front bead into the drop center portion. The rear bead should not be allowed to start on the rim.

When the front bead is on the rim, insert the tube starting with the valve stem, pushing it through the valve stem hole in the rim. Pull the

After attaching the wheel to the painting stand, it may be rotated to any position for painting.

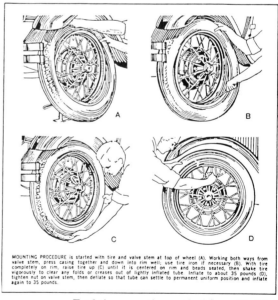

MOUNTING PROCEDURE is started with tire and valve stem at top of wheel (A). Working both ways from valve stem, press casing together and down into rim well; use tire iron if necessary (B). With tire completely on rim, raise tire up (C) until it is centered on rim and beads seated, then shake tire vigorously to clear any folds or creases out of lightly inflated tube. Inflate to about 35 pounds (D), tighten nut on valve stem, then deflate so that tube can settle to permanent uniform position and inflate again to 35 pounds.

Ford tire-mounting method from Model A owners manual.

stem fully through the hole until the base of the stem contacts the rim. Remove the valve core at this time.

Start the rear bead over the rim at the area away from the valve stem. Be very careful not to pinch the tube between the bead and rim. Slowly walk with the heels at least half of the bead over the rim edge. Squeeze the rear bead into the drop center to allow the rest of the bead to be walked over the rim. Use the heels on alternate sides, periodically compressing the bead into the drop center to gain room for the last portion of the bead to get over the rim.

When the bead is fully over the rim, turn the tire and rim over to check the name alignment with the valve stem. Rotate the rim inside the casing until the alignment is correct.

Lay the tire face up and apply about twenty pounds of air to seat the bead to the edge of the rim. Deflate the tire fully and insert the valve core. Reinflate the tire to thirty-five pounds.

Clean the tire and install the hubcap, making sure that the Ford script reads horizontally when the valve stem is at the top. If desired, the wheels may be balanced at a good tire shop. The early rims may require the stick-on-type balance weights used on some custom wheels. The later nineteen-inch rims will probably use the modern weights.

The brake system

The brake system on the Model A is of the mechanical type. This means that there is a direct mechanical connection between the brake pedal and the brake shoes as opposed to the hydraulic system found on all modern cars. The mechanical system was considered perfectly acceptable in its day when even the most expensive cars such as Cadillac had mechanical brakes. The hydraulic systems of the day were not very reliable and could fail very easily.

The brakes on the Model A took two basic forms. When the car was introduced in December of 1927, it had a four-wheel brake system with

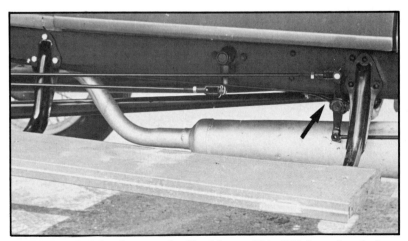

Brake cross shaft bracket on underside of frame. This 1931 frame has the later-style emergency brake cross shaft.

the parking brake lever mounted on the left side of the frame actuating all four service brakes.

By January of 1928, many states had declared the Model A brakes illegal and Ford had to redesign the system to incorporate a separate parking brake. Ford initially was going to mount the brake on the driveshaft, but decided on a system which added two additional brake bands on each rear wheel actuated by a lever mounted in front of the shift lever.

The functioning of the brakes begins at the brake pedal which, when depressed, pulls a rod connected to a cross shaft mounted under the center crossmember. The early 1928 cars had a complicated equalizing system using about ten parts. In November of 1928, this was replaced with a one-piece shaft mounted on bearings held to the frame with flat steel brackets. The special bearings in the end of this cross shaft served to keep the pull of the brakes equal when the frame of the car twisted while the car was being driven.

The cross shaft has a double-ended lever attached to each end which pulls rods to operate the arms of the front and rear brakes. The front brakes are operated by the lever turning a shaft with a pawl that pushes down on the front brake operating pin forcing a wedge downward that spreads the brake shoes.

The rear brakes are operated by the lever rotating the brake camshaft which contains the cam that spreads the brake shoes. All Model A brake shoes are internal expanding; that means that the shoes are pushed tightly against the drums which, if all goes well, causes the car to stop. The rear brake drum also contains the actuating mechanism for the parking or emergency brake. This consists of a single brake band operated by a set of levers to expand the band against a separate part of the brake drum.

It is obvious when it is considered that the brake system contains about sixteen clevis pins, twelve levers and about fifteen bushings that the condition of this mechanism has to be excellent if the system is to function properly.

Rebuilding of the brake system

The rebuilding of the brakes will follow the same sequence as the functioning of the system with the pedal and shaft first, the cross shaft, and then the brake assemblies themselves. It is important that all systems are done right if the brakes are expected to work like they did when the Model A was new; therefore, nothing should be left undone in the rebuilding process.

Removal of the pedal and shaft

1. Remove the brake pedal by removing the cotter pin and collar pin from the pedal collar and remove the collar. Disconnect the pedal-to-cross-shaft-rod clevis pins and remove the rod. Pull the clutch pedal, spacer washer and brake pedal off the pedal shaft. The pedal shaft and bushings should be replaced as shown in the transmission chapter.

If the pedals do not have grease fittings, it is a good idea to drill and tap the bushing housing and install fittings. Ford used them in the early 1928 pedals and again in the later models.

2. The cross shaft rod, like all the brake rods, has probably been worn to the point where the holes do not fit the clevis pins very well. The answer is to either replace the rods with reproduction parts or drill the holes to an oversize and use the oversize pins available from vendors.

Another answer is to braze the holes closed on the rods and redrill the holes to original size. If reproduction brake rods are used, they will probably be too wide at the eye to fit the brake levers and will require grinding to fit.

Rebuilding of the cross shaft

The service brake cross shaft took on two different designs. The early brake system, used from the beginning of production until February of 1928, consisted of an equalizer bar and multi-piece cross shaft assembly mounted to the universal-joint cap. The parking brake was mounted on the left side of the frame and actuated the service brakes by a rod attached to the cross shaft. In February to June of 1928, depending on the plant, the parking brake was redesigned and made a separate system with a solid cross shaft mounted behind the center crossmember.

In November of 1928, the equalizer bar and multi-piece cross shaft were eliminated and replaced by the solid cross shaft A-2485-D, which was used until the end of production. This shaft was mounted in bearings hung on brackets under the frame.

The last change to the brake system was the change of the parking brake shaft to a through-the-frame design in about April of 1930. This change eliminated the two grease fittings in the frame for the old cross shaft.

Since the solid service brake cross shaft is the most common type, it will be the only style dealt with here.

Service brake cross shaft bearing. The lever must be removed to replace this bearing.

1. Disconnect the clevis pins and pedal-to-cross-shaft rod if they are not already off. Remove the four service brake rods from the levers. Remove the four bolts, nuts and lockwashers from the cross shaft bracket and lower the shaft to the floor.

2. The bearings at the ends of the cross shaft should be removed and replaced with new bearings.

The levers are removed from the ends of the cross shaft by removing the pins. Grind the heads off the pins and drive them out with a punch. Many times these pins are very tight and will require drilling to get the levers loose. After the levers are removed, the ends of the cross shaft should be rebuilt to their original size. The only way to do this is to have the shaft built up with weld and turned on a lathe by a machine shop. Check the size of the shaft against the new bushings to find the correct diameter. Be sure when purchasing new cross shaft bushings that they are brass rather than aluminum. The aluminum bushings that have been available from some suppliers have been found to seize.

The holes in the ends of the levers will have to be either redrilled to an oversize or brazed and redrilled as with the brake rods. Oversize clevis pins are available in 0.340 inch diameter. The original pins were 0.310 inch. The original cross shaft brackets are usually good and may be reused. If necessary, reproduction brackets are available.

Removal of the brake assemblies
1. Raise the car with all four wheels off the ground and block firmly with jackstands. Remove the wheels and place the lug nuts back on the studs so they will not be lost or damaged. Remove the cotter pins and remove the axle nuts on all four wheels. Remove the brake drums from the front wheels by pulling them off. The rear drums will probably require a wheel puller. It is highly recommended that a proper wheel puller be used rather than the knock-off type so widely found. Use of the knock-off-type puller carries the risk of damaging the threads on the axle. The puller that Ford service departments used was shaped like a cup and fit around the groove on the rear hubs. A screw tightened against the axle and broke the drum loose easily. If any drums are difficult to remove, the brakes will probably need to be backed off at the adjusting wedges to release them.

2. Pry the lower ends of the front brake shoes loose and disconnect the springs. Slide the brake-adjusting shaft out of the adjusting housing and remove the shoes. If it is difficult to remove, tap it out with a hammer.

3. Disconnect the clevis pins and rods from the brake lever. Remove the nut and lockwasher from the front brake shaft housing. Remove the shaft and housing by removing the spindle locking pin and driving the spindle up slightly from the axle. This will loosen the brake shaft housing to where it can be removed without damaging the threads.

4. Remove the nut and cotter pin on the lower rear of the backing plate and remove the brake operating wedge, washer and stud. The brake operating pin will drop out of the spindle as the wedge is removed. Turn the adjusting wedge all the way into the adjusting housing on top of the backing plate and strike the wedge sharply with a hammer to remove it and the housing cover.

5. Remove the four nuts with cotter pins from the back side of the backing plate and remove the backing plate from the spindle.

6. Remove the clevis pins and disconnect the brake rods from the service and parking brake levers. Remove the bolt and lockwasher from the parking brake lever, pry the lever from the shaft and remove the retracting spring and woodruff key. The brake shaft is usually frozen to the bushings, so it will probably be necessary to disconnect the connecting link from the toggle lever to remove the parking brakes. Disconnect the retracting springs and pull the band and lining out of the backing plate. If the parking brake shaft does not come out with the band, it will come out when the carrier plate is removed and can be taken out later with the help of a torch and hammer.

7. Pry the brake shoes off the cam, as was done with the front brakes, and remove the retracting springs. Pull the adjusting shaft out of the housing and remove the brake shoes.

8. Remove the cotter pins and special castle nuts from the inside of the backing plate and pull the backing plate off the axle by turning the brake lever to a forward position, tilting the backing plate forward and slipping the lever through the radius rod opening (for May 1928 and later cars). The front two bolts may be left in place to secure the radius rod to the axle.

9. Turn the brake adjusting wedge all the way in and remove as was done for the front brakes.

Inspection and cleaning

Clean all the backing plates of rust and grease and have them sandblasted or dipped if a nice finish is desired. Remove the camshaft bushings from the rear brakes by driving them out with a chisel or punch. Check for bent or twisted backing plates. Good backing plates are not

Typical wear found on the roller tracks.

difficult to locate if they are needed. The front plates will interchange with all years. The rear plate for the earlier cars, A-2211-CR, will only be used for the cars without a separate parking brake. Replace the camshaft bushings in the rear backing plates.

The most important part of rebuilding the backing plates is to rebuild the roller tracks to their original specifications. The front tracks are available new, but it is usually best to just rebuild the old ones.

The roller track is rebuilt by building the track portion up with weld and grinding the edge down flat and smooth with a hand grinder and file. The edges of the tracks should conform to the original specifications so the brake rollers will ride in the correct location.

Remove the lever from the camshaft by grinding the head off the pin, centerpunching it and drilling it out. Mark the levers so that they can be identified as right or left if they are not already marked.

Check the brake adjusting wedges for wear and replace them if necessary. Good ones are available from Snyder's Antique Auto Parts or from Auto Hardware and Supply. Be careful of poor-quality reproductions that do not fit well.

The brake rollers are usually in good condition, but the roller pins will most often be worn on one side where they have ceased to roll on the tracks. These pins are extremely important and should be replaced. Most reproduction pins do not seem to be of good quality. If good, original pins cannot be found, it may be possible to have new ones made at

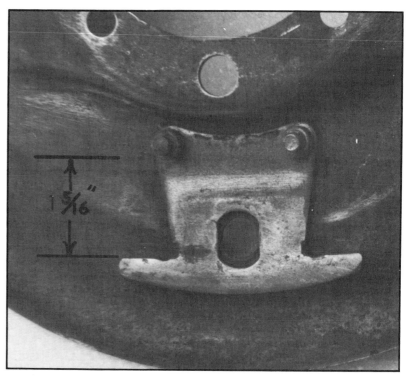

Roller track height is checked on the welded and finished track for the front brakes. The track should be 1 5/16 inches below rivet. Rear track should measure one inch for same dimensions.

31

a machine shop to original specifications. These must be made of hardened steel or they will wear out very quickly. The roller pins at the adjusting shaft end are not critical and may be reused.

Check the adjusting shaft for wear. These shafts may be refinished very easily with a file. They should have a sharp edge to seat into the adjusting wedge for accurate adjustment clicks.

Check the brake shoes to see that they are not bent or the clevis pin holes are not worn oversize. The old brake lining should be removed from the shoes and the shoes cleaned thoroughly of rust and dirt.

Inspect the rear brake cams and front brake wedge for excessive wear or damage. They can usually be reused by dressing them with a file as was done with the adjusting shaft. The two rear camshafts will probably be worn and will have to be refinished or replaced. The only way to reuse a worn shaft is to have it built up with weld and turned to original size. The replacement camshafts are sometimes very poor and the quality should be checked very closely before buying.

The emergency or parking brake carrier should be cleaned and inspected for bends or cracks. The bushings are usually rusted and worn badly because they have not received any lubrication. The parking brake shaft is usually well worn and should be replaced with a better one if possible. These are not available as new replacement parts so the old ones must be reused or reconditioned. A way to prevent this wear in the future is to drill a hole down the center of the shaft to about the middle of its length and then cross-drill another hole in the shaft to meet the first. Tap the hole on the end of the shaft for a 1/8 inch pipe thread and install a grease fitting. Replace all bushings in the carrier and paint it with black enamel.

The brake drums are the next point of inspection. The original drums are probably worn badly and possibly scored. For the brakes to operate properly, the drum surface has to be smooth and free of gouges

Filing the operating wedge for the front brakes. The adjusting wedge is also filed this way.

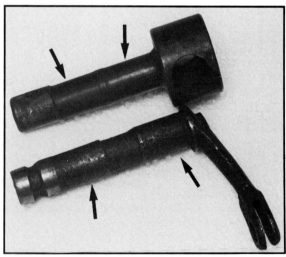

Typical wear on rear camshaft and emergency brake shaft.

and grooves. The best remedy is to take the drums to a good brake shop and have them turned to an oversize. Be certain that the drums have not been turned more than 0.100 inch oversize as they will become weak and easily warped. The original pressed steel drums are thin and when they are worn and old they can only get worse.

If the drums can be turned and reused they may be strengthened by the addition of reinforcing bands available from Varco, Inc. These will help to prevent distortion of the drums. Bands should be installed before drums are turned.

It is a good idea when having the drums turned, to have a wheel installed which will help to maintain the proper drum shape. Some Model A mechanics keep an old wheel that has been cut down to the hub, just to use when turning brake drums.

If the drums seem to be beyond use, they may be replaced with new cast iron drums available from The Plasimeter Corporation. These are very good quality and will give much better service than overground used drums.

While the drums are off, it is a good time to check the condition of the wheel bearings and rear wheel grease seals. These seals should be replaced to prevent oil and grease from getting on the brake shoes. These seals are removed by prying out the snap ring holding the seals and driving the seals out of the drum from the inside, or using a slide hammer puller. If the wheel bearings are pitted or worn badly they should be replaced.

Some other parts of the brake system worthy of attention are the front brake shafts. These are removed from the housing by grinding off the head of the retaining pin and driving or drilling it out so the lever may be removed and the shaft taken out of the housing.

Drive the bushings out of the housing and install new ones. The shaft is usually found to be in good shape and in most cases will not require replacement. Replacement shafts have not been found to be of

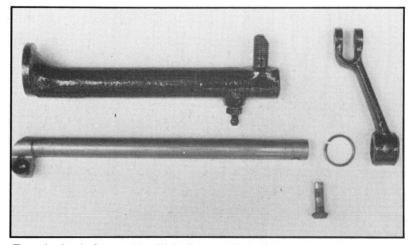

Front brake shaft assembly. Right front brake shaft B-2076, housing BB-2078, dust ring B-2087, and lever A-2084 (late 1931). The housing contains two brass bushings, B-2082, which should be replaced if worn.

very good quality and are probably not worth considering.

The front brake operating pin should be checked for excessive wear on the tips. See that the shaft is the correct length of 7 3/16 inches. Try to find the best original pins possible as most of the reproduction pins do not fit well.

The original springs may be reused if they are not rusted or broken. Some care should be taken in purchasing reproduction springs. Some of them do not fit properly or they are completely unusable. Check any new springs to see that the ends are at a ninety-degree angle to each other.

New linings should be installed on all brake shoes, being sure that only the soft woven high-friction type is used. This lining will wear faster, but it will give the best braking power. The linings are installed by cleaning out the counterbore with the special tool that comes with the riveting set. Start all linings on the center of the shoe and hold them in place with clamps as the rivets are installed. Install the rivets with an anvil-type rivet tool available from most Model A parts suppliers.

The tips of the lining should be chamfered with a grinder to take down the high spots. The fitting of the linings is a tedious process and a good choice is to take the drums and shoes to a good brake shop where they can be fitted and matched on special equipment. The shoes must be kept with the drums as a matched set once they are fitted.

If the shoes are fitted at home, the lining should be marked with chalk and turned inside the drum by hand. The high spots will show so they can be ground off with a grinder or a file. This process is repeated until there is the greatest possible contact of the shoe to the drum. If the drums have been turned excessively, the shoes may need to be shimmed to fit. This step is very important if the brakes are to work well. When all drums and shoes are fitted and mated, the brakes are ready for assembly.

Assembly of the brakes
1. Begin by installing the brake adjusting wedge and cover in the adjusting wedge housings of the rear brake backing plates. Pack the housing with brake lubricant before assembly. Install the dust cover by tapping it into the housing.
2. Install the brake camshaft into the backing plate and replace the dust ring and lever to the shaft. Be sure to identify the left and right levers and match them to the left and right backing plates. The levers should point toward the center of the frame. They are held in place by pins A-2238.
3. Turn the brake lever all the way forward, slip the lever through the radius rod and mount the backing plate on the axle. Replace the front two bolts and nuts temporarily.
4. The brake shoes should be assembled with the adjusting shafts installed with beveled edges facing to the backing plate. All cotter pins face outward for the service brake shoes. Install the brake shoes by slipping the adjusting shafts into the adjusting wedge housing and attaching the long brake spring to both shoes. Add the short spring to the opposite end of the shoe and slip the other end of the spring over the stud.

5. Install the cam on the camshaft and push it into the backing plate bushings, being sure that the edges of the cam are positioned correctly to open the brake shoes as the cam turns.

6. Force the ends of the brake shoe rollers over the cam, being sure that the heads of the roller pins are riding on the roller track. Use plenty of brake lubricant on all parts.

7. Remove the temporary nuts from the backing plate and install the parking brake carrier assembly with shaft to the axle. Replace the two bolts and four nuts to the axle and tighten them securely. Be certain that the parking brake carriers are installed to the left and right sides respec-

The short springs are attached by pulling the shoe toward the center and then back into place after the spring is hooked to the pin on the roller track.

Make sure that the cam is installed in the correct position to open the brake shoes.

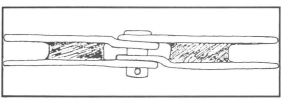

Alignment of emergency brake toggle links.

tively, as they are different. Replace the cotter pins in the nuts.

8. Assemble the parking brake band assembly which should have had a new lining installed. The cotter pins on the parking brake should go toward the inside of the car with the heads of the clevis pins visible. Be certain that the toggle links are assembled so that they form a straight line. If these links are installed incorrectly, the brake band will not align with the carrier.

Emergency brake carrier in place on the backing plate.

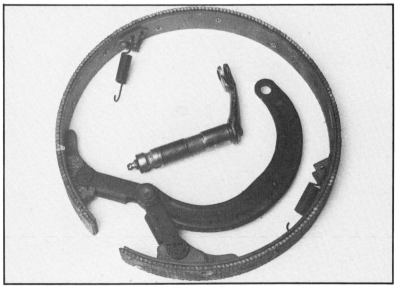

Emergency brake band, toggle links and shaft. Notice the newly installed grease fitting on shaft.

9. Replace the parking brake levers on the shaft being sure to put the left and right levers on the correct side. These levers should be marked. Replace the retracting spring with the lever, and hook it over the shaft. This spring is sometimes difficult to install but a good method is to use a piece of heavy cord or wire and construct a hook to pull the end of the spring over the lever.

Completed rear brake assembly. Notice that cotter pins are to the inside.

Completed front brake assembly.

10. Replace the brake drum and check to see if the drum contacts the backing plate. If this condition exists, it will be necessary to use a shim around the axle to increase the clearance. Check the axle key and key- way to be sure that they are not damaged or worn. This key must fit tightly to prevent the drum from shifting on the axle, causing the key or the axle to be broken. Replace the fiber washer and wheel nut on the axle and torque the nut to 80 to 90 foot-pounds and replace the cotter pin. Check the torque of this nut often to be sure it has not loosened.

11. Move to the front brakes and begin reassembly by replacing the ad- justing wedge and cover as in the rear, using plenty of brake lubricant. Place the backing plate and grease baffle on the front spindle with the adjusting housing at the top and insert the bolts through the backing from the outside. Replace the special castle nuts and cotter pins on the back of the spindle.

12. With the spindle bolt loose and raised slightly, slip the brake shaft and housing assembly pawl end into the ball on the spindle with the cup portion facing down. Slip the stud on the shaft housing into the perch and replace the nut and lockwasher. Push the spindle bolt back down and replace the spindle locking pin by driving it in until the threads appear through the rear of the axle. Replace the special locking pin nut and tighten it slowly while tapping the pin in place to prevent damag- ing the threads.

13. Slide the operating pin with felt washer into the spindle from the bottom and insert the operating wedge under it with the stud through the backing plate. Be sure that felt washer is between bottom of spindle bolt and backing place. With the pin seated in the wedge, tighten the castle nut on the back of the backing plate to secure the wedge and allow it to move freely.

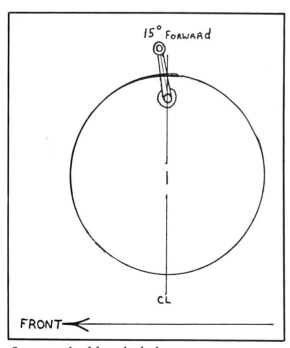

Correct angle of front brake lever.

14. Fasten the assembled brake shoes to the backing plate by inserting the adjusting shafts with the beveled edge facing into the adjusting housing. Attach the long brake spring to both shoes. Connect the short springs to the lower holes in the brake shoes and the stud on the backing plate. Pull the brake shoe up over the operating wedge by hand until the rollers slip over the top of the operating wedge and the head of the roller pin is riding on the roller track. Be sure to use plenty of brake lubricant on all moving parts.

With everything in place, check to see that the front brake lever is in a forward position when the wedge is all the way up. If the lever is not forward, use brake "pills," available from parts suppliers, under the operating pin to raise it and move the lever to the proper position, which is about fifteen degrees from the vertical.

15. If the front wheel bearings have been inspected or replaced, pack them with wheel-bearing grease and slip the drum and hub over the axle. Replace the nut and washer, tighten it to 15 to 20 foot-pounds, back off one castellation and replace the cotter pin. Some restorers like to use the Rocky Mountain brake drums. These are reputed to help in the cooling of the brakes during heavy use.

Adjusting the brakes

1. Make sure that the brakes are cold when adjustments are made. Raise the car and disconnect all the brake rods at the adjusting end and loosen the lock nuts on the adjusting clevis. Make sure that all brake retracting springs (called "anti-rattlers" by most people) are properly installed on the frame and rods.

2. Adjust each wheel with the adjusting wedge until a distinct drag is felt, then back off one or two notches. Make sure that the adjuster is

Slotted Rocky Mountain drums help to cool the front brakes during heavy service.

between the high spots when checking the wheel. On the front brakes, check the lever to make sure that it is forward of a vertical position. If it is not, then brake pills should be added to the operating wedge.

3. See that the levers are vertical on the brake cross shaft and the brake pedal is all the way up. Take up all the free play in the rods until the pins can just be installed in the clevis. Leave the cotter pins out until the final adjustment is completed.

4. For an accurate measurement, mark the brake pedal with chalk or tape, or use wooden blocks cut to size to check the brake pedal travel. Have a helper depress the brake pedal exactly one inch and adjust the rear brakes until a firm drag is felt. At this point, the front brakes should just begin to engage. Depress the pedal 1 1/2 inches, and the rear brakes should have a heavy drag but not be locked. The front should have a firm drag. At two inches, the rear brakes should be solidly applied and the front should have a heavy drag but not be locked.

If the brakes do not operate as described, adjust the rods at each wheel until the proper adjustment is reached. When the adjustment is complete, replace the cotter pins and tighten the lock nuts at the clevis eyes.

Test drive the car and check the brake action. If the brakes do not respond evenly, adjust the wedges at each wheel to fine tune the system. After driving the car several hundred miles, repeat the adjusting procedure. After that point, all future adjustment should be done at the wedges only. If the brakes are good and properly adjusted, they should respond to a panic stop situation with at least two inches of pedal above the floor board.

As the service brake adjustment is completed, attention should turn to the parking brake. If the car happens to be a late 1928 or early 1929 with the lever in front of the gear shift, a problem will be encountered if the lever-to-cross-shaft rod needs to be replaced. This particular rod is not available from suppliers and one will need to be made. This rod uses an eye on the front which is the same as the service brake eyes. Use the rear end of the replacement rod and modify it by cutting and replacing the front with the eye end of an old service rod. Weld the rod closer to the rear and the change will not be noticeable. The length of this rod is 20 3/4 inches, compared to 18 3/4 inches for the later style.

Adjusting the parking or emergency brake rods
1. Make sure that the retracting springs are properly installed at both the frame and at the lever.
2. Pull the hand-brake lever back about two notches and check to see that the rear wheels have a slight drag. Adjust the clevis ends to equalize the pressure. At three notches, both wheels should have a heavy drag. The brakes may be checked by driving the car on a level surface and slowly applying the hand brake while someone watches the wheels to see if one locks up before the other. Do not apply the hand brake too quickly unless in an emergency as the carrier can be damaged.

Remember that the brake pressure is increased by turning the eye down on the rod and lessened by turning it off the rod end.

The brakes are now completed and the car may be driven for many hundreds of miles in confidence and safety.

Chapter 4

FRONT AXLE AND STEERING

THE condition of the front end and steering components of any automobile is extremely important to safe operation and pleasurable driving. If the steering is worn the car will not track well and will be difficult to turn and control. Worn steering is not responsive to the desires of the driver and will cause the vehicle to be unsafe to anyone on the road with it.

Because loose front end components such as spindles or steering balls contribute much to making a car handle poorly and unsafely, the rebuilding of the front end is an area of restoration that should not be short-cut in any way. A dangerously worn front end and what it does to a car's handling presents a very bad image of the old car hobby to everyone who sees the car or rides in it.

The front axle and steering system of the Model A consists of the front axle assembly, which includes the spindles and front radius rod, and the steering gear and wheel assembly.

The front axle of the Model A was basically the same for all model years. The only modification was the change of the design of the spindle bolt locking pin nut which was changed from a large bolt and castellated nut to a tapered, headless pin with a stop nut in August of 1929.

Inspection of front end and steering

Check for play in the spindle bushings by raising the front of the car to see if there is movement in the front wheels. Grasp the wheels at the top and bottom and try to move them while looking for play at the spindle bolt. If there is more than 1/64 inch of play in the spindles they should be replaced. Be sure that the play is not from loose wheel bearings.

Check for play in the steering mechanism by having someone move the steering wheel while the linkage is observed for movement. The steering wheel should not have more than one inch of play or backlash at the rim. Check for looseness in the steering system by moving one wheel while the car is up. If the wheel will move more than 1/4 inch without moving the other wheel, there is excessive play in the system and the cause will need to be located and repaired.

The parts that generally need replacing are the tie rod ends, the steering balls, the spindle bolts and bushings and the worm, sector and bearings in the steering gear.

Removal of the front axle

1. Raise the front of the car with a jack from the frame and place a two-inch block of wood under the front spring hangers. Lower the weight of the car back down on the hangers and remove the the cotter pins and nuts from the hangers. Drive the hangers out with a punch or rod, and raise the front of the car back off the axle.
2. Disconnect the drag link from the left steering arm by removing the large cotter pin and unscrewing the plug with a special tool which is available at good auto parts stores. The drag link will be able to be lifted off the steering arm ball and pulled to the side.
3. Disconnect shock absorber arm from shock absorber by removing bolt and nut from arm and slipping it off the shaft. Disconnect the brake rods from the actuating arms by removing the cotter pins and clevis pins and pulling the rods away.

Left front of axle assembly on 1931 Ford.

4. Remove the front radius rod ball from the clutch housing by removing the two cotter pins, nuts, springs and sleeves and lowering the cap. If the car is raised enough, the ball should fall out of the socket. The front axle assembly is now ready to be rolled from under the car. It may be necessary to remove the wheels to allow the axle to roll under the front bumper.

Disassembly

1. Remove the brake drums by removing the dust cover and cotter pin and loosening the large nut holding the drum to the axle and pulling the drum off. If the drum is tight, the brakes may need to be loosened by unscrewing the adjusting wedge on the backing plate.

2. Remove the brake shoes by pulling the lower end of the shoe away from the backing plate and releasing the springs holding the shoes together. The brake shoes may then be removed from the backing plate. Remove the cotter pin and nut from the lower back side of the backing plate and pull out the operating wedge. The brake operating pin will fall out of the opening in the backing plate. Remove the four castle nuts with cotter pins from the backing plate back side and pull the bolts out. The backing plate and grease baffle may now be removed from the spindle.

3. Remove the plugs on both sides of the tie rod and remove the tie rod from the steering arms. Notice which way the grease fittings are facing on either end.

4. Remove the cotter pin and spindle arm nut from the front of the spindle on each side and remove the spindle arms.

5. Remove the spindle bolt locking pins from both spindles and drive the spindle bolts from the bottom out the top using a bushing driver or a tool made from an old water pump shaft or brass rod. Sometimes, the spindle bolts are frozen in the axle and require heating of the axle to remove them.

6. Remove the cotter pins and nuts from the bottom of the axle and remove the spring perches by driving them out the top of the axle. Remove

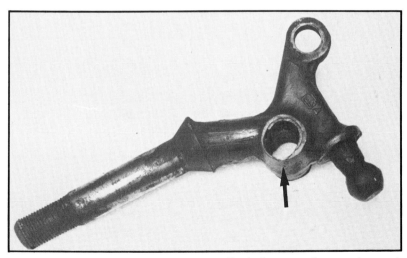

Typical wear on front spring perch.

43

the cotter pins, unscrew the plugs and remove the shock absorber arms from the balls on the perches. The front axle is now disassembled.

Inspection and restoration

Have the axle checked to be sure that it is not bent. It will be much better to find out that the axle is unusable now than after all the rebuilding work is completed. If the axle is bent, it may be straightened by a

Typical wear and damage to front spindles. Notice worn threads on right example.

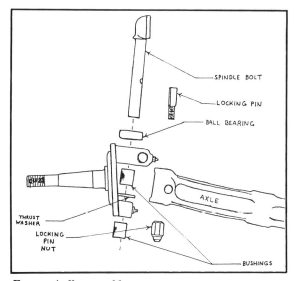

Front spindle assembly.

frame or truck front end shop, but it would be much simpler and probably less expensive to find a better one.

Check the bushing bore in the spring perch after removing the bushing with a driver. If the bore is worn excessively, a new perch should be obtained.

Inspect the ball ends of the steering arms. There are three on the two arms. If they are worn to an oval or egg shape, they must be replaced or rebuilt. This work is best sent to an expert such as N/C Industries, Inc., which will take the old steering arms and install new balls. If these balls are not perfectly round, the steering will not operate smoothly and it will be difficult to get all the play out. This rebuilding should also include the ball on the Pitman arm.

If the spindle bolts and bushings are worn, it is advisable to rebuild the spindles with new bolts, bushings and bearings. This is one of the most important operations in acquiring safe, tight steering in the Model A. New spindle-bolt kits are available from all Model A parts suppliers. Be sure that the parts are USA made and of the best quality. Some do not fit or wear well for a car that is to be driven very much. Only the later-design spindle bolts are available new, so if the car is an early 1928

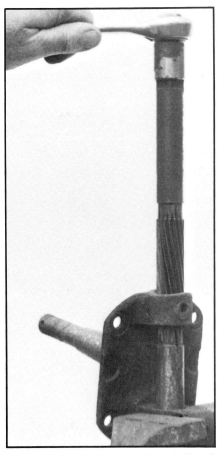

Use a bushing reamer to fit the spindle bolt to the bushings.

Ensure that the holes in the bushing align with the grease fitting holes.

with the castellated nut, it will not be possible to replace it with a new kit without losing the proper appearance of the nut and pin. The new kits will work if all new parts are used. (See the Ford Service Bulletins, page 378, for information about the change.) Inspect the axle portion of the spindle for damage to the bearing surface or the threads.

Rebuilding the front spindle assembly

1. Clean the spindle of all rust, grease and scale. It may be sandblasted or beadblasted if necessary. Remove the old spindle bushings with a bushing driver or chisel.

2. Install the new bushings by driving the top one in from the top and the bottom one in from the bottom. Be sure that the bushings are installed with the grease holes aligned with the holes in the spindle for proper lubrication. Using a reamer of the proper size, ream the bushings for a snug fit and alignment. Be sure to grease the spindle bolts before installing them.

3. Be sure to follow the proper order of assembly of spindle bolt components, whether using a kit or not.

4. Keep the spindle bolts assembled to the spindles until the time comes to install them on the axle so that the fit of the pieces is not lost. When the spindles are installed on the axle, check for easy turning and smooth operation. Although spindles are interchangeable side for side on all models, the spindle bolts are not and must be installed on the proper side with the ball socket facing to the front.

5. The spindles may now be reinstalled on the front axle and the spindle bolt locking pins reinstalled and tightened. Install the rebuilt steering arms, tighten the steering arm nuts and install cotter pins. The remainder of the front axle may be assembled in the reverse order of disassembly. Check all parts for easy movement and fit. Remember to check and grease the wheel bearings before installation. Torque the nut to 15 to 20 foot-pounds, back off one castellation and replace the cotter pin.

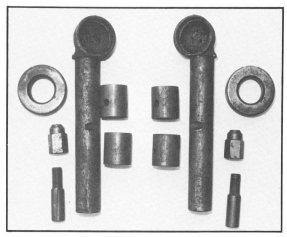

Parts supplied with spindle bolt repair kit include new bushings, spindle bolts and bearings.

Tie rod and drag link ends

The ends of the tie rod and drag link contain an assemblage of springs and cups that must be replaced if the front end has very much wear. The ends are removed from the shaft by loosening the 5/16 inch lock nuts on the shaft end and screwing the end off the tie rod.

The ends are disassembled by using a special tool for the slot in the plug end and unscrewing the ball plug out of the housing. Inside the housing will be a spring and two cups. Notice the position of these parts as they are removed; they go back in different positions on each end of the drag link. These parts may be replaced with rebuilding kits available from all Model A parts suppliers.

Pay attention to the quality of the parts in the rebuilding kit. Many times, the new spring does not have the tension that even the old one does and should not be used if the old looks good and is not broken or bent. Grease these parts well when reassembling.

A new choice is the Steer-Eze kits with Teflon seats available from some parts dealers. These are reputed to make the steering operate more easily. They cost almost three times the original parts, but they might be worth asking about.

Alignment of the front end

1. Make sure that the car is on a level surface to check alignment. Check the height of the car at the frame and the bumpers to see if any defects exist. If the frame or the axle are found to be bent they should be repaired or replaced if the car is ever to steer properly.

2. The only alignment factor that can reasonably be adjusted by the restorer is the toe-in. The caster and camber are built into the axle and can only be corrected by a frame shop or a truck front end shop. Remember that the caster can be affected by the motor mounts on a Model A. If the motor mounts are loose, the front radius rod ball will not seat in the proper location and the angle of the front axle will be changed. The more an engine sags, the more positive the caster will appear at the axle. Have the caster and camber checked at a front end shop. The caster should be five degrees for the A chassis and 3 1/2 degrees for the AA chassis. The camber is set at 1 13/16 inches.

3. The toe-in is checked by using a tape measure long enough to reach between the rear of the tires. Measure the distance between the center line of the rear tires with the tape no higher than the level of the radius rod. Mark this measurement on the tire with chalk and be sure to use the same spot on each tire. Roll the car backward until the spot is exactly the same height from the floor as in the rear and take the measurement again in the front. The front of the tires should be 1/8 inch plus or minus 1/16 inch closer together than the rear.

This adjustment is obtained by loosening the bolts on the tie rod ends and turning the tie rod in or out until the proper toe-in measurement is reached. Remember to retighten the bolts when the alignment is completed.

The steering gear

The steering gear on the Model A was made in two basic types. The first type was the seven-tooth irreversible worm-and-sector design

47

which had a one-piece housing welded to the steering column. The second type of steering gear was introduced in February of 1929 and was known as the two-tooth worm-and-sector which was a Gemmer-design gear.

Both of these steering gears were designed for balloon tires and were of the irreversible type. Although the two-tooth gear is considered to be the better operating of the two, they were both a great improvement over the Model T which had a planetary gear under the steering wheel.

Removal of the steering gear

1. Remove the floor mat and floor boards. Disconnect the battery ground cable.
2. Remove the pin and collar from the pedal shaft. Disconnect the brake rod and clutch clevis and remove the clutch and brake pedals from the shaft.
3. Disconnect the spark and throttle rods from the levers on the steering column.
4. Disconnect the battery cable from the starter switch and unscrew the starter switch rod. Remove three 3/8 inch hex-head cap screws and washers, and remove the starter.
5. Unhook the light switch bail and disconnect the light switch assembly from the steering column.
6. Remove the large cotter pin and loosen the drag link ball plug at the Pitman arm and pull the drag link off the Pitman arm. Remove the clamp bolt and nut and remove the Pitman arm from the sector shaft.
7. Remove the two bolts, nuts and washers holding the steering gear to the frame. Remove the two fillister head screws at the tank clamp and remove the clamp and anti-rattler rubber. The steering gear may be lifted out of the car.

Disassembly of the seven-tooth steering gear

1. Remove the light switch spider and retainer by pushing up on the spring at the bottom of the steering column and removing the retainer.

The seven-tooth sector is lifted from the housing.

The light switch tube may then be pulled out of the column from the top.

2. Remove the steering wheel nut and remove the steering wheel by using a knock-off-type puller sold for the rear axle. If the wheel is difficult to remove, sit on a high shelf and place the wheel between the knees with the column hanging unsupported. Strike the knock-off puller firmly and the wheel should come off. Do not use the steering wheel nut to remove the wheel as the threads on the steering shaft may be damaged.

3. Remove the three cap screws from the housing cover and drain the lubricant. Lift out the sector shaft.

4. Remove the four cap screws from the bottom of the housing and remove the lower bearing assembly. Do not lose the shims that come out with the bearing assembly.

5. Screw the knock-off puller on the steering shaft again and tap the shaft out of the housing from the bottom. A thrust bearing is at each end of the worm. The lower thrust bearing will probably come out with the shaft, but the upper bearing will most likely stay in the housing to be lifted out separately. Remove the loose sector-shaft thrust washer if it did not come out with the sector shaft. Remove the upper bushing from inside the housing. This bushing may be difficult to remove but it should be checked for excessive wear or damage.

6. Remove the sector bushings from the housing by driving them out with a bushing driver. Inspect the sector and worm gears at this time for excessive wear, galling or pits. If they are defective they should be replaced. If they look usable, it will not be necessary to remove the worm gear from the shaft. If either gear is replaced, it is a good idea to replace the other so that they will wear evenly.

7. Remove the worm gear from the steering shaft by using a two-jaw bearing and gear puller available at a good tool supply or tool rental store.

8. Remove the spark and throttle rods from the steering housing by shearing the pins out of the levers. Turn the steering column upside-down with the quadrant end of the levers resting on a wood block. Strike

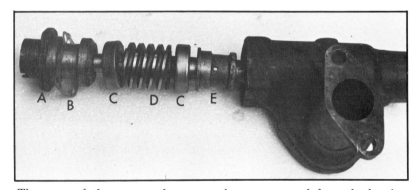

The parts of the seven-tooth gear as they are removed from the housing:

A. Lower bearing assembly	*A-3551 BR*
B. Shim, lower bearing	*A-3558 and A-3559 AR*
C. Steering worm thrust bearing	*A-3123 AR*
D. Steering shaft and worm assembly	*A-3524 BR*
E. Steering gear housing bushing	*A-3553 AR*

the levers sharply while holding a small socket over the ends and drive them down the shaft about 1/8 inch and remove the pin pieces with a pin punch. Remove the levers and springs.

9. Remove the two #10-32 flathead screws holding the upper bushing in the column and drive the bushing out the top by using a long rod inserted from the bottom of the column.

Inspection and restoration

Inspect all bearing and gear surfaces for wear, pits and chips. Check the lower bearing for excessive wear. Clean all parts with a good solvent. Replace all thrust bearings and bushings in the housing. If the sector shaft is replaced with a later type that does not have an oil groove, the shaft housing must be drilled and tapped for a grease fitting. The 21/64 inch hole should be drilled 2 3/32 inches from the center line of the housing flange and tapped for a 1/8 inch pipe thread grease fitting.

If the bushing in the lower bearing assembly is worn or scored badly, the bushing must be replaced. The steering shaft will have to be machined to a smaller size and a new bushing will have to be made to fit. The bushing has to be drilled for lubrication. The original bushing has a spiral groove.

Reassembly of the steering gear

1. If worm gear has been removed, have it replaced by a machine shop or use a driver.

2. Replace the bushings in the sector housing and ream to fit the sector shaft.

3. Install the upper bearing, control rods, springs and levers in the steering column. Replace the small pins securing the levers. Remember that the spark rod ball faces forward and the throttle rod ball faces to the rear

Grease fitting for sector shaft. Drill and tap for 1/8 pipe thread.

The grooved bushing in the lower bearing assembly should be checked for wear.

when the levers are installed.

4. Assemble the steering shaft bearings and bushings in place. Make sure that a thrust bearing is placed on each end of the worm gear with the moving race of the bearing facing the worm.

5. Insert the shaft into the housing until the thrust bearing is seated against the upper bushing. Slip the lower bearing shims over the lower bearing assembly as they were removed. These shims are made in three thicknesses (0.0025, 0.005 and 0.010 inch), and are used to adjust the end play in the steering shaft.

6. Slide the lower bearing assembly over the shaft, making sure that the slot for the light switch is facing down. Bolt the lower bearing assembly loosely in place. Install the steering wheel and tighten the bolts, checking for binding. If the steering wheel is difficult to turn, a shim should be added. If the end play is excessive, shims should be removed.

7. Center the sector shaft and insert it into the housing with the thrust washer grooves toward the gears. Make sure it meshes with the worm.

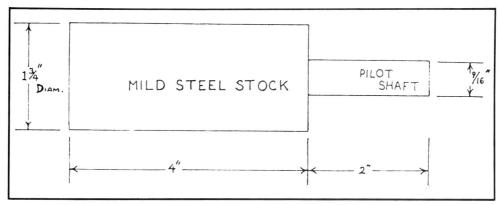

Worm installation tool.

This screw adjusts end play in the seven-tooth sector shaft.

Turn the housing on its side and fill it with 7 3/4 ounces of 600W gear lubricant. Make sure all other parts are lubricated as they are assembled.

8. Put the housing cover back on the housing with a new gasket with the adjusting screw backed off. Tighten the screws holding the cover in place and check the end play of the sector shaft with a Pitman arm attached, while tightening the adjusting screw until there is no end play and no binding.

9. Paint the steering gear with black enamel and complete the remainder of the assembly in the reverse order of disassembly. The steering gear is now ready to be installed in the car.

Disassembly of the two-tooth steering gear

1. Remove the light switch and steering wheel as described in steps one and two of the seven-tooth section.

Two-tooth steering gear housing assembly.

Parts identification of two-tooth steering gear:		*E. Steering gear adjusting screw*	*350607-S*
A. Lighting switch bracket	*A-3569*	*Lock nut*	*33927-S*
B. Housing end plate	*A-3568*	*F. Worm roller bearing assembly*	*A-3571*
C. Felt seal	*B-3528*	*G. Steering shaft and worm assembly*	*A-3524 D*
D. Steering gear housing	*A-3548*	*H. Worm adjusting sleeve*	*A-3553 D*

52

2. Remove the two 1/4 inch cap screws and lockwashers holding the steering gear lighting-switch bracket and housing end plate to the housing. Remove the grease seal and cup-shaped washer from the end of the steering gear housing.

3. Remove the four nuts and washers holding the sector housing on the steering gear housing and pull them apart. Sometimes the sector shaft will come out with the housing. If it does not, then remove the sector shaft.

4. Loosen the two bolts and nuts securing the steering column clamp and the upper bearing cup clamp. Pull the steering column off the steering shaft and lay it aside. Remove the steering gear adjusting screw, drive a wedge into the slot in the housing and remove the steering shaft, bearings and worm adjusting sleeve.

5. Remove the worm adjusting sleeve and bearing from the steering shaft. Remove the lower bearing cup from the housing by using a small punch in the two threaded holes for the end plate screws. A flat pin punch of 3/16 inch or less works best.

6. If inspection shows the worm and sector gears to be worn or damaged beyond use, then the worm gear will need to be removed from the steering shaft with the use of a two-jaw gear and bearing puller. The worm and sector gears should only be replaced as a pair.

Inspection and restoration

Clean all parts in a good solvent and inspect all bearing and gear

Look for pits and galling in worm gear and bearing cup surfaces.

Use a sharp punch to remove the lower bearing cup from the gear housing.

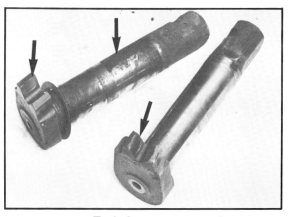

Typical wear on two-tooth sector gear.

surfaces for wear and pits. It is best to replace all bearings and bushings with new parts if the steering is to perform as it should.

If the gear is a 1929 or 1930 model, the worm should be checked to see if it is the old A-3524-CR design with a twenty-five-degree taper (as shown on page 517 of the December 1930 Ford Service Bulletins). If this worm is present, the new bearings, cups and adjusting sleeve cannot be used. All of these parts will need to be replaced together as the reproduction parts are only made for the new-design A-3524-D worm. All parts catalogs today should show the replacement A-3524-CD worm which will replace the 3524-D and CR.

The inside of the worm gears have serrations similar to splines on the inside. The original gears had eight of these splines, but the replacement gears all have ten. The reason for the difference is to allow for a better fit of the gear on the shaft.

One of the best improvements that can be made to the steering of a Model A Ford is the installation of needle bearings and oil seals in the sector housing of the two-tooth gear. These bearings replace the original bushings and greatly increase the ease of steering.

There are a few craftsmen installing these needle bearings around the country, but none better than Willis Schwent. Willis first machines the face of the old housing for alignment and machines the bore to receive three sets of Torrington needle bearings followed by a C/R seal on the frame side of the housing. This modification also eliminates the problem of lubricant leakage at the frame. For best results, perform this modification when a new sector shaft is to be installed.

Another modification liked by many restorers is the use of a tube installed in the housing end plate to prevent the leakage of grease into the lighting switch. If one of these tubes is used, be sure that the tube has a tight fit in the end plate or it will leak. Willis Schwent uses a shoul-

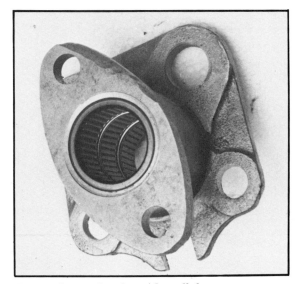

Two-tooth sector housing with needle bearings installed for smoother steering action.

dered press fit on all tubes that he uses when rebuilding steering gears for customers.

Reassembly of the steering gear

1. Begin reassembly by installing the worm gear on the steering shaft. The end of the worm gear that goes on the steering shaft is counterbored slightly larger than the shaft so it generally will require the use of a brass shim to align the gear with the shaft for installation. Check the size of the shaft and of the inside of the gear with a vernier caliper to determine the shim needed. Measure the shaft about 2 3/4 inches from the end, or where the end of the gear will seat. The shim should be wrapped around the shaft to help center the gear as it is installed.

Clamp the steering shaft firmly in a vise to install the gear. Tap the gear onto the shaft at first to determine where it will seat. Remove the gear and use a mill file to make lineal flats in the shaft taking off about 0.003 to 0.005 inch where the splines or serrations make contact with the shaft. This will aid in assembly of the shaft and gear.

Heat the gear uniformly to about 300 degrees to expand it so it will fit more easily onto the shaft. (Do not overheat the gear or the hardness will be affected.) Drive the gear onto the shaft while aligning the keyway. Use gloves when handling the hot worm gear. The gear is best driven on with the use of the special tool shown earlier. (This tool will need to be made on a lathe.) Remember that the gear goes on the shaft with the serrations on the bottom end.

2. Drive the lower worm bearing cup into the steering gear housing by using a special driver.

3. Insert the lower roller bearing into the housing. Place the upper roller bearing over the steering shaft followed by the worm gear adjusting sleeve and insert the clamping bolt and nut. Install the sleeve adjusting screw and lightly force the adjusting sleeve to just remove the end play in the worm shaft, then tighten the clamp bolt.

4. Place the sector shaft back into the gear housing with the sector thrust washer in place. Place a new gasket in the sector housing and install it over the sector shaft. Replace the four nuts, lockwashers and tapered sleeve and tighten the nuts. Install the sector adjusting screw and turn it in against the sector, then back it off just enough to allow the sector to rotate freely.

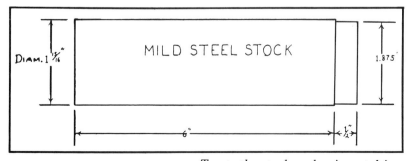

Two-tooth sector lower bearing cup driver.

5. Install the end plate and light switch retainer with a gasket and two 1/4 inch hex-head screws.

6. Install the upper bearing, control rods and levers in the steering column and replace the steering column over the steering shaft. An important point to mention here is that many of the reproduction spark and throttle control rods made for the 1930-31-style cars are not bent properly at the lever end and do not fit the upper column notches well. The bend on the rod should be a sharp one. Tighten the bolt and nut at the steering column clamp after aligning the column.

7. Paint the steering column and gear with black enamel. They are now ready to be installed in the car. Remember to fill the gear with 7 3/4 ounces of steering gear lubricant.

Adjusting the two-tooth steering gear when installed in the car

There are four adjustments which can be made to the two-tooth sector steering gear: sector shaft end play, steering shaft end play, mesh of worm and sector gears and centralization of tooth contact. When any adjustment is made the other two should be checked. Adjustments should always be made in this order.

When making any adjustments to the steering gear, the front wheels should be raised or the drag link disconnected from the Pitman arm.

1. The first adjustment is the end play of the sector shaft. Begin by insur-

Two-tooth steering gear installed in chassis. Notice special bolt.

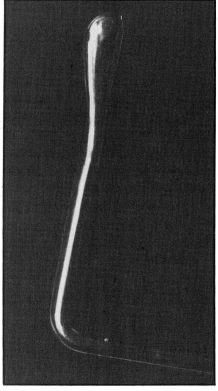

Original spark and throttle control rod. Notice sharp angle.

ing that the nuts on the sector housing cover are tight. Turn the steering wheel to either extreme and back it off one eighth of a turn. Grasp the Pitman arm at the shaft and check to see that there is no end play and that the wheel turns freely without binding.

If adjustment is necessary, loosen the lock nut on the engine side of the gear housing and adjust the sector thrust screw.

2. To adjust the end play in the steering shaft, turn the steering wheel to either stop and back it off one eighth of a turn to where lash appears in the steering arm. This frees the steering shaft bearings of side thrust.

Loosen the housing clamp bolt, which is the lower one on the column, and loosen the lock nut on the sleeve adjusting screw. Tighten the adjusting screw to just remove shaft end play. When adjustment is completed, tighten the lock nut.

3. To adjust the mesh of the worm and sector gears, turn the steering wheel to mid-position and check the Pitman arm for looseness by shaking it firmly. If adjustment is required, loosen the three housing cover nuts exactly one-quarter turn. Loosen the adjusting stud nut exactly one-half turn and then turn the eccentric adjusting sleeve clockwise very gradually while checking the movement of the Pitman arm. Adjust until all lash is eliminated in the steering arm and no more. Be sure to finish movement of the eccentric adjusting sleeve in a clockwise direction.

Turn the steering wheel throughout its full travel to check for smooth, free operation. If the wheel is too tight, turn the eccentric sleeve counterclockwise to free it and adjust again, more carefully.

When adjustment is completed, tighten the adjusting stud nut and follow by tightening the housing cover nuts. It is important that the ad-

Adjustment of sector shaft end play.

57

justing stud nut be tightened before the cover nuts.

It is likely that these adjustments will be sufficient in most cases but sometimes, even after all these adjustments have been made, there may still be unequal lash in the steering gear at opposite ends of the travel. In this case, the tooth contact must be centralized. This adjustment must be made with the gear removed from the car. This adjustment should be made any time the gear is completely disassembled or rebuilt.

This adjustment must be made with the sector shaft teeth meshed at the center of the worm. To find the center of the worm, turn the steering wheel to the left as far as possible then turn it to the right 1 1/2 turns. From this point, turn the shaft by the shortest direction to where the keyway aligns with the adjusting screw.

Turn the steering shaft one-half turn to the right and check the steering arm, noting the amount of play at this point.

Turn the shaft back to the left one complete turn and check the steering arm to compare the play with the first check. If there is less lash or play when the steering shaft is turned to the left, turn the eccentric rivet on the sector housing in a clockwise direction.

If there is less lash when the shaft is turned to the right, move the eccentric rivet in a counterclockwise direction.

When the lash of the steering arm is equal when the wheel is turned in both directions one-half turn from center, adjust the mesh of the sector teeth in the worm. After securing a final adjustment, tighten the cover adjusting stud nut, then tighten the housing cover nuts. It is important that the adjustment stud nut be tightened first.

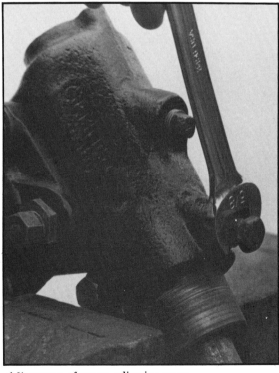

Adjustment of worm adjusting screw.

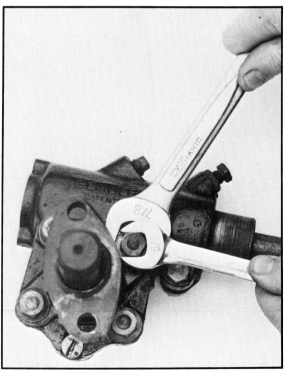

Adjustment of eccentric on two-tooth steering gear.

Chapter 5

REAR AXLE

THE rear axle provides the means of transmitting the power of the Ford engine to the wheels and to the road. In addition, the rear end contains the differential which changes the direction of the power and also allows the rear wheels to turn individually at different speeds when the car turns a corner.

The Ford Model A employs a built-up type, three-quarter floating, bevel gear rear axle assembly. The manufacture of the Ford rear axle employed some of the most interesting methods of fabrication of any Model A part. The housing was constructed using a combination of hot-metal spinning and electric welding. The differential housing was made on an automatic welding machine that was operated by one man and could produce sixty pieces per hour. This machine was adopted in mid-1928 to replace the old operation which required three men and twenty-five percent more floor space.

The differential housing weighs eight pounds twelve ounces and has a test strength of twelve tons to crush and eighty tons expansive force.

Model A sales literature for 1930 listed the following specifications for the Ford axle:

Drive gear and pinion—Steel forgings with heavy spiral-type bevel gears matched and lapped.

Teeth on pinion and drive gear—1 3/16 inches long. Ratio 3.78:1

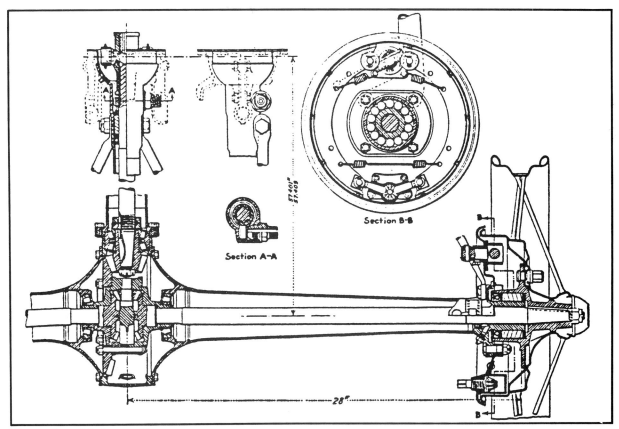

Rear axle and hub assembly.

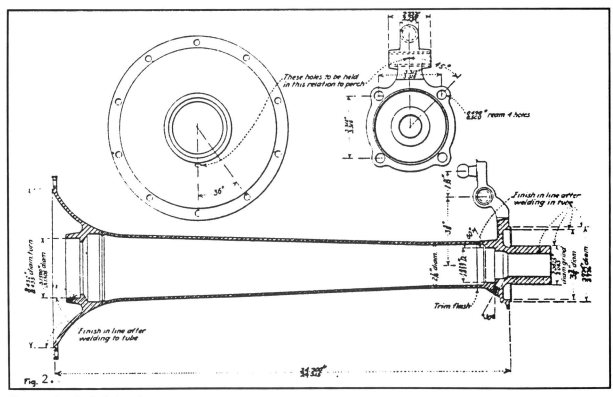

Rear and axle-shaft housing.

(earlier ratio was 3.70:1).

 Differential bearings—Taper roller bearing on each side.

 Differential spider—Steel forging. Pinions—three.

 Differential gears—Forged integral with axle shaft.

 Axle shaft—1 1/8 inches diameter. Special Ford carbon manganese steel.

 Wheel bearings—Spiral roller running on end of forged steel axle housing hardened and ground.

 Driveshaft—Special Ford Manganese drawn steel perfectly aligned to eliminate whip.

Inspection and troubleshooting

 If the rear end is generally quiet and does not make any excessive noise, it may be possible to leave this assembly together and get away with it. The gears and bearings in the rear axle are strong and sturdy and if they have been well lubricated, may very well be in good condition.

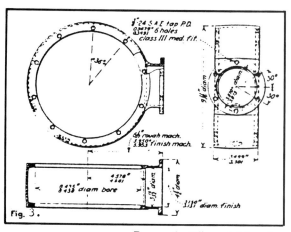

Rear axle differential housing.

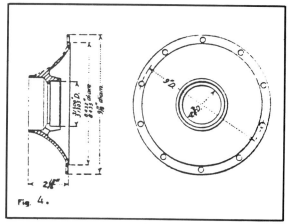

Rear axle-shaft housing bell.

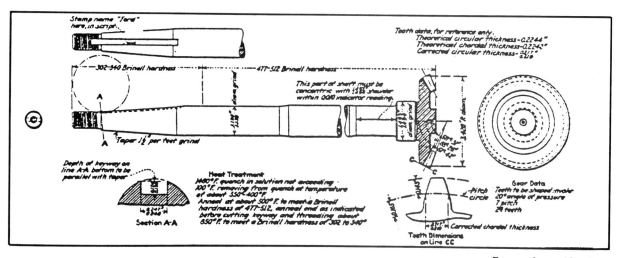

Rear axle specifications.

If the car is running, the first thing to do is check to see that the lubricant is filled to the proper level. Next, drive the car on a smooth, asphalt road (to eliminate any possible tire noise) and listen for sounds from the rear. Keep the speed of the car below 30 mph and see if noises appear. Rear axle noises are usually not present at this speed and the sound, if any, is probably tires.

Noises caused by a worn or damaged wheel bearing are often the loudest when the car is coasting at low speeds, and usually stop when the brakes are gently applied. To find the noisy bearing, jack up each wheel and check each bearing for roughness while the wheel is rotating.

If all possible external sources of noise have been checked and eliminated and the noise still exists, test the car under all four driving conditions: drive, cruise, float and coast. Any noise produced by the side gears and pinion gears in the differential will be most noticeable during turns. A continuous whine under a light load at 20 to 35 mph indicates a rough or Brinelled (dented) pinion bearing. If the tone of drive, coast and float noise differs with speed and if the noise is very rough and irregular, then worn, rough or loose differential or pinion shaft bearings are indicated. The axle should be removed and repaired if these conditions exist.

Removal of the rear axle assembly

1. Drain the lubricant from the rear end by removing the lower plug on the differential housing. Disconnect the service and emergency brake rods from the brake levers by removing the cotter pins and clevis pins.
2. Disconnect the brake retracting springs from the radius rods by removing the 5/16 inch nuts and bolts from the brackets. Disconnect the shock absorber arms from the shock absorbers by removing the clamp

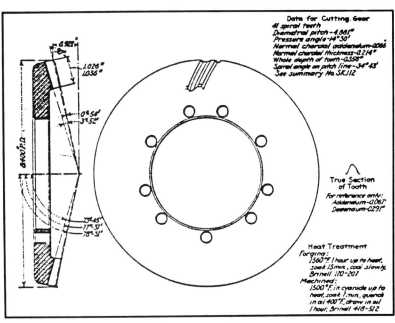

Differential ring gear.

bolt and pulling the arm off the shaft.

3. Raise the rear of the car by the frame enough to put a block of wood under the spring hangers on both sides, then lower the car back down to put weight on the spring. Use a spring spreader to release the pressure on the hangers and remove the 7/16-20 nuts and cotter pins holding the spring hangers on both sides. With a large punch or rod, drive the spring hanger out on the side with the spreader in place. Release the spreader and allow the spring to compress toward the center.

4. Place the spreader on the opposite end of the spring and remove the other hanger in the same manner. Raise the car again and support it with blocks or jackstands for safety.

5. Remove the speedometer drive cable from the right side of the driveshaft tube by unscrewing the cable retainer.

6. Remove the cotter pins from the six castle nuts around the universal-joint housing half-caps. Remove the six 3/8 inch nuts and bolts joining the caps to the transmission. Remove the two 3/8 inch nuts and bolts with lockwashers holding the two U-joint half-caps together and remove the caps. Raise the car enough to clear the rear wheels and roll the rear axle out from under the car, supporting the front of the driveshaft. Remove the wheels and place the rear axle assembly on a stand or on the floor for disassembly.

Disassembly

1. Remove the rear brake drums with a wheel puller. Remove the backing plate and brake assemblies as described in the brake chapter. Remove the speedometer drive gear cap assembly. Remove the lock ring from inside the torque tube and slide the speedometer driving gear off the shaft followed by the spacer and roller bearing assembly.

2. Cut the safety wire and remove the six 3/8 inch bolts, securing the torque tube. Remove the backing plate bolts, remove the large bolt and nut in front and remove the radius rods. Slide the torque tube off the driveshaft.

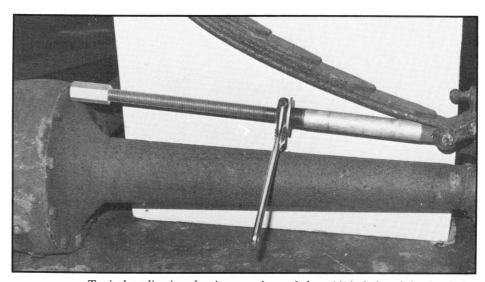

Typical application of spring spreader made from 3/4 inch threaded rod and pipe.

3. Remove the ten 3/8 inch bolts from the left axle housing and pull the housing off the differential housing. Pull the axles, ring gear and carrier assembly out of the housing and lay it aside. The other axle housing may now be removed from the differential housing by removing the other ten bolts.

4. With a large pipe wrench or adjustable wrench, remove the lock nut, nut locking plate and adjusting nut from the driveshaft and pull the

Axle and differential carrier removed from differential housing.

The driveshaft is removed from the differential housing from the inside. The parts shown are: A. lock nut, B. locking ring, C. adjusting nut, D. front pinion bearing, E. driveshaft.

front pinion bearing out of the front of the differential housing. The driveshaft may now be pulled from the inside of the differential housing.

5. Cut the safety wire and remove the nine 3/8 inch nuts holding the two halves of the differential carrier together. Before separating the carrier sections, mark them with a punch or scribe so they can be reassembled in the same position. These two parts are machined to match and must be replaced the same way they come out. When these two parts are separated, the spider and spider gears will fall out. The carrier, axle shafts and ring gear may be separated and laid aside for inspection.

6. Remove the nut from the end of the driveshaft and, using a gear puller, remove the pinion and bearing from the shaft.

Inspection and restoration

Inspect all the gears for chips and broken teeth. Look at the ring gear to see if there is any excessive wear or pits on the gear surface. Check the outer roller bearing surfaces of the axle housings to be sure that they are perfectly round. Refer to the proper original dimensions given at the beginning of this chapter.

Check the spider gears and spider for chips, pits or excessive wear.

Look at the tapered hub end of the axle shaft and look for damaged keyways or badly scored hub surfaces. Check the back side of the axle gears for scoring and damage. Look at all bearings and races for any signs of galling, pitting or excessively worn bearings. Replace any bearings or gears that do not look like they are in good condition. Most gears and bearings are available new and it is much easier to replace them now than after the car is together.

If the double bearing cup in the differential housing appears to require replacement, it may be removed with a heavy-duty hydraulic jack. Place the housing on the floor with the bearing area facing down and

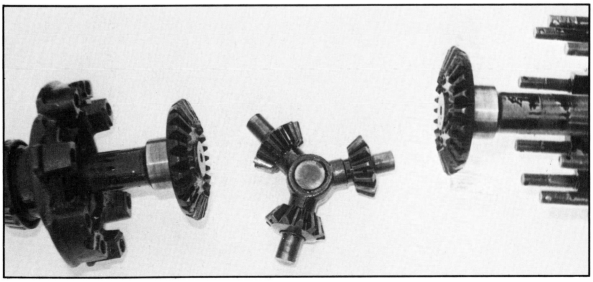

As the two halves of the differential are separated, the spider and pinion gears will fall out easily.

place the jack inside with a block of wood on top to protect the housing. Place an old bearing or some other type of spacer on the bottom against the race and slowly push the bearing race out of the bottom of the housing.

The bearing races in the axle housings must be removed by driving them out from the outer end or, if a proper puller is not available, they can be removed and replaced by any good machine shop. If the differential bearings must be replaced, they can be removed by using a gear-and-bearing puller available at any tool supply or rental store. Refer to pages 273 and 274 of the Ford Service Bulletins for a description of the original tools used by Ford service departments.

Remove the seals in the ends of the axle housings by driving them out with a rod or wooden shaft. They are driven to the inside of the housing. To replace the seals, use a threaded rod with two washers that are slightly smaller than the diameter of the seals. Lock the seal in place on the rod with two nuts on either side and insert it carefully into the housing, being careful not to compress it or force it too much.

When the seal is in place, remove the lock nuts and washers and pull the threaded rod out of the housing. Be very careful of the quality of these seals as some of the reproductions are not very good. The number of this seal is A-4245 and it may be available from some standard seal and bearing suppliers in a better quality than from some Model A parts dealers.

Before reassembly, clean all parts of grease and rust and paint the outer housings with black enamel.

Look for pits and galling in the spider and pinion gears. This gear would not turn on the spider.

Typical defects found on bearings and bearing races.

Reassembly of the rear axle

1. Install the rear bearing and pinion gear on the driveshaft and tighten the pinion gear nut and cotter pin. Bend the cotter pin around the sides of the nut (rather than over the front as usual) to prevent it from binding against the ring gear carrier and affecting the adjustments. Slip the driveshaft into the differential housing and install the front bearing, spacer, adjusting nut, locking plate and lock nut. Adjust the adjusting nut to provide 20 inch-pounds of preload on the bearings if they are new and about 12 to 15 inch-pounds if they are good used bearings. The preload is checked by turning the driveshaft with a torque wrench and 1 1/16 inch six-point socket. When preload is adjusted, tighten the lock nut and bend over the tabs on the locking plate.

2. Assemble the spider gears to the spider and place in the carrier half See that the gears turn freely with a clearance of about 0.005 to 0.010 inch. If possible, try to find the later pinion gears (introduced in January of 1930) with oil holes drilled in them. These will decrease the chance of the gears seizing on the spider. (See page 410 of the Ford Service Bulletins.)

3. Assemble the two halves of the differential carrier and the axle shafts. Make sure that the marks made during disassembly match on the carrier housing. Torque the bolts to 35 foot-pounds and replace the safety wire.

4. Fasten one axle shaft in a large vise and turn the other back and forth to check for the proper amount of backlash, which should not exceed 0.010 to 0.015 inch. While in the vise, check the end play of the axle to see that it does not exceed 0.015 to 0.020 inch. Check both axles in the same manner and if the play does exceed these allowances, check the carrier to see that it does not have any dirt or pieces of metal holding

The bearing preload is adjusted by turning the adjusting nut on the front of the differential housing.

the two halves apart. Wear on the old gears will cause the backlash to exceed these limits if new spider gears were not installed.

5. Install the axle and carrier assembly into the differential housing making sure that the ring gear is on the driver's side of the axle assembly. Install the right axle housing with a gasket of 0.004 to 0.006 inch thickness and secure with the 3/8 inch bolts. Attach the left housing in the same manner and torque all bolts to 35 foot-pounds.

6. With a helper on the opposite side, turn the axles in the same direction and check for a heavy drag which should be present if the bearing preload is correct. Turn the driveshaft in both directions and check for a backlash of about 0.005 to 0.010 inch. To adjust the backlash of the pinion and ring gear, add or remove gaskets from the right and left axle housings. A thicker gasket on the left housing increases the backlash, a thinner gasket decreases it.

7. Install a new seal in the torque tube. This is the same seal that was installed in the ends of the axle housing and should be pushed into place in the same manner. Remember that the angled rubber side of the seal goes toward the source of lubricant, in this case, the driveshaft front bearing. Install a new roller bearing race in the end of the torque tube. This race may be installed easily by compressing it and wrapping it with light wire. Slide it into the tube carefully and when it is in place, cut the wire and remove it with needle-nose pliers. V-slot on bearing race should be up, and dimple on bearing race should line up with indentation in torque tube housing.

8. Install the torque tube over the driveshaft and replace the bolts and safety wire. Lubricate and replace the driveshaft bearing, spacer washer, speedometer gear and lock ring. Be sure that the gear end of the

Reassembled carrier with safety wire in place.

68

speedometer gear is toward the rear. Replace the lubricant in the differential housing with either 600W as original or a good 140 gear lubricant. Do not mix the two oils, and do not pull the 140 into a rear end that has not been disassembled and cleaned or rebuilt. Do not overfill the lubricant as it will run into the brake drums and ruin the shoes. The lubricant should be to the level of the filler hole when the axle is installed in the car.

9. The rear axle assembly is now ready to install in the car. If the rear spring has been off and rebuilt, a good way to reinstall it is to secure the main leaf to the axle housing with new hangers and bushings, then replace the other leaves using a long center bolt and spring U-bolts as described in the frame chapter. When the spring is assembled and secured, the axle can be replaced under the car. Be sure to replace all cotter pins on the spring hangers and clamps. The rear brakes may be reassembled to the axle before or after it is under the car. Replace the radius rods and speedometer drive cable to the torque tube. Fasten the brake retracting springs to the radius rods with 5/16 inch bolts, nuts and lockwashers.

After the rear axle is installed in the car, test drive it to be sure that all components are working properly and quietly. Recheck the lubricant level at the intervals shown in the lubrication chart.

Although the 3.70 or 3.78 gears provide for the best all-around driving conditions, some restorers who drive their cars on tours like to replace the original ratio with high-speed gears of 3.54:1. This ratio will give a higher top speed, better gas mileage and help the engine to last longer, but on anything but a light roadster or pickup the hill-climbing ability and acceleration will be noticeably affected. While the rear end is apart, these gears may be easily installed in place of the original set. The speedometer will not read the proper speed after the new gears are in place.

A well-built rear axle in the Model A will give many years of good, quiet service and make the car as dependable and smooth as when it was new.

Chapter 6

THE FRAME

FIVE major sections and several minor parts make up the Model A frame. The minor parts include the fender and running board brackets and other tributary parts. The main sections are made of No. 9 USS gauge hot-rolled open-hearth steel held in thickness between 0.140 and 0.160 inches. The steel has an elastic limit of 42,000 pounds per square inch minimum. The Brinell hardness is held to 131 minimum. The Model A frames were originally made on electrically driven blanking presses that produced 2,000 frames during each eight-hour shift. The front crossmembers were blanked-out at a rate of 300 per hour on Bliss, Hamilton and Ferracute presses.

The Model A frame is what is known as ladder-type construction consisting of two long sidemembers and three crossmembers. The front and rear crossmembers serve as mounts for the springs, and the front crossmember supports the engine mounts. There were three basic frames used on the Model A passenger cars and eight used on AA trucks. The first major change came in November of 1928 when the front crossmember was altered by removing the solid engine mount which had been part of the crossmember. In October of 1929 the front crossmember was again altered by adding a slight depression on both ends where the radiator was fastened. There were many minor changes made in the relocation of holes to facilitate new body designs and equipment.

Specifications of Model A and AA frames

Material—pressed steel   Sidemembers—Length—113 7/16 inches
Thickness of material—5/32 inch   Width—1 3/4 inches; Depth—4 inches

AA Frame

Thickness—7/32 inch
Length—Short wheelbase—(early) A-5005-B—171 5/16 inches
                      (late) A-5005-B—169 13/16 inches
             Long frame A-5005-D—181 5/16 inches
          Long wheelbase— A-5008—210 3/8 inches
Depth—Short wheelbase—6 inches   Width—2 3/4 inches
       Long wheelbase —7 inches

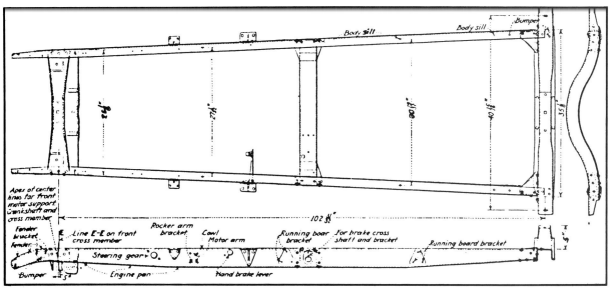

Frame assembly of early 1928 Model A.

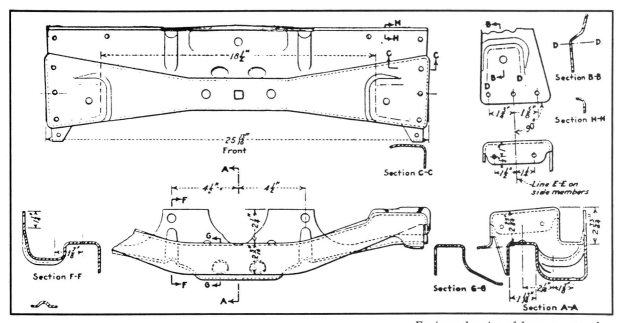

Engineer drawing of front crossmember.

The function of the frame is to support the body and to be an attaching point for the suspension components. Because the alignment of all of these parts is critical to the safe and smooth operation of the car, the alignment of the frame members is the most important consideration for selection of a frame to use for a restoration project.

Many times these old frames have been bent and badly damaged from wrecks and bad roads for over fifty years of abuse. It cannot be assumed that the frame has not seen other use before being placed under that Model A body. Farmers in many areas found that the Model A frame made a good base for hay wagons and put them to that very use after removing the bodies and engines and disconnecting the brake mechanisms. Two or three thousand pounds of hay and rough fields took their toll on that light-duty component and usually left them beyond repair.

Inspection of the frame

The first step in inspection of the Model A frame is to check for straightness and alignment of the rails and crossmembers. This is accomplished by measuring the frame diagonally with a tape measure and comparing the measurements.

The most difficult damage to identify is vertical twisting of the frame members. The best way to determine this is to place the frame on a level floor supported by evenly sized jackstands or blocks and measure the distance to the floor from side to side.

If there appears to be an excessive amount of deflection in the frame members it will be impossible to get a good body fit or a good front end alignment. Any variance of more than 1/8 inch in any direction should be considered excessive and steps should be taken to correct it. Any automobile frame or body shop should have the equipment necessary to straighten the Model A frame, but if a shop of this kind is not available a frame may be straightened in the home shop with the use of a Porta-Power or a hydraulic jack and heavy beams of wood or steel. If the damage is severe, a better choice would be to find another frame. They are usually available for a very nominal price from restorers who have stripped cars for parts. Make sure that the new frame is one that matches the year of the car being built. Any frame may be used on any

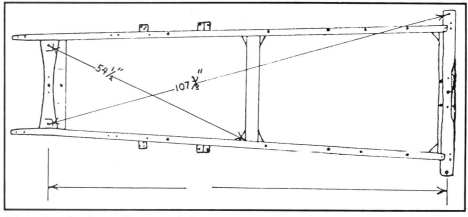

Dimensions for frame-alignment check.

car, but if authenticity is important, the frame should have the proper components and design. An early 1928 frame with a solid front engine mount would not be appropriate for a 1931 body.

Another area of inspection of great importance is the rivets mounting the crossmembers and brackets to the frame rails. If these rivets are loose, they will need to be replaced with new rivets. These rivets are available from various suppliers, but they are better installed by professionals with the proper equipment and skills. Some restorers like to replace the rivets in many parts with bolts. If this method is chosen, be certain that the bolts are grade five or six hardened bolts and that they fit very tightly in the holes. It is probably best to drill the holes to fit the bolts. The proper rivets for fastening frame members are available from Gene Renninger.

Do not for any reason weld the frame members together. The frame and body structures on old cars were riveted so that there would be a certain amount of flexibility and movement between the parts. If these structures are welded, they will not give and the frame will creak and groan at every turn, in addition to causing damage to the body mounts and framework.

After the frame is inspected and found to be usable, the next step is cleaning. The areas around the motor mounts and steering gear usually are encrusted with dried grease which is best removed by tedious scraping with a putty knife. Sometimes this grease may be loosened by generous application of a good degreaser or solvent before scraping.

The most common problem with a Model A frame is rust and pits from the rust. The best method of removing rust is dipping the frame in a rust-removing solution such as Redi-Strip or an inhibited acid process. These methods are usually better than sandblasting because the solution will get under the joints and inside the holes everywhere on the frame. Both of these processes should also leave a protective coating on the metal to prevent it from rusting prior to painting. Be certain that the pro-

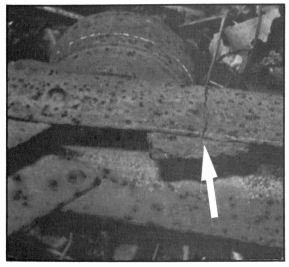

An example of a cracked and repaired frame. This frame should not be used.

tective coating is removed with a metal prep solution before the primer and paint are applied or it may seep through to the finish.

When the frame is thoroughly cleaned check it again for cracks or damage.

To prevent rust and provide a base for repairs, use a zinc chromate primer before continuing with the restoration. Be certain that the primer gets under the joints as much as possible to prevent the formation of new rust. Make sure that the running board brackets have been checked for straightness and cracks. The stamped brackets are available new from most parts vendors and suppliers, so it is not worth the trouble to try to repair them. The early forged brackets found on the 1928-29 models may be bent back into shape if they are not too badly deformed. The reproductions of these brackets are cast iron and do not have the same strength and flexibility as the originals. Do not try to bend reproduction cast brackets. The replacement side-mount brackets are also cast iron and have the same type of weaknesses.

Use a good-quality fiberglass or epoxy filler to fill all pits and rough places in the frame rails, then sand the frame smooth. Remember that the frame was not finished to the quality of the body so it should not be necessary to strive for a mirrorlike finish when the frame restoration is completed. The frame should be painted with a good-quality black enamel. Many restorers like to paint the top of the frame first and then the bottom because the bottom is what the show judges will see, and will have the better finish if painted last as it will not be as likely to get scratched.

If garage space is limited, the frame may be stored out of the way by securing it to the ceiling with chains and toggle hooks until the time comes for reassembly when it can be lowered to the floor and placed on level blocks.

Springs

Included in the supporting structure of the frame on the Model A

This frame has been bent at the side rail and is not useable.

Ford are the spring assemblies. The supension design of the Model A is called transverse semi-elliptic and is similar in design to that used on the Model T for over nineteen years.

Springs Used Under Model A Chassis

A-5310-A	10 leaves	A chassis front
A-5310-B	12 leaves	A chassis special equipment after November 1930 front
A-5560-A	10 leaves	55A, 55B, 295A, 140A rear (straight ends on main leaf)
A-5560-B	8 leaves	35A, 35B, 180A, 45A-B-C, 50A, 50B, 68A, 68B, 190A rear
A-5560-C	7 leaves	(with spacer) 40A, 40B rear
A-5560-D	10 leaves	155A-B-C, 165A-B-C, 170A-B, 160A, 160B, 160C, 130D, 200A, 00A-B-C
A-5560-E	10 leaves	79A, 79B, 225A, 78A, 150A, 150B, 66A, 76A, 76B, 82A, 82B rear

The springs are fastened to the axles of the Model A with flexible couplings known as hangers which allow for movement of the spring and axle assemblies, independent from the frame rails to provide for safe, comfortable ride and handling.

Rear spring removal

1. Raise the rear of the car enough to place a piece of two-inch wood under the rear spring eyes on both sides. Lower the car back down to put pressure on the spring and the wood. Remove the cotter pins and 7/16 inch nuts from the spring hangers on both sides and install the special spring spreader as shown in the rear axle chapter. This spreader is made from 3/4 inch threaded rod and iron pipe. Be sure to build the spreader in such a way that it will have about eight inches of deflection. Make the threaded rod about twelve inches long and the iron pipe about ten inches long. Also needed are a nut and a 3/4 inch flat washer.
2. Screw the spring spreader apart to relieve pressure on the hanger on one side and drive the hanger out the rear of the car with a large punch or soft rod.
3. Turn the spring spreader back in to let the spring draw inward toward the center and remove the spreader. Remove the spring hanger on the opposite side which should now be relieved of pressure.
4. Raise the rear of the car again from the frame to allow the spring to clear the rear axle and place jackstands or blocks under it for support.
5. Remove the four cotter pins and castle nuts from the spring-to-frame U-bolts and remove the spring clip bars from the bolts.
6. The spring may now be pulled free of the frame and removed from under the car.

Disassembly of the spring

1. Great care should be used in the disassembly of the rear spring as the leaves are pressed together under a great deal of pressure and it could be extremely dangerous should they escape control. A good method is to use a pair of rear spring U-bolts and clip bars fastened firmly around the spring on either side of the center bolt. Cut the center bolt with a

cold chisel and carefully loosen the U-bolts, which will slowly relieve pressure on the spring leaves. Carefully remove the spring clamps on either side of the spring assembly.

2. The spring hanger bushings should be pressed out and the bores cleaned of all rust. If the bushings are difficult to remove, they may be cut lengthwise with a hacksaw and removed in pieces.

Repair of the spring

Once the spring has been disassembled it should be inspected for broken leaves and wear. The spring's point of wear is principally where the ends of the leaf push into the spring leaf below and cause a dished-out area to form which prevents full movement of the leaves.

These dished-out areas are repaired by grinding the tip of the spring causing the wear. This will prevent future wear from occurring so quickly. The dished-out area on the lower spring leaf should also be ground smooth, and all spring surfaces cleaned either with a wire brush or sandblasting. The cleaning of the spring surfaces is important if the reasonably smooth ride of the Model A when new is to be regained.

New spring bushings should be installed in the spring eyes. These bushings are included with the spring hanger rebuilding kits available from parts vendors. Sometimes, the bores of the spring will need to be reamed slightly for the new bushings to fit properly. Beveling of the end of the bushing should help to make installation easier.

After the spring is cleaned well, it should be sprayed with a rust preventative primer and allowed to dry thoroughly. It is best not to apply the final coat of black enamel until the spring is assembled as it will probably be damaged during assembly.

Assembly of the spring

1. A new spring center bolt should be acquired from a parts vendor.

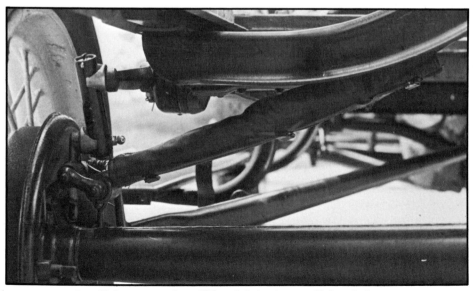

Spring covers installed on rear spring will keep lubrication supplied to the leaves.

These are special bolts of hardened steel with fine thread and special square heads which are usually made longer than necessary to facilitate assembly of the spring. Insert the new center bolt through the stack of springs and start the nut on the bottom side.

2. Replace the spring clips and U-bolt around the spring as in the disassembly. Apply a good-quality grease and graphite mixture to the spring leaves so the springs will move easily.

3. Tighten the nuts on the U-bolts slowly alternating side for side while the center bolt is being tightened snugly against the spring. Do not try to pull the spring together with the center bolt as it could break and release pressure on the stack of spring leaves and cause injury. Paint the entire spring with a good black enamel and allow to dry thoroughly.

4. When the springs have been brought together enough, replace the rebound clips on either side of the spring being sure to place the nuts on the outside and the clips inside the notch in the spring. There is a front and rear to the spring leaf with the notch holes for the clamps. The spring is installed in the car in the reverse order of removal.

5. The front and rear springs may be improved by installation of spring covers like the ones that were available from Ford when the cars were new. The spring covers will keep the lubrication in the springs and keep out water and dirt.

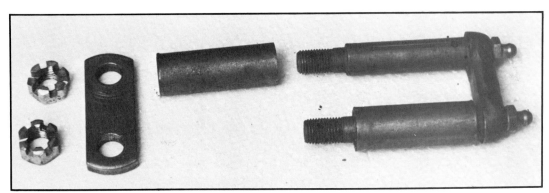

Spring hanger components are similar for the front and rear except for size. The grease fittings always face to the outside of the car.

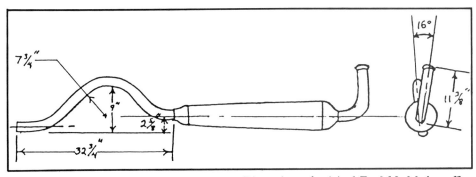

Dimensions of original Ford Model A muffler.

Removal of the front spring

The front spring is removed in a similar way to the rear spring but a spring spreader is unnecessary because there is not so much pressure on the front spring as on the rear.

The front spring should be rebuilt and finished in the same fashion as the rear spring. Be sure that the spring clamp nuts face to the front so that the bolts may be removed from the rear.

Check to see that the car sits at the correct height in the front. The front axle should be entirely visible on all models if the front spring is good. The height of the center of the front bumper on all cars except the station wagon should be eighteen inches. The wagon should be 18 1/2 inches. The rear bumper center should be approximately 16 1/2 inches from the ground on all models. If the springs show excessive sag, new spring assemblies are now available from many parts suppliers. Be sure to use the proper rear spring application for the body style being built.

Muffler

The muffler is usually considered to be part of the engine but Ford included it with the chassis parts, so it will be discussed here.

Good replacement mufflers are available from many suppliers so it is not necessary to be concerned with the old muffler. It is important to check the dimensions of the new muffler, as many of them do not fit well when received. Many times, the arch at the rear has been compressed during shipment which causes the tail pipe to hang low.

The most common problem for most restorers is leakage of the connection between the muffler and the manifold. This can be remedied by bending the front of the muffler pipe until it aligns with the manifold. Leave the rear tail pipe clamp loose while tightening the front clamp to allow the pipe to align itself properly.

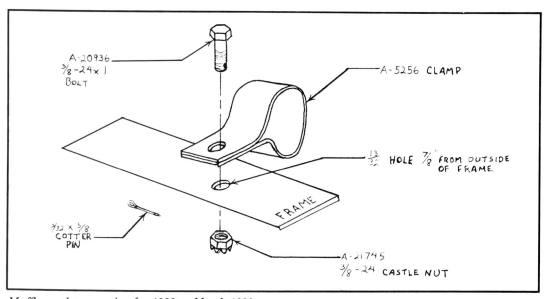

Muffler outlet mounting for 1928 to March 1929.

An area of confusion among many restorers is the carriage bolt that comes with the rear exhaust clamps (A-5256). The answer is to discard this improper fastener and install the clamp with the proper A20936 or A20953 bolt.

Before installing the exhaust system, clean the muffler with a metal prep or a grease remover, and paint with a good, heat-resistant paint. Allow the paint to dry thoroughly before starting the engine.

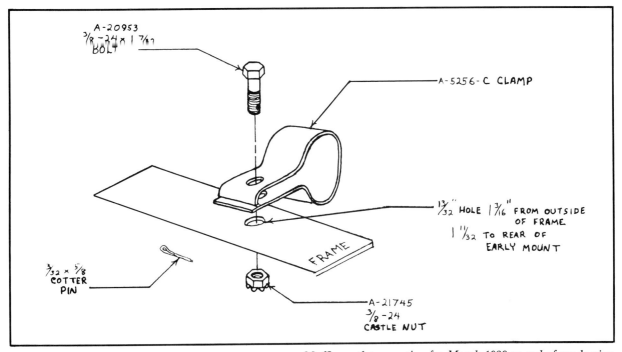

Muffler outlet mounting for March 1929 to end of production.

Chapter 7

ENGINE ASSEMBLY AND INSTALLATION

AS in any automobile, the heart of the Model A Ford is its engine. Regardless of the quality of all the other restoration factors, only a properly built and adjusted engine will provide the driving enjoyment and reliability that a Model A should give.

The Model A engine is of four-cylinder "en bloc" construction. It is of L-head design like its predecessor the Model T. The cylinders have a bore and stroke of 3 7/8 and 4 1/4 inches respectively. The rated horsepower according to the SAE (Society of Automotive Engineers) standard is 24.03, but the maximum horsepower developed at 2200 rpm is 40. The piston displacement is 200.5 cubic inches and the compression ratio is 80-gauge or 4.22:1. (At the end of this chapter is a list of the critical specifications of the Ford powerplant.)

The Model A crankshaft is made of hot-rolled, heat-treated steel. It is a forged component, made on a 5,000-pound Erie hammer and upset on a four-inch Ajax forging machine.

Ford Model A pistons are aluminum alloy. They are 3 29/32 inches long and should weigh 1 pound 1 7/8 ounces each within one dram. They are equipped with three rings. Model A connecting rods are forged with the studs integral with the rod.

Engine removal

1. Drain the radiator and the engine oil pan, replacing the plug after

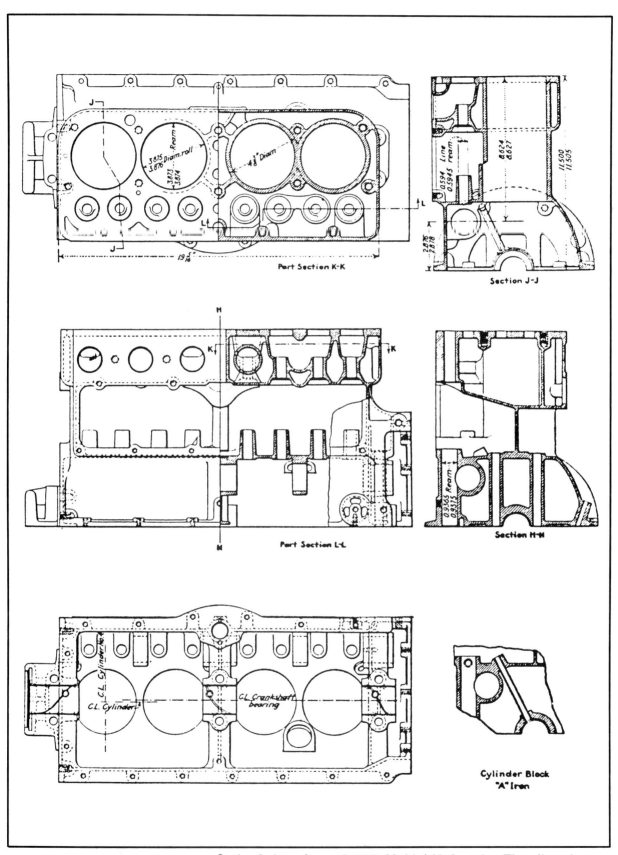

Part Section K-K

Section J-J

Part Section L-L

Section M-M

C.L. Cylinder No.4

C.L. Crankshaft bearing

C.L. Cylinder

Cylinder Block "A" Iron

Sectional views of an early 1928 Model A block casting. These dimensions are important for checking alignment and condition of components.

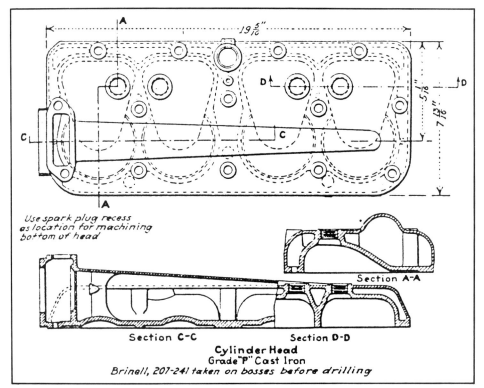

Sectional views of cylinder head of an early 1928. Certain portions of this design (and that for the block casting) will be different for later models.

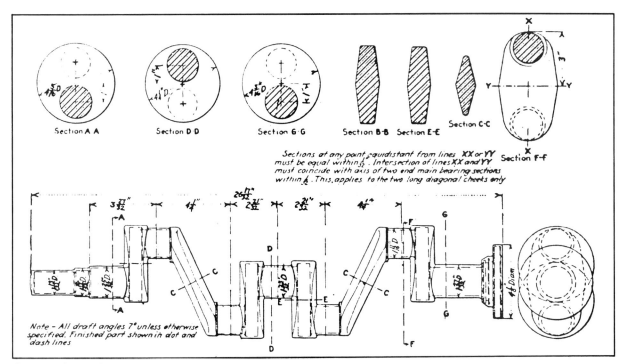

Crankshaft specifications.

draining. Move to the inside of the car before getting dirty and cover the seats with a protective material if the interior is to be preserved.

2. Remove the floor mat, accelerator cap and floor boards. Disconnect the battery ground strap.

3. Under the hood, right side, remove the throttle rod linkage, choke rod and spring.

4. Under the hood, left side, remove the spark control linkage, hand-throttle linkage and starter push rod.

5. Inside the car remove the choke rod, accelerator linkage from the rear of the engine (two 7/16 inch cap screws), the five top clutch housing bolts (3/8 inch cap screws) and the engine mount at flywheel housing

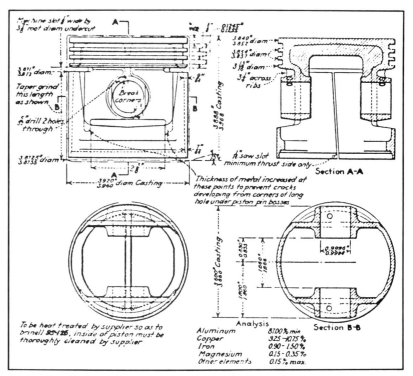

Model A piston specifications.

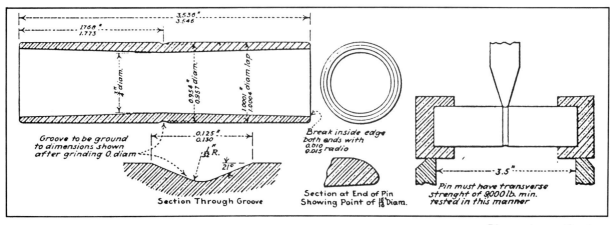

Piston pin specifications.

83

bolts (four 1/2 inch cap screws). The safety wire must be cut before removing these bolts.

6. Under the hood, left side, remove the engine wire at the generator, the wire at the starter switch, the water inlet clamp (3/8 inch hex screws), the starter (three 3/8 inch cap screws), the generator (1/2 inch bolt), oil cap and dipstick, left 1/2 inch screw from engine front yoke, the upper radiator hose with two clamps, the lower hoses, clamps and inlet pipe and the left headlamp conduit connection. Disconnect the horn, pulling the two wires back through the conduit. Remove the radiator support rods (1/2 inch nut at front, 9/16 inch nut at rear), pull radiator forward one inch and remove the hood assembly, placing it on end of a carpet to protect the finish.

7. Under the hood, right side, remove the fuel line (two 1/2 or 9/16 inch fittings), the manifold-to-muffler clamp (two 3/8 inch nuts and bolts), tying the pipe to the rear engine mount to keep it away from the flywheel housing. Remove the right 1/2 inch cap screw at the engine front yoke. Remove the manifold assembly (four 7/16 inch nuts and special washers). Remove the coil wire and the distributor by loosening the lock nut and screw at the head, removing the 7/16 inch head nut and clamp, and tapping the distributor up gently. Unscrew the cable, tying it up behind the coil on the firewall. Remove the right headlamp and pull the wires back from the conduit.

8. Under the car remove the cotter pins from the two front radius rod nuts and remove the nuts, springs, spacers and lower cap by tapping the rod solidly. Lower the radius rod a few inches and remove the upper cap. Remove the remainder of the clutch-housing-to-flywheel-housing 3/8 inch cap screws. Remove the radiator-to-frame 3/8 inch bolt, nut, cotter pin and springs by holding the bolt head under the frame and using a U-joint and extension with a deep 9/16 inch socket. Slide the radiator to one side to clear the fender and lift the free side. Retrieve the mounting pads from the mounting flange and/or frame. Store the radiator in a protected area to prevent accidental damage. Remove the front engine yoke cotter pin, nut, spring and brass bushing. Remove the engine side pans by removing the three 1/4 inch cap screws on the top side of the lower frame rails and flatwasher, lockwasher and 1/4 inch square nut on the bottom of the pans. Loosen the two or four pan bolts securing the side pan ears under the oil pan and remove pans.

9. In the engine compartment remove the water pump and fan assembly (four 3/8 inch hex nuts and lockwashers) and the fan belt.

The engine is now ready to be hoisted. Place a jack under the rear of the front radius rod and raise approximately one inch or until a slight gap appears between the clutch and flywheel housings. Be careful not to raise it too much or the clutch disc hub will be bent out of alignment and rendered useless.

The balance point of the engine in this condition is the number three spark plug. Secure a cable or chain on the number four manifold stud using a washer and nut. The other end can be secured around the water inlet or by removing the two 7/16 inch bolts. The inlet can be removed and a bolt and washer inserted through a chain link. An additional support can be secured to one waterpump stud and run to the chain over the number three spark plug for extra strength.

Attach hook to chain above the number three spark plug and start raising the engine. Raise the front slightly more than the rear, being careful not to touch the crank pulley on the handcrank guide, as the pulley is easily broken. Raise the jack under the radius rod at the same time to prevent distortion of the clutch disc. The transmission and clutch housing should be raised only until the flywheel housing contacts the firewall edge. At that point, the front crank pulley should clear the crank guide and the clutch will be fully clear of the transmission shaft.

The engine may now be carefully raised until the oil pan clears the headlight bar. Be careful not to allow the flywheel and clutch pressure plate to touch the terminal box or coil. Lower and remove the transmission jack, roll the car back from the engine and roll the engine hoist away from the car. Lower the engine to disassembly work surface or engine stand.

Engine disassembly

1. Remove the twelve 5/16 inch hex bolts holding the clutch pressure plate to the flywheel and remove the pressure plate and clutch disc. If the engine is a 1928 model with the multiple-disc clutch the clutch will have remained with the transmission.

2. Remove the safety wire and four bolts holding the flywheel to the crankshaft. Remove the flat, metal dowel-pin retainer plate and carefully lift the sixty-three-pound flywheel from the engine.

3. Remove the safety wire and four bolts holding the flywheel housing to the block. As the housing is lifted from the block, there should be two small, flat metal shims between the top of the housing and the block. These shims were used to provide for alignment of the housing and the block. Many times these shims are missing and the housing frequently becomes cracked at the bolt-mounting holes.

4. Remove the fourteen 7/16 inch nuts and lift the head and water outlet from the block. The head gasket may require prying loose from the block or head surface.

5. Using a suitable stud-removing tool, remove the fourteen cylinder-head studs from the block. These may be saved but it is more desirable to replace them as they are inexpensive and they probably have become stretched from repeated tightening. Many times the studs are broken when removal is attempted. The studs near the exhaust ports are especially vulnerable, and great care must be taken while removing them. If any studs are broken, they should be removed by a shop experienced in this type of work. Do not try to use an "easy out" or some other type of tool, because if it becomes broken in the stud the job is made much more difficult.

6. Turn the engine over and remove the twenty 5/16 inch hex screws holding the oil pan to the block. Pry the pan and gasket loose and remove them from the block assembly. Remove the baffle from the oil pan and prepare them both for cleaning.

7. The oil pump may now be carefully removed by tapping it gently from the block. There is a pin which secures the pump to the block and prevents it from turning. This pin may be broken very easily, so great care must be taken during removal. The oil pump usually requires very little work other than cleaning and replacing the gasket, but if wear is evi-

dent, rebuilding kits are available for small cost. Some pumps have soldered covers which must be made airtight when replaced if they are removed and repaired.

8. Remove the cotter pins from the rod nuts using a 17 mm socket, and remove the rod nuts. The rod caps may now be tapped loose from the rods one at a time as the rod and piston assembly is removed from the engine. Before removing the piston and rod, the tops of the cylinder bores should be checked for ridges which could damage the pistons or prevent their removal. These ridges may be removed from the bores with a ridge reamer. As the rod and piston assemblies are removed from the engine the caps must be placed back on their respective rods in the same direction and position as removed. Be sure that the rods are numbered according to the cylinders from which they were removed. Do not rely on the numbers stamped on the rods, as many times these were replaced and renumbered by different methods and may not match their locations.

9. Remove the bolts securing the main bearings to the block (9/16 inch head bolts with 3/4 inch nuts and cotter pins). Remove the main bearing caps and place them aside in numbered order in the same position as removed. It is a good idea at this time to keep track of any shims that may have been under the main bearings in case the bearings and crank

The valve spring retainers can be removed with the fingers as the spring is compressed.

Using a special valve-guide-removing tool will assist in getting the old guides out of the block.

are to be used again.

10. Carefully lift the crankshaft out of the main bearing saddles and set it aside. Place the main bearing caps back into their respective positions.

11. Remove the two 5/16 inch screws and special washers, securing the oil-return pipe to the valve chamber cover, and lift the pipe from the block. Remove the valve chamber cover so that the valve train is accessible.

12. Using a suitable valve spring compressor remove the spring retainers and pry the valve springs out of the valve chamber. The retainers may be removed with the fingers, or a needle-nose pliers may be utilized to save the fingers.

13. The valves may be removed at this time by using a valve guide removing tool and driving the guides out into the valve chamber. Keep the valves and valve guides together and marked in case they will be used again. Lift the valves from the block and place them in a board with numbered holes for identification.

14. Remove the nine 3/8 inch bolts holding the side cover and front timing cover to the block and pry the covers loose. Do not lose the plunger and spring from the front of the camshaft. In many cases, the plunger will be stuck in the timing cover and will have to be soaked with penetrating oil and pried from its socket.

15. With the engine resting on its top side, carefully remove the camshaft from the block. The lifters will now be able to be removed from the block and placed with their respective valve gear components.

Cleaning and inspection

Now is the time to decide whether the engine will need a complete rebuild or whether some of the components may be used again. There are different schools of thought on this decision and both have their good and bad points. One group feels that if the original pieces are not

Cracks in the area of the valve seat and cylinder are sometimes difficult to locate. They are usually found in this location.

worn beyond acceptable limits they should be reused. Many times the quality of original parts far exceeds that of some of the reproduction parts available, and using the original parts will save money on the building of the engine. The other group believes that the relatively small cost of the new parts compared to the loss if the original parts fail or do not perform satisfactorily is not worth using the old components. The original parts may be unknowingly fatigued to the point of failure. The decision is up to the individual restorer, but I feel that the best way to go is a complete rebuild with as many new parts as possible. There are quality reproduction parts available if the restorer is careful about choosing the dealer from which they are purchased. Higher quality parts are worth the confidence of knowing that the car will not be left stranded somewhere on a tour.

Inspection of the block

The first step is to determine whether the block is serviceable. The block should be carefully inspected for cracks that may have been caused by overheating or freezing. Many of the cracks are very difficult

Typical crack in water jacket.

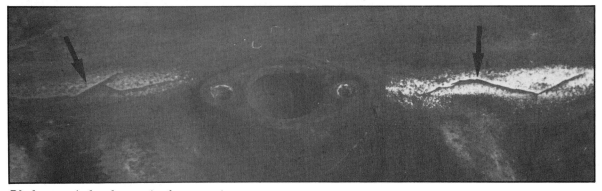

Block water jacket damage is often extensive.

to see so it is important that the area to be inspected is clean. Be especially thorough in looking at the area between the valve seats and cylinder wall. A crack in the valve seat may be repaired, but it is better to find a better block if at all possible.

The next area to check is the concentricity of the cylinders to determine if they will need reboring and if so, how much. This check requires the use of an inside micrometer. Measure the cylinder diameter at various points about halfway down the cylinder and compare. If the difference in these measurements is excessive, then the cylinders will need to be rebored to a standard oversize and fitted with new pistons. New pistons are available in standard oversizes of 0.010, 0.020, 0.030, 0.040, 0.060, 0.080, 0.100 and 0.125. It is recommended that the amount of bore be as small as possible so that a sufficient amount of cylinder wall thickness is left to prevent weakening and possible overheating. The original bore of the Ford engine is 3.875-3.876.

New pistons should be selected prior to the boring operation so the machine shop will be able to properly size the bore for the required clearance of 0.002 inch. Most builders like to leave the last 0.001 inch of clearance to be accomplished through the honing operation for a more accurate piston fit. If a block is either out-of-round excessively or has already been bored in excess of 0.125 inch, the alternatives are to either select a different block or to have that block bored and new

Block damage in the early Model A necessitates replacement blocks such as this one. Notice the markings.

sleeves installed to bring the cylinders back to standard size. A good machine shop or competent engine rebuilder should be consulted on this decision.

If the block appears usable at this point, the next thing to check for is broken castings or damaged threads. Broken castings usually occur at the oil pan flange or the valve chamber bolt ears. When it has been determined that the block is good and all damage has been repaired, it should be taken to a good machine shop to be cleaned, cylinders bored, head and deck surfaced and the valve seats ground to the proper angles and depth. These operations must be carried out prior to the bearing work because the caustic solution used for the cleaning process will damage the main bearing Babbitt material beyond use.

Inspection of the crankshaft

The backbone of any engine is the crankshaft. Proper checking of the crankshaft is a task that will probably best be left to the skills of a good crankshaft grinder. The first important dimension is the straightness of the shaft. The grinder or machine shop will know how to check this point. The next important check is the run-out and diameter of the main and rod bearing journals. The original diameter of the main bearing journals was 1.624 inches. Maximum allowable run-out is 0.002 inch. The original diameter of the rod journals was 1.499 inches. Tolerances in excess of this amount indicate that the crankshaft should be reground to a standard undersize. If the crankshaft is reground, then the bearings must be repoured and refitted no matter how good they may look. Most Model A engines found now have already been reground and

The rear oil slinger must be turned to receive a Chrysler rear main seal.

rebored. Marks to indicate this repair will usually be found on the crank or on a tag attached to the block.

While the crankshaft main and rod journals are being turned by the crankshaft grinder, the rear main-bearing oil slinger should be turned down to a diameter of 2.140 inches. This modification will allow for the installation of a Chrysler rear main oil seal which will provide better oil control than the original Ford configuration. Rear main seal leakage is a common problem with the Ford engine and anything which decreases the oil loss in this area will ensure a cleaner and more dependable engine. The Chrysler seal is available as FEL-PRO BS6378.

This is the time to inspect the crankshaft timing gear for wear and damage. It is recommended that this gear be replaced along with the camshaft timing gear. The crankshaft gear will have to be changed by the machine shop because it requires a gear puller or press to remove.

Camshaft service

It is a good idea to have the camshaft checked for wear and damage by a camshaft grinder. The camshaft may be reground, but it is possible that this regrinding may change the valve timing slightly and affect engine performance. (Camshaft specifications are found at the end of this chapter.) The camshaft timing gear should be replaced with a high quality gear of laminated construction for greater wear and strength.

Connecting rod service

The pistons are removed from the connecting rods by removing the

Timing gears become worn and chipped through years of use and must be replaced.

Notice the laminated construction of the new fiber timing gear. Always replace both timing gears for better service.

lock rings that are located on either side of the piston and pushing the pin out. The rods will be fitted to the new pins that should come with the pistons. This fitting will be done by the machine shop and must be performed on a special reamer. The rods will be checked for proper alignment at this time and realigned if necessary. This process is illustrated elsewhere in this chapter.

If the builder is considering using the old rod bearings and the rod journals on the crankshaft have not been turned, then this is the time to inspect the bearings for pits and galling. If the bearings show any of these defects, or show black areas, a sign of burned bearings, they should not be reused. The rods will need to have new Babbitt poured and fitted to the crankshaft journals. When the rods are returned from the machine shop, they will be fitted to individual crank journals and numbered for proper installation. Shims should be installed in the rods to allow for future adjustment.

Cylinder head service

The cylinder head does not usually require much attention other than a good cleaning by hot tank to remove rust and chemical deposits in the water jackets. The head should be resurfaced on a surface grinder to ensure a perfectly flat mating surface and good gasket adhesion. The material removed will slightly increase the compression ratio, but the increase will probably not be noticeable to the driver.

General preparation

Many builders feel that the best way to achieve a good finish on the block, head and other castings is to have them glass bead blasted.

Typical defects of rod and main bearing Babbit material in engines after many years of use and neglect.

This will also help to uncover any hidden defects not found by other methods. It is also a good idea to consider having the block and crankshaft magnafluxed while at the machine shop. A complete balance job will also cost a little more, but will provide for a smoother-running and longer-lasting engine. Remember that the parts have been changed and the original Ford balance is no longer valid.

After cleaning, all cast parts should be painted Ford engine green. There were at least two shades of engine green used on the Model A. Although either shade is acceptable, all parts should match. All sheet metal parts such as the oil pan, oil filler tube and flywheel housing shield should be painted with black enamel after cleaning. Refer to the current MARC/MAFCA Judging Standards for proper finish on all engine components. Be sure that all necessary parts are ready for assembly and that all new gaskets, fasteners and washers are available.

Reassembly

The first step in the reassembly of the block is pouring new Babbitt and fitting the main and rod bearings. These operations are best left to specialists because specialized equipment is required that is not found in most shops. The technician must be provided with the block, crankshaft and rods. After pouring the bearings, they must be align bored to the exact diameter to fit the journals with a clearance of 0.001 inch. A

Rods should be checked for twist and corrected on straightening fixture.

The rod-straightening fixture also corrects bends in the rod. Notice the deflection at the right.

detailed description of this operation may be found in *Engine Rebuilding by the K. R. Wilson Process* by Doc Wishon, in the May-June 1982 issue of the *Model A News*, published by the Model A Restorers Club. At the same time the main bearings are fitted to the crankshaft, the rod bearings will be fitted to the rod journals and piston pins. When the pistons are fitted to the rods, the rods should be checked for straightness on a special rod straightening fixture.

When the block is returned from the machine shop, the crankshaft should already be installed, the main bearing caps torqued to 50 foot-pounds and the cotter pins replaced on all nuts. The rods and pistons should have been assembled, but if they were not, the operation is accomplished as follows: Heat the pistons in boiling water for a short time to allow them to expand so that the pins may be pushed easily through the fitted bores by hand. Do not force or try to beat the pins into the bores as the fit in the rod end is only 0.0003 inch and in the piston boss 0.0002 to 0.0005 inch. Replace the piston pin lock rings on either side of the piston. If the cylinders have been bored to an oversize of 0.100 or more, the piston tops should be beveled on a lathe to keep them from contacting the head gasket. Cut a forty-five-degree bevel on the piston top to a width of about 0.135 inch.

Before the pistons are installed in the block it is very important that the exact size of the bore be determined from the shop that performed the boring operation. Some shops will bore the piston clearance into the cylinders and others will leave the last 0.001 or 0.002 to be gained through honing.

The honed finish of the cylinders is important because it determines how well the rings seat into the cylinders. A crosshatch pattern of approximately sixty degrees is usually found to work very well. The crosshatch pattern is controlled by the speed of the up-and-down movement of the stone during the honing operation. Be sure that plenty of oil is used while honing the cylinders.

The next step in the reassembly is to thoroughly clean the cylinder bores of all foreign matter that might damage the pistons or rings. A good cleaning may be accomplished with hot water and laundry detergent. When the cylinders are clean to the touch of a white cloth, they should be coated with a film of fresh oil to preserve the finish and prevent rust from forming.

1. The first parts to be installed into the block are the valve lifters into the lifter bores. It is recommended that adjustable lifters be installed rather than the solid, nonadjustable lifters that were originally in the Ford engine. These lifters will allow for a more precise adjustment of the valve lash and make it easier to take up the difference caused by resurfaced valve seats and reground camshaft. This is a good time to mention that all parts installed in the new engine should be coated with lots of Lubriplate or STP to ensure that they are properly lubricated when the engine is first started.

2. After coating all the bearing surfaces with lubrication, the camshaft is inserted into the block. The timing gear should then be installed on the camshaft with the timing mark in line with the timing mark on the crankshaft gear (as shown on page 228 of the Ford Service Bulletins of February 1928). To facilitate easier timing of the engine later, it is help-

ful to slightly enlarge the timing pin hole on the timing gear with a drill bit so the timing pin will slip into it more positively. The timing gear nut should then be tightened securely.

3. The next step is the assembly of the valves and valve guides. The guides should have been numbered by the technician who resurfaced the valve seats. If this job is done properly, the guides should have been in place as a pilot for the valve grinding equipment and each will have been matched to its own bore and marked. The valves should be ground into their seats at this time using a hand grinding tool and Prussian blue until an even seat shows on both the valve and the valve seat. The valve seat should be 1/16 to 3/32 inch wide.

Place each valve guide into the bore and insert the valve, slipping the valve spring and retainer in place using a valve spring compressor. Be sure that the valve guides remain in position and seated against the block inside the valve chamber as the springs and retainers are put in place.

4. Separate the piston rings into sets and arrange them in the order in which they will be installed on the pistons and by the cylinders in which they will be used. One at a time, insert the rings into the cylinder and

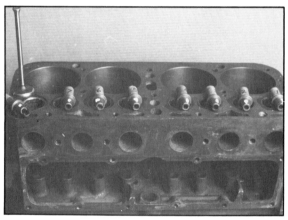

The valves and guides should be matched to their bores when the valve seats are cut. Notice the numbered guides.

The valve grinding or lapping tool is turned back and forth between the hands to seat the valves. A valve-grinding compound is used to lap the valves which are then checked with Prussian blue for seat contact.

level them with a piston head. Using a feeler gauge, check the end gap of the rings for the following limits:

Lower ring gap —0.008 to 0.010 inch
Center ring gap—0.010 to 0.012 inch
Upper ring gap —0.012 to 0.015 inch

If the ring gap is too small, file the ends of the rings until it is correct.

5. Install the rings on the pistons, being sure to stagger the ring gaps so that none of them are in line. Check to see that ring groove clearance is 0.001 inch.

6. Using a ring compressor, carefully install the lubricated piston and rod assemblies into the cylinders. Be sure that the split in the skirt of the piston, if present, is toward the driver's side of the engine. To be sure that the rods and pistons are correctly assembled, be sure that the dipper on the rod's big end faces toward the camshaft. The rods should have already been numbered by the technician who fitted the bearings to the crankshaft journal. As the rods are being lowered into the crankcase, care should be taken that the rod bolts do not strike the crankshaft journals. As each rod is assembled to the crankshaft, the bearing cap should be torqued to 30 to 35 foot-pounds and cotter pins installed to lock the nuts. Remember to use plenty of lubrication as the rods are installed. All rod bearings should have shims at this time so that they might be adjusted at a later date as wear occurs.

7. Assemble the rear main-bearing oil-drain pipe to the rear main bearing cap. If possible locate a late rear main cap (A-6327-B) because it provides for a larger (3/8 inch) drain pipe which allows for better drainage and leakage control. The later cap is also better because it has a thicker boss for the bolts and may provide more strength than the older design. Use of this cap requires the longer (four A-21214-B 3/16 inch) bolts.

8. Assemble the oil-pump drive gear assembly and spring into its bore in the valve chamber. This is a very important gear and it is critical that it be in excellent condition. This gear drives both the oil pump and the distributor.

9. The valve clearance should now be adjusted using the procedure described on page 338 of the April 1929 Ford Service Bulletins for determining that the valves are on the heel of the cam. The valves should be adjusted to 0.010 for the intake valves and 0.013 for the exhaust. Some adjustable pushrods can be adjusted only when on the toe of the cam rather than the heel. If there is any error, it is better to be on the loose side because valves will be burned if the clearance is too tight.

10. Assemble the valve chamber cover to the side of the block with ten 5/16 inch cap screws and lockwashers. Ensure that the proper gasket is in place and sealant is used to prevent leakage. Torque the valve chamber bolts to 15 foot-pounds.

11. Assemble the crankshaft oil slinger to the crankshaft, making sure that the cup side faces out. Assemble the crankshaft pulley and ratchet to the crankshaft. Many restorers like to use the new-style two-piece pulley because it can be removed from the engine while it is in the car and makes any necessary service easier to perform.

12. Install the front seal packing and the camshaft thrust plunger and spring to the front cover. Install the front cover and gasket to the front

of the engine with six cap screws and washers and the timing pin with washer.

13. Assemble the oil pump spring to the oil pump and install the oil pump to the engine being sure that it is seated firmly in the block, and that the gear slots and pin are aligned.

14. Assemble two gaskets to the oil pan with gasket sealer and install the oil pan on the block using twenty 5/16 inch cap screws and lockwashers. If the pan is an early 1928, install the clean-out plate and gasket with six cap screws and washers. Be sure the main bearing seal packing is installed in the oil pan before assembly.

15. Assemble the two gaskets to the block using gasket sealer. Be especially heavy with the sealer at the camshaft bearing to prevent leaks at that point. This gasket only goes on one way so that the camshaft bearing is covered. Install the flywheel housing to the block, aligning it with the locating dowels. Install the four cap screws and lockwashers around the center of the housing, torque them to 35 foot-pounds and run heavy wire through all the bolt heads. The upper two bolts are the longer ones and should not be tightened at this time. These housing with the block. Be sure the main bearing seal packing and dipper tray are installed in the oil pan before assembly.

16. Assemble the two dowel pins onto the crankshaft and install the flywheel assembly to the crankshaft. The flywheel should have already had a new starter gear installed. If this gear has not been replaced, the old one may be removed by knocking it off with a heavy hammer and punch. The new gear is installed by heating it in a fireplace or barbeque (an oven probably would not be large enough or hot enough) until it expands and is able to be dropped onto the flywheel. Make sure that the bevel of the gears is toward the rear. Install the four bolts holding flywheel to crankshaft and torque to 80 foot-pounds. Secure these bolts with a lock wire. If there is a problem aligning the flywheel with the crankshaft, use a couple of head studs screwed into the crank as guides to slide the flywheel into position.

17. Install clutch pilot bearing in flywheel and pack with grease if not a sealed bearing.

18. Assemble the oil return pipe to the valve chamber side cover with two cap screws, gaskets and special washers.

19. Assemble the flywheel housing shield to the flywheel housing with three 1/4 inch capscrews.

20. Install the cylinder head studs to the block using a stud-installing tool to prevent distortion. It is a good idea to run a 7/16 inch coarse thread tap into the stud holes to clean the threads before screwing in the studs. Oil the threads and turn the studs in as far as possible by hand to be sure that the threads are good. To accomplish a uniform height of 1/32 inch above the nut, as called for in the Judging Standards, the eleven short studs should protrude 2 3/4 inches above the block. The stud between the number three and four spark plug should protrude 3 1/2 inches for the earlier cable clamps and 2 29/32 inches for the later clamps. The two long studs for the water outlet should protrude five inches from the top of the block.

21. Using a copper-asbestos head gasket sprayed with manifold and head gasket sealer, assemble the head and gasket to the block and secure

with fourteen 7/16-20 head nuts. Torque all nuts to 30 foot-pounds. Torque a second time to 45 foot-pounds following the same sequence. Torque the nuts a third time (while the engine is still hot) to 50 pounds. After the engine has been installed and run for about twenty minutes, torque all nuts again to 50 pounds. It is a good idea to put radiator sealer in a new engine before it is run the first time to prevent leakage around the head studs and gasket. In many cases the head will leak no matter how well the engine has been built. Torque the head nuts again after about 100 miles of driving.

An antiseize compound should be used on all cylinder-head studs to prevent seizure in the block should they ever have to be removed for any reason.

22. Attach the manifold assembly to the block using a metal asbestos gasket and the special washers and 7/16 inch nuts. The manifold assembly should be surfaced by a machine shop before installing to ensure a good fit to the block. This is a common point of exhaust leakage on the Model A engine. The glands may or may not be used as original. Many restorers find a better fit by using a one-piece gasket and leaving the gland rings out. Use an antiseize compound on all manifold studs to prevent problems later if the unit has to be removed.

23. After installation of the oil filler tube and dip stick, the engine is now ready for installation into the chassis.

Engine installation

If the car is still in an assembled condition, the engine may be installed in the same way it was removed. The easiest and most common condition of the car at this time is a bare frame which gives a few alternative methods of installation.

The original method of engine installation at the Ford plant was to lower the engine into the frame with the transmission attached. This works just as well now as it did then. Many restorers like to install the engine before the rear axle and driveshaft which simplifies the assembly. If a hoist is not available, the block without the head and flywheel may be lifted into the frame by two people rather easily. The front engine yoke should be secured to the frame with new springs, nut, bushing and cotter pin before attaching the engine.

Another method of installing the engine is to place the engine on

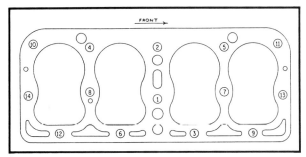

The cylinder head nuts must be torqued in the proper sequence to prevent warpage of the head.

the shop floor and block in a vertical position. The frame may then be lowered over the engine and slipped under the flywheel housing mounts. One person may now easily lift each end of the frame up under the engine and block it in position. The engine mounts can now be secured. Be sure to safety wire the four bolts holding the rear mounts to the frame. Regardless of which method of installation is used, new rear mounts will usually make it necessary to spread the frame rails apart to allow the flywheel to fit between the engine mounts on the frame. This may be done with a hydraulic jack and a piece of wood or with a Porta-Power.

Before the transmission may be installed, the pressure plate and clutch disc must be in place. Align the disc with an old main drive gear. Be certain that the long side of the clutch hub is facing the transmission when the disc is installed.

Remember when preparing to start the new engine for the first time to pour the last two quarts of oil down the distributor hole to be sure that the rods pick up oil as soon as the engine turns. Five quarts of oil will fill the engine.

Adjusting rod and main bearings

After the Model A engine has been run for a time, whether it be an original unrestored engine or a recently rebuilt one, it may become necessary to adjust the Babbitt bearings. If the rod or main bearings are allowed to become loose enough to cause a knock, damage to the bearings will occur very quickly.

The clutch disc must be aligned with a main drive gear as a pilot shaft. Tighten the pressure-plate cover bolts after the alignment.

With nothing more than a few simple tools and some time, adjustment may be accomplished by anyone with a little patience. It is not necessary to remove the engine from the car to adjust the bearings, but the front must be raised and braced with jackstands for safety.

1. Drain the oil pan and remove the flywheel housing shield. Remove the dip stick and twenty 5/16 inch bolts holding the oil pan and remove the oil pan from the engine.

2. Remove the carburetor, manifold, oil return pipe and valve chamber cover. Remove all four spark plugs.

3. Remove the cotter pins from the main and rod bearing nuts. The nuts for the front main bearing are located behind the generator and below the water pump. The center bearing nuts are found in the valve chamber and below the water inlet above the dip stick.

4. Remove the rear main bearing cap using a 3/4 inch socket and 9/16 inch square socket on the bolt heads. Remove shims from each side of the bearing so that they are equal in thickness. These shims are laminated and may require a sharp knife to separate. Add or subtract shims until there is a slight drag on the engine when it is cranked by hand. Add shims until there is the proper 0.002 inch clearance on the bearing. This clearance may be checked accurately with the use of a Plastigage, which may be purchased at a good auto parts store. This material will give an accurate measurement of the bearing clearance.

Proceed with the center and front bearings in the same manner, leaving the bolts loose after adjusting each one. If there are no shims, or not enough to adjust the bearings, carefully file the cap until the proper clearance is achieved.

5. Adjust the rods using the same method as the main bearings.

6. Tighten all bearing caps to the proper torque as called for in the engine assembly section. Be sure that all bearing surfaces have been lubricated. Replace all cotter pins with new ones.

7. When all bearings are tight, be sure that the engine will turn and that no bearings are adjusted too tightly.

8. Clean all gasket surfaces and coat them with sealer. Install all gaskets and put front and rear main bearing seals in the oil pan. Install oil pan and tighten all bolts.

9. Install flywheel housing shield, valve chamber cover, oil return pipe, manifold and carburetor. Replace the spark plugs and refill the engine with oil. Start the engine and let it warm up and idle for a few minutes to check for leaks.

Engine specifications and tolerances

Unit construction

Cylinders—4, cast en bloc—L-head type
Bore—3 7/8 inches
Stroke—4 1/4 inches
Weight complete with clutch and transmission—473 pounds

Displacement—200.5 cubic inches
Torque—128 foot-pounds
Horsepower—40 at 2200 rpm
Piston compression—76 pounds gauge
Firing order—1-2-4-3

Sets in frame at 3 1/3-degree angle
Flywheel—cast iron with starter ring gear shrunk on
Weight—63 pounds with gear
Diameter—outside over ring gear, 14.2 inches
Ring gear—112 teeth
Ring gear ratio to engaging gear—11.2:1
Offset of cylinders—1/8 inch
Crankshaft
Material—drop forged, special Ford manganese steel
Weight—28 pounds finished
Main bearings—3
Diameter—1 5/8 inches
Length—No. 1—2 inches
No. 2—2 inches
No. 3—3 inches
Connecting rod bearings—all 1 1/2 inch in diameter; 1 5/8 inches long
Length—22 1/8 inches from front of front bearing to rear of rear bearing
Rear flange thickness—3/8 inch
Total square inches of main bearing surface—11 1/2 square inch
Gear—25 spiral teeth
Connecting rods
Material—steel forging I-beam section
Weight—1 pound 6 ounces
Length—7 1/2 inches
Bearing—(lower) Babbitt—1 1/2 inches diameter x 1 5/8 inches long
Piston pin bearing—bronze 1-inch diameter x 1 5/8 inches long
Piston, ring and pin
Material—aluminum
Weight—1 pound 7/8 ounce
Weight with rings and pin—1 pound 8 3/4 ounces
Weight with rings—1 pound 4 1/4 ounces
Diameter—3 7/8 inches
Length—3 29/32 inches
Ring groove width—upper two, 1/8 inch; lower, 5/32 inch
Ring groove depth—7/32 inch
Pin hole—1 inch diameter
Skirt—split for expansion
Three rings per piston—2 compression and 1 oil
Material—cast iron, cast singly

Diameter—3 7/8 inches
Width—compression—0.1235, oil—0.1550
Type—one-piece diagonally cut
Piston pin material—machined seamless steel tubing, hardened, ground, honed and polished
Diameter—1 inch
Length—3 inches
Oil Pump
Material—body malleable casting
Type—gear, gears fitted to 0.001 inch
Drive—spiral gear on center of camshaft
Shaft—steel, mounted in bronze bushings
Capacity—1 gallon per minute at 1000 rpm
Valves
Material—chrome silicon alloy
Lift—0.287 inch
Opening—1 3/8 diameter
Seat angle—45 degrees
Spring pressure—36 pounds
Stem diameter—5/16 inch
Stem seat diameter—1/2 inch
Timing—Intake opens 7 1/2 degrees before TDC; intake closes 48 1/2 degrees after BDC; exhaust opens 51 1/2 degrees before BDC; exhaust closes 4 1/2 degrees after TDC
Tolerances
Piston in cylinder—0.002 inch maximum
Piston ring gap—lower, 0.008 to 0.010; center, 0.010 to 0.012, upper, 0.012 to 0.015
Ring groove clearance—0.001
Piston pins—0.0003 maximum
Pin in piston—0.0002 to 0.0005 shrink fit
Connecting rod side play—0.008 to 0.012 (lower end of rod)
Clearance between piston bosses—0.040 to 0.053 (upper end)
Connecting rod to crankshaft—0.001
Crankshaft end play—0.002 to 0.004
Main bearing clearance—0.001
Camshaft bearing clearance—0.003 maximum
Camshaft tension—35 pounds approximately
Exhaust valve in valve guides—0.002
Intake valve in valve guides—0.001 to 0.0015
Timing gear backlash—0.004
Flywheel wobble—not more than 0.005

Ford Engine Power Chart

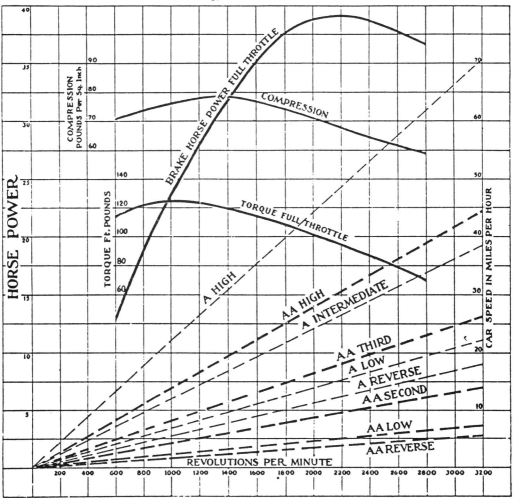

This chart shows the curves resulting from a recent test of the Ford engine.

At the left, near the top, is a notation "Lbs. Per Sq. In." reading 60, 70, 80, 90. Opposite this is the "Compression Curve." At the foot of the sheet are figures that number the perpendicular lines. These are Engine R.P.Ms. Thus the Compression Curve indicates compression developed at various R.P.Ms.

About the center is a notation "Torque Ft. Pounds." reading 60, 80, 100, 140. Opposite this, a curve marked "Torque Full Throttle," shows the Torque, or turning power, that the motor develops at various R.P.Ms.

It will be seen that the Torque Curve and Compression Curve are almost parallel. This shows that Compression and Torque exist in direct ratio to one another and explains why a motor that is leaking compression stalls easily because as compression decreases, torque also decreases.

At the left margin and beginning at the bottom is a column "Horse Power" reading from 5 to 40.

The curve marked "Brake Horse Power Full Throttle" shows the B.H.P. developed at various R.P.Ms. Comparing this with the other Curve it will be seen that H.P. depends directly on R.P.Ms., while Torque and Compression do not gain by an increase in R.P.M.

The dotted Transmission lines are self-explanatory. The figures at the extreme right indicate M.P.H. and those at the bottom R.P.Ms. Since it is shown that "Pulling Power" as indicated by the Torque Curve is greatest at 1000 R.P.M., a comparison of the charts shows the truck to have its greatest pulling power in low gear at about 2.5 M.P.H., in second at 4.5 M.P.H., in third at 8 M.P.H., and in high at 14 M.P.H.

This information is of utmost value in determining the speed at which the truck, with a big load, will climb a hill.

The Compression Curve shows the speed at which the motor has the greatest braking power. This is of tremendous value when descending a hill with a big load.

Engine power chart from 1930 sales catalog.

Chapter 8

TRANSMISSION AND CLUTCH ASSEMBLY

THE transmission of the Ford Model A is of the selective-sliding-gear type. It has three speeds forward and one reverse with a standard shift pattern. The case and gears are designed with a view to compactness and high mechanical efficiency. All the gears are made of heat-treated chrome-alloy steel, laid out and manufactured in the most careful manner. The main shaft runs on ball bearings and the reverse idler on a bronze bearing.

The ratios of the various gears of the Model A three-speed transmission are 3.75:1 in reverse, 3.12:1 in low, 1.85:1 in second and 1:1 in third. These gears permit a speed of approximately 15 mph in low gear at 2000 rpm, about 26 mph in second and about 46 mph in third at the same rpm. This will vary slightly according to the rear tire size. (A chart indicating power and speed in the different gears is shown elsewhere in this book.)

A properly functioning transmission is essential to the smooth operation and driving pleasure of the Model A Ford. The care taken in the selection of the components and accurate assembly of this unit will prevent the occurrence of such problems as noisy operation and jumping out of gear. Because of the considerable effort required to remove the Ford transmission for repair, it is important to ensure that the restoration is done correctly the first time.

The first area to be covered will be the removal of the transmission assembly.

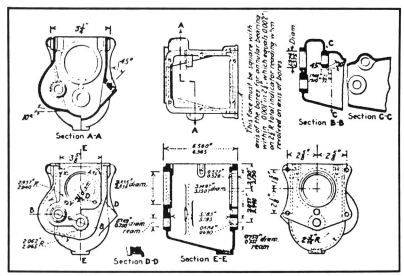

The transmission case. The iron from which the case is cast is of a special grade, indicated in the Ford plant by the letter B. The maximum hardness of the casting must not exceed 228 on the Brinell scale.

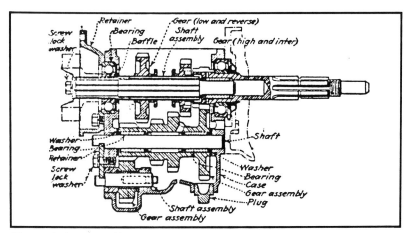

Transmission assembly.

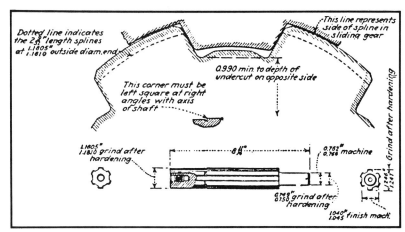

Transmission mainshaft. This shaft is annealed at 1,500° F, cooled in the furnace to 1,150° F and allowed to cool in the air to produce a hardness of from 187 to 217 Brinell. It is again heated to 1,500° F in cyanide and then quenched in oil. It is drawn in oil at 400° F. The hardness is from 477 to 532 Brinell. The shaft is mounted in ball bearings of ample size.

Removal with engine previously removed from chassis

1. Remove lower transmission plug to drain lubricant and replace plug. Remove the brake pedal to cross shaft rod by removing the cotter pins from clevis pins and removing clevis pins at brake pedal and at brake cross shaft from underside of frame crossmember. Remove the emergency-brake lever to cross shaft rod by removing cotter pins from clevis pins and removing clevis pins from hand-brake lever and cross shaft. Remove pedal shaft collar pin and shaft collar. Remove clutch trunion clevis pin and slide pedals off shaft being careful not to lose the antirattler spring washer between the pedals.

2. Place the transmission lever in neutral and remove six 5/16 inch cap screws holding the transmission top to the case. Lift the transmission top with shift lever and emergency-brake handle straight up and off transmission.

3. Remove cotter pins from the six castle nuts around the U-joint housing half-caps. Remove the six 3/8 inch nuts and bolts joining the caps to

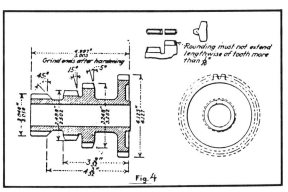

The cluster gear.

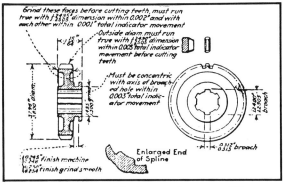

The low- and reverse-sliding gear.

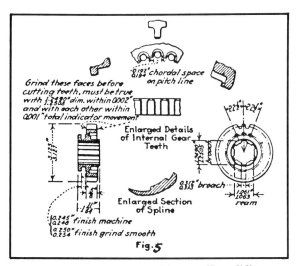

The high- and intermediate-sliding gear.

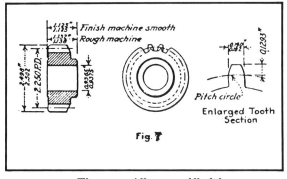

The reverse idler gear. All of these gears are made from annealed forgings and are heated to 1,500° F in cyanide and quenched in oil. They are then drawn in oil at 400° F for one hour.

the transmission. Remove the two 3/8 inch nuts and bolts with lock-washers holding the two U-joint half-caps together, and remove the caps.

4. Firmly grasp the clutch housing and transmission assembly and slide forward, off the driveshaft splines. Remove the transmission from under the car for disassembly.

Removal with engine in car

1. From inside car, remove floor mat and floor boards. Disconnect battery ground cable and battery-to-starter cable using a terminal puller. Remove battery hold-down clamps and remove battery from car.

2. Remove cotter pins and remove the four castle nuts from the rear spring U-bolts securing the rear spring to the rear crossmember. Remove the two spring-to-frame retaining bars from under the rear spring. Remove the rear shock arms from shock absorbers by removing the cotter pin, bolt and castle nut. Remove the bolt from arms and slide arm off the shock absorber shaft. Remove cotter pins and clevis pins from both emergency and service brake rods at the rear backing plates. Remove the brake rod return springs from the rear radius rod bracket by removing the 5/16 inch nut and bolt. Disconnect the speedometer drive cable from the torque tube by unscrewing the cap at the gear case and pulling out the cable.

3. Remove the front radius rod cap nuts by removing cotter pins and two nuts, two springs, two sleeves and the lower cap. Pull the front radius rod down and place a two-by-two block of wood between the flywheel housing and radius rod to permit removal of the lower two 3/8 inch cap screws securing the clutch housing to the flywheel housing.

4. Refer to removal with engine out of chassis and complete steps one, two and three.

5. Raise the rear of the car approximately eight to ten inches until the top of the rear spring will clear the rear spring U-bolts and (important!) support the frame or rear bodysill adequately to permit the rear axle to be rolled forward approximately five inches to disengage the driveshaft from the U-joint. On 1929-31 models the brake cross shaft will support the driveshaft. On early models the driveshaft may be held up with wire to prevent it from dropping the forward end to the floor.

6. Remove the universal joint by using a 9/16 inch socket and extension to remove the bolt securing the front yoke to the transmission shaft.

7. Remove eleven 3/8 inch cap screws securing the clutch housing to the flywheel housing, being careful to support the weight of the transmission when the last screws are removed to prevent the possibility of warping the clutch disc. If the disc is to be reused, the warpage could cause the clutch to drag.

8. Firmly grasp the clutch and transmission assembly and pull rearward. Sometimes the main drive gear may be stuck in the pilot bearing and some careful prying may be necessary to slide the assembly off the engine.

9. Lower the transmission to the floor and remove from under the car.

10. Remove the fourteen 5/16 inch pressure plate cap screws two turns at a time so as not to distort the pressure plate. Remove the pressure

plate and clutch disc.

11. Cut wire and remove the four flywheel cap screws.

12. Remove starter and carefully pry the flywheel off the crankshaft dowel pins by prying slightly, then turning the engine one-half revolution and prying again until the flywheel is free. Use caution as the flywheel weighs sixty-three pounds!

Basic transmission disassembly

1. Remove clutch inspection-plate screws and plate from clutch housing.

2. Remove clutch bearing hub spring and slide hub and bearing forward off sleeve.

3. Tap old clutch release bearing off hub and discard bearing.

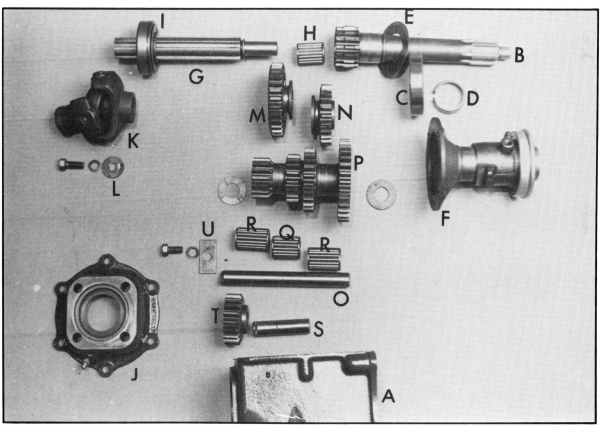

Transmission parts identification			
A. Transmission case	A-7006-B	K. Universal joint	B-7090
B. Main drive gear	A-7017-B	L. U-joint front knuckle retainer	B-7095
C. Main drive gear ball bearing	A-7025	M. Low-reverse sliding gear	A-7100
D. Bearing retainer snap ring	A-7045-B	N. Second-high sliding gear	A-7101
E. Bearing oil baffle	A-7040	O. Countershaft	A-7111
F. Main drive gear bearing retainer	A-7050	P. Countershaft gear	A-7113
G. Mainshaft	A-7060	Q. Bearing	B-7118
H. Mainshaft pilot bearing	A-7118	R. Bearing	B-7121
I. Mainshaft ball bearing	A-7065	S. Reverse idler shaft	A-7138-AR
J. Bearing retainer	A-7085-BR	T. Reverse idler gear	A-7141
		U. Countershaft & reverse idler retainer	A-7155

4. Remove four 7/16 inch cap screws and lockwashers inside the clutch housing securing housing to transmission case. Carefully tap the housing to separate.

5. Remove four 5/16 inch cap screws securing the clutch hub sleeve to the transmission and pull sleeve off over the main drive gear shaft.

6. Using a soft brass rod, tap the main drive gear and bearing out through the front of the transmission case. Discard the mainshaft pilot bearing.

7. Carefully spread the main drive gear bearing retainer collar and slide off the main drive gear.

8. Tap the main drive gear ball bearing off the gear using a soft iron or brass rod. Do not strike the bearing directly, as it is hardened and could chip and cause injury. Discard the bearing but save the grease slinger washer.

9. Remove the U-joint if not already removed by using a 9/16 inch socket to unscrew the cap screw securing the forward yoke to the mainshaft. Engaging both sliding gears on the cluster gear will prevent the mainshaft from turning while removing the bolt.

10. Cut wire securing four 7/16 inch cap screws holding the rear bearing retainer to the case, and remove the cap screws and retainer.

11. Tap mainshaft and bearing out of rear of transmission case using a soft mallet or rod. Slide second and high gear (small) and low and re-

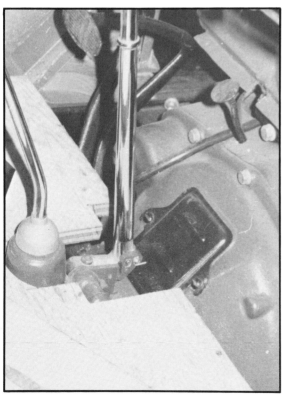

A-7222 BR transmission top cover for late 1928 to early 1929 cars.

A-7222 C transmission top cover for late 1929–31 cars.

verse gear (large) from mainshaft as shaft is pulled out from the rear of the case.

12. Tap mainshaft bearing off mainshaft as in step 8. Discard bearing and save grease slinger washer.

13. Remove 3/8 inch cap screw and retainer plate securing reverse idler shaft and cluster shaft at back of transmission. Pull reverse idler shaft out of rear of transmission case.

14. Tap cluster gear shaft out of front of transmission case as the front hole is reamed 0.0005 inch larger than the rear to reduce lubricant loss from the rear hole.

15. Remove the cluster gear and thrust washers (on 1928 and early 1929 only) and reverse idler gear.

Disassembly of transmission top and shifter assembly

1. Remove hand-brake assembly on 1929-31 models by removing two 7/16 inch cap screws on side of top cover. On mid-1928 to early 1929 models, remove cotter pin and 3/8 inch castle nut and special head bolt securing hand-brake lever to housing. Remove lever and flat-head machine screw securing brake ratchet to housing, and remove the ratchet.

2. Secure shift lever in a vise and clamp locking pliers to the end of the lever to avoid the possibility of the shift lever spring accidentally snapping out while the spring retainer is being removed.

3. Using a large screwdriver depress the shift lever spring while using another screwdriver to pry the spring retainer from the lever seat.

4. Using a 1/8 inch drive, drive the shift-fork retaining pins from the shift forks. Save these pins.

5. Remove shift rails one at a time from the front of the shifter housing

Removal of shift lever spring retainer.

Removal of pedal shaft using hammer and punch.

by using a nail in the pin holes to push the rails out of the housing.

6. Remove screw slot plug on the left front of the shift housing and tap out shift rail detent plugs and spring.

7. Shift-lever spring tension should now be fully released so that locking pliers may be removed from the lever and the spring allowed to be easily removed.

8. Remove any pins and retainers that may have dropped inside the shift housing tower.

Clutch housing

1. Remove pedal shaft by cutting the head off the retainer rivet and riveting on through the housing using a 3/16 inch drift. Using a long punch, drive the pedal shaft out of the clutch housing.

2. Remove clutch-release fork by driving groove pin up from bottom of fork. The 1928-29 models use a 1/4 inch pin and woodruff key, while the 1930-31 models use a 5/16 inch pin only. Slide the clutch-release fork off the right side of shaft and slide shaft out of left side of housing.

3. Remove shaft bushings from housing using a bushing driver or collapse the thin-wall bushings using a sharp pin, tapping lightly with a hammer. Be careful not to damage the cast iron bore.

4. Remove clutch trunion from clutch pedal by unscrewing trunion and sliding trunion nut from pedal.

5. Remove pedal bushings as in step three.

Cleaning and inspection

1. Degrease all parts in a suitable safety solvent. Do not sandblast gears, shafts or bearings. Exterior of housings may be sandblasted but be very cautious in thoroughly washing all abrasives from all cavities or serious

Use a sharp-pointed punch to remove thin-wall bushings.

Clutch pedal trunion nut wear.

damage could occur when the unit is put back in service.

2. Inspect all cases for stripped threads, cracks, chips or excessive wear where parts are pressed together. Carefully dress all flat machined surfaces with a broad flat file to remove any burrs or nicks. Inspect all gears and shafts to be reused for galling on wearing surfaces indicating a breakdown of the hardened surfaces. Good-quality replacement parts are available or good, used original parts can usually be found.

3. Normally, the following parts should be replaced: pedal shaft, pedal bushings, clutch trunion nut, clutch trunion clevis pin, clutch release shaft and bushings, front ball bearing, mainshaft pilot bearing, cluster gear bearings, cluster gear shaft, clutch release bearing, clutch disc, ring gear and pilot bearing.

4. Clutch inspection

A. Check pressure plate levers for excessive wear at bearing contact point. Check also for scoring or cracking at clutch disc contact surface. Lightly scored plates can be resurfaced or a rebuilt pressure plate may be purchased.

B. The clutch disc used should be a spring center type. If reusing the old clutch disc be sure that there is no indication of grease on the lining. The clutch lining faces should not even be touched with the fingers.

C. The flywheel should be inspected for scored clutch surface and resurfaced if necessary. If a machine shop resurfaces the clutch face, be sure that an equal amount of material is removed at the pressure-plate bolt surface to maintain the original dimensions for flywheel depth from the pressure plate. Check the starter ring gear for wear. Most wear will be on five or six teeth in two locations 180 degrees opposite each other, due to the fact that the Model A engine will always come to rest with all four pistons about halfway up the bore. This means that the starter always hits the ring gear in the same two areas. To remove the ring gear, place the flywheel over some blocks so that the ring gear can be driven off using a heavy hammer and a soft iron rod. Remove the pilot ball bearing from the flywheel by tapping it out with a soft iron rod. The old pedal shaft is ideal for this purpose. Do not use an old cluster gear shaft since it is hardened steel and a chip could cause serious injury in addition to damaging the hammer face.

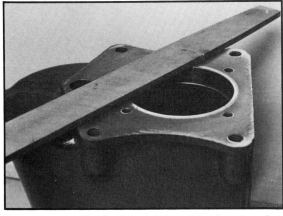

Typical hand filing of machined surface.

Some common defective transmission parts.

Transmission reassembly

1. Paint the exterior of all case parts Ford engine green except for the following parts, which should be painted black: U-joint half-caps, clutch inspection cover, clutch release lever, clutch adjusting trunion and nut, clutch and brake pedals. All nuts, bolts, washers, screws, clevis pins and collars are plain or cadmium plated. For current finish acceptability, check the MARC/MAFCA Judging Standards.

2. Screw drain plug into transmission case and clamp square end of plug in a sturdy workbench vise very tightly to support the transmission for reassembly.

3. Check the bore of the cluster gear to see if it is machined all the way through. If it is, insert a lightly oiled long roller bearing, then a short roller bearing and another long bearing into the cluster gear bore. If the bore is not machined smooth at the center, use a long roller bearing in the small gear end, a spacer in the center and a short roller bearing in the large gear end. Set the cluster gear in the transmission case. If the case is the 1928 style that uses thrust washers on each end of the cluster gear, slip the washers between the case and gear on both ends. Remove transmission from vise and set the rear face down on a clean bench. Insert a long, narrow screwdriver into the cluster gear bore and align the thrust washers and gear with the case bore. Insert the new cluster gear shaft from the front of the case but do not drive it all the way through the rear bore. Using a feeler gauge, check that the cluster gear end play is no more than 0.020 inch. If greater than that, a shim washer will have to be made and inserted at the rear of the cluster gear.

4. Replace the transmission in the vise and apply a light film of non-hardening brush-on gasket sealer to the cluster shaft rear bore in the case. Rotate the shaft so that the lock bar flat will face the reverse idler bore, and tap the shaft flush with the front face of the transmission case. The cluster gear shaft is always removed and installed through the front of the case because the rear is reamed 0.0005 inch smaller than the front to reduce lubricant leakage.

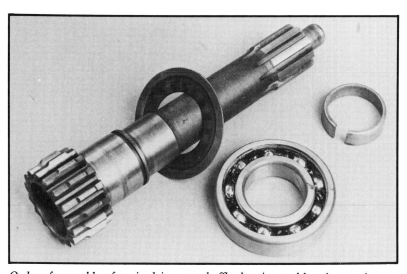

Order of assembly of main drive gear, baffle, bearing and bearing retainer.

5. Place reverse idler gear in rear of case with beveled edge of teeth facing to the front and with gear shaft bushing oiled. Press the reverse idler shaft into the rear bore and align the gear with the shaft. Be sure that the lock plate groove faces the cluster gear shaft. Apply a light film of gasket sealer on the last 1/2 inch of reverse idler shaft and press shaft in until the lock plate groove is flush with the rear of the case. Apply gasket sealer to the lockplate bolt threads, use a new lockwasher on the bolt and tighten to approximately 15 foot-pounds using a 9/16 inch wrench. Check the gears for free-spinning condition with a slight clearance or backlash.

6. Warm the front ball bearing by placing it on a 100 watt light bulb for ten to fifteen minutes. Some replacement bearings come with an external groove and snap ring. Remove and discard this snap ring. If the bearing is shielded, leave one shield in place but remove the shield on the side of the bearing facing the oil baffle. Place the bearing oil baffle over the main drive gear with recessed center away from gear.

Early cases with a cast shoulder for bearing stop use an oil baffle with a 2 3/4 inch outside diameter. Later cases using a retainer ring in case groove use a 2 7/8 inch outside-diameter oil baffle. Incorrect oil baffles can cause oil leaks or the baffle will scrape the transmission case. (Refer to Model A Service Bulletins page 379.)

7. Using insulated gloves, slide the warm ball bearing on the main drive gear with oil baffle between gear and bearing.

8. Tap bearing fully on shaft using a soft iron or brass rod. The bearing outer race must not touch the oil baffle. If it touches, then the baffle is

Typical bearing installation using soft iron or brass rod to tap home.

bent or installed backward. If the bearing is heated enough, it will go on without tapping and would be removable.

9. Slightly spread the main drive gear bearing retainer using snap-ring pliers and set in place on gear. Make sure that the retainer fits into groove on drive gear.

10. After the bearing has cooled, use a plastic-face mallet to tap the bearing into the front of the transmission case until the bearing stops against the retainer ring in the case.

11. Using four 5/16-18x3/4 inch cap screws and lock washers, secure the main drive gear bearing retainer to the front of the transmission case with a new gasket and gasket sealer. Be sure that the oil-return notch in the gasket is at the bottom to align with the hole in the case. Ensure that the clutch release bearing spring hole is at the top. Torque the retainer bolts to 10 foot-pounds.

12. Slide an oiled, short roller bearing into the bore on the inside of the main drive gear.

13. Assemble oil baffle to rear side of mainshaft and collar assembly with recessed center away from collar. Early cases with cast bearing retainer shoulders use a 2 7/16 inch outside-diameter oil baffle. Later cases using retainer ring in case groove use a 2 9/16 inch oil baffle.

14. Warm and install the rear ball bearing in the same manner as the main drive bearing. Check baffle for clearance between bearing outer race.

15. Check mainshaft for pilot bearing spacer ring on front or a machined-in-place shoulder between pilot bearing portion and start of splined portion.

16. After bearing has cooled start the mainshaft into case, pilot bearing first. Slide the low-reverse (large) gear onto splines of mainshaft being sure that the collar portion of gear for shifter forks faces to the front of the transmission. Slide the second-high (small) gear onto mainshaft, being sure that the collar portion faces to the rear. The collar portion of both gears should be adjacent to one another. Carefully slide the assembly into position in the transmission case. The pilot portion should slide easily into the main drive pilot bearing. The rear bearing may need careful tapping to seat it into the case.

17. Check the operation of all gears at this time. Slide the low-reverse gear to neutral between the reverse idler, and third from the front of the cluster gear. Slide the second-high gear fully forward over the main drive gear. Rotate the main drive gear and the mainshaft should turn at the same speed with no scraping or binding. This is third or direct drive. Slide the second-high gear to the rear to a position between first and second front cluster gears. (Rotating the main drive gear should not result in mainshaft rotation.) Slide the second-high gear rearward to engage the second gear from the front of the cluster gear. (Rotation of the main drive gear should result in slower rotation of the mainshaft in the same direction.) Slide the second-high gear back to neutral position between first and second from front cluster gear. Slide the low-reverse gear forward to engage the third from front gear on cluster gear. Rotate the main drive gear; the mainshaft should rotate much slower than the main drive gear in the same direction. Slide the low-reverse gear fully

to the rear and rotate the main drive gear. (The mainshaft should rotate much slower and in the opposite direction from the main drive gear.)

18. If all positions check out correctly, apply gasket sealer to the rear bearing retainer cap and transmission case rear and install retainer with the grease fitting on the bottom side using four 7/16-20x1 inch drilled head cap screws and lockwashers. Torque to 35 foot-pounds. Safety wire these bolts making sure that the twisted wire ends are pushed close to cap.

19. Place the universal joint on the mainshaft splines. Place heavy washer locating tab in U-joint and secure to shaft using a 3/8-24x1 inch hex-head cap screw and new lockwasher. Torque to 22 foot-pounds. The basic transmission is now complete.

Transmission shifter and tower assembly

1. Paint casting Ford engine green.

2. Examine both shifter rails for excessive wear in the area of the lever ball contact. In particular, the second-high rail sustains a great deal of wear. Resting a hand on the shift lever while driving causes wear at this point. Using a file, square the ball contact faces and remove sufficient material from the other fork for equal hole size on both. These forks are interchangeable, so if a better one can be found, either fork could be used. The shift-lever ball should be built up on both front and rear portions with weld—but do not build up the sides. Carefully file the ball round to fit the shift-fork opening with a minimum of looseness but with no binding. Clean and plate the shift lever. See MARC/MAFCA Judging Standards for proper finish.

3. Place the top cover casting on bench with open bottom facing you and with shifter-shaft bore openings facing up. Slide low-reverse shift shaft (one with evenly spaced plunger notches) into the left-hand bore with the notches to the top. Slide the shaft into the casting while passing it

Wiring of rear bearing retainer. Notice grease fitting opening faces down.

115

through shift forks until retainer pin hole in fork aligns with hole in shaft. The shift-lever-ball notch in fork should face to the center of the housing. Insert pin from top side of fork and, using a long rod through the housing lever opening on the pin head, tap the bottom tubular portion with a tapered punch to slightly expand it.

4. Slide shift shaft plunger into plunger bore with round end toward shifter shaft. Follow plunger with spring and other plunger with round end facing out. Position first shift shaft even with top of housing, with detent notch facing plunger.

5. Start remaining shift shaft for second-high gear (with unevenly spaced plunger notches) into housing bore with notches facing previously installed shift shaft. Using a narrow screwdriver depress shift shaft plunger to allow shaft to be slipped into the housing. Pass shaft through remaining shift fork being sure that shift-lever-ball notch faces the other shift fork. Using a needle-nose pliers, insert pin from top side of fork after aligning hole in fork with hole in shift shaft. Expand bottom of pin as done for the first shaft.

6. Push each shift shaft to the last of the three detent positions.

7. Using a large vise, clamp the shift-lever spring between the jaws and carefully compress it while firmly holding the coils to prevent the spring from snapping out of the vise and causing injury. (Eye protection is advised during this operation.) When the spring is fully compressed, release the vise just enough to expose one third of the coil face. Using sixteen-gauge mechanics wire, secure the exposed coils tightly with one wrap of wire. Twist the wire near one end and cut off excess to leave a 1/4 inch twist.

8. Slightly loosen the vise and, while firmly grasping the spring to prevent it from snapping out, rotate it one-third turn. Tighten the vise and again wire as before.

9. Apply a third tie of wire as before. When finished, there should be a

Compression of transmission shift-lever spring in vise. Notice addition of third wire.

Compressed shift-lever spring in top cover.

fully compressed spring with three equally spaced tie wires. Handle with care to prevent an accident.

10. Drop the compressed spring into the transmission top with the twisted wire ends facing the shift shafts.

11. Insert the newly plated shift lever into the transmission top, passing the ball end through the compressed spring. Clamp the casting in the vise and, using needle-nose pliers, slip the spring retainer into the groove located one inch above the lever ball. Be sure that the retainer is set in the notch with the spring seat portion lower than the notch portion so that the retainer will not slip out when the spring is released. Cut the retaining wires and, using locking pliers, jerk the wires out of the housing, making certain that the retainer is correctly centered.

12. Push one shift shaft up to the first notch so that the shaft protrudes from the housing. Push the other shaft in the opposite direction until the lever ball drops into the slot on the shift fork. Push the lever to move the shift fork to the second notch, or neutral position. Push the other shift fork to the second notch. Both shafts should then be even with the forward face of the top casting.

13. Screw the plug into the shift-plunger thread hole on the top left side of the housing.

Clutch housing assembly

1. Paint the clutch housing Ford engine green. The inspection plate, collars, pedals, clutch linkage and front radius rod caps are black. Consult the current MARC/MAFCA Judging Standards for finish on nuts, bolts and washers as various options are available to the purists.

2. Some new pedal shafts are rough finished and poorly sized. Dress the shaft with emery paper if required. Align the hole one inch from shaft end with hole in clutch housing. Lightly oil the shaft and housing bore. Using a hardwood block to protect shaft end, tap the shaft into the housing until pin hole lines up with hole in housing. Secure with new pin and peen-in to lock when inside of housing.

3. Using a bushing driver and vise, press bushings into pedals. A slight chamfer on the edge of the bushing bores will greatly ease this operation.

4. If pedals were originally equipped with grease fittings, knock them out with a cold chisel and drill a grease hole through the newly installed bushings. Grease fittings may be added to pedals not originally equipped if desired. Drill and tap a hole for threaded fittings or use new 5/16 inch drive-in fittings.

5. Ream pedal bores to allow easy rotation on the new shaft. A machine shop can do this on a piston-pin reamer in short order.

6. Slide the brake pedal on the pedal shaft with the spring-type spacer washer.

7. Clutch-pedal trunion-nut bore may require boring out to oversize to accommodate a new oversize trunion nut to compensate for wear. Again, a machine shop would be able to do this operation along with making an oversize trunion nut.

8. Slide rebuilt clutch pedal on shaft and apply collar on end while aligning collar pin hole with hole in pedal shaft. Insert pin and cotter pin to secure collar.

9. Chamfer clutch-shaft bores on housing and, using a bushing driver, carefully drive bushing in place. If desired a grease fitting can be added to reduce wear on the clutch shaft. Drill and tap to bushing boss as required on the bottom side to permit use of a grease gun from the underside of the car. Align ream these two bushings until the shaft is snug but rotates freely in the bores. The 1929 shafts had clutch-release lever pinned and keyed to shaft. The 1930-31 models used a larger grooved pin only. To use 1929 levers on replacement shafts the lever holes will have to be drilled out to 5/16 inch. Do not drill oversize, as groove pin must be a tight fit. For accurate alignment, drill lever while on shaft and do not drill completely through opposite side. Leave just enough clearance for a press fit of the pin.

10. For an easier-operating clutch an early multidisc-clutch release arm may be used. It is approximately 3/4 inch longer than the standard 1929-31 arm and provides more leverage. A slight bit of filing is required on the pedal for trunion rod clearance when this arm is used.

11. Install clutch release arm on clutch release shaft and pin securely. Slide shaft into clutch housing with lever facing to rear and guide shaft through clutch release fork. Be certain that the machined face of the clutch release fingers faces forward to engage clutch bearing hub surface. Tap release shaft fully into housing and align hole in fork with pin hole in shaft. Again, pin these parts securely, checking that the external release arm faces to the rear. Install pedal trunion nut and screw trunion into nut. Periodic lubrication of these parts will reduce wear.

12. Apply gasket sealer to the transmission face of the clutch housing and to the front of the transmission case. With a new gasket between the castings, secure the clutch housing to the transmission using four 7/16-14x1/2 inch hex head bolts and lockwashers. Torque to 35 foot-pounds using a 5/8 inch socket.

13. A vise and wood blocks can be used to press a new clutch release bearing on the clutch bearing hub. Be sure that the flat thrust face of the bearing faces the front toward pressure plate.

14. Apply a thin film of grease to the hub sleeve and slide it over the

Installation of bushing using hand bushing driver. Notice location of optional grease fitting for pedal.

transmission main drive gear retainer and engage clutch fork into the hub using grease at all contact points.

15. Using pliers, hook spring into hub hole near grease fitting and secure the other end into hole on main drive gear retainer.

16. Slip front radius rod bolts through holes in bottom of clutch housing. A new felt oil wick should be installed in the large hole between the bolts. Align notches in the bolt heads and slide lock pin in place to secure bolts and felt. If bolts drop below the lock pin the bolt holes are worn and washers will be required under the heads.

17. Support the transmission and clutch in a level position and pour in enough 600-weight or SAE No. 250 lubricant to come to the level of the filler plug on the right side of the case.

18. Make sure that the transmission sliding gears are both in neutral position, and that shift forks in the transmission top are in neutral position. Using a new top gasket, carefully engage forks with sliding gear grooves.

19. Set top on transmission and secure with four 5/16-18x3/4 inch and two 5/16-18x1/2 inch hex-head bolts and lockwashers. Torque to 11 foot-pounds.

20. Transmission must be maintained in a level position once lubricant is installed or leaks will occur at front and rear bearings or top cover vent hole.

21. Clutch, flywheel and pressure-plate assembly are covered in chapter on engine assembly.

Installation of transmission top cover and alignment of shift fork with sliding gear.

Chapter 9

COOLING SYSTEM

THE power-producing medium of the Ford Model A engine, as it is in any internal combustion engine, is heat—the heat produced by the compression of the fuel-air mixture, the heat produced by the exploding gases and the heat produced by the friction of metal parts moving against one another at hundreds of feet per second. If this heat were not transferred away from the engine, the operating components would glow red hot, the oil would ignite and the pistons and rings would expand and seize, welding themselves to the cylinder walls.

It is important that the heat of any gasoline engine be kept within the bounds which will provide the greatest operating efficiency, and at the same time be below the danger point of engine damage. The medium which controls the dissipation of this heat is the cooling system.

Cooling of the Model A is accomplished by a centrifugal water pump mounted on the front of the cylinder head and driven by the fan-and-pulley assembly with a V-belt from the crankshaft. Water enters the block centrally on the left side. As the water is circulated through the jackets in the block and head, heat is transferred to the water which then travels out of the head back into the radiator through the outlet on the front of the engine. The radiator cools the water by circulating it through the three rows of tubes which are exposed to the air being pulled through it by the fan and by the movement of the car.

Overheating causes

The overheating of the cooling system can serve as an indicator of many problems in the engine and a knowledge of these causes of overheating will help the driver to locate and repair many serious faults before they become big problems. Some of the common causes of overheating in the Ford Model A engine are:

Lack of coolant—Keep the coolant in the radiator filled to the proper level. Be sure to use a good antifreeze rather than plain water because the boiling point is higher.

Lack of oil—Low oil level in the engine will increase friction and create more heat. The oil also serves as a heat transfer medium and must be kept full.

Loose fan belt—The fan belt should be kept adjusted to a deflection of one inch by loosening the generator bracket and moving the generator out to tighten the belt.

Incorrect spark timing—If the spark is set in a retarded condition, it will cause overheating and a loss of power.

Loose fins on the radiator—If the tubes on the radiator are not in contact with the fins they cannot transfer the heat from the coolant effectively.

Brakes out of adjustment—When the brakes are dragging, the engine will be pushing against them and will cause a strain on the cooling system.

Leaks—When the system leaks, the level of the coolant will be lowered and overheating will occur. Leaks around the radiator-cap gasket will allow coolant to be thrown out on the hood and windshield and cause the appearance of overheating even at normal temperature. The system should not be overfilled as this will also cause the appearance of over-

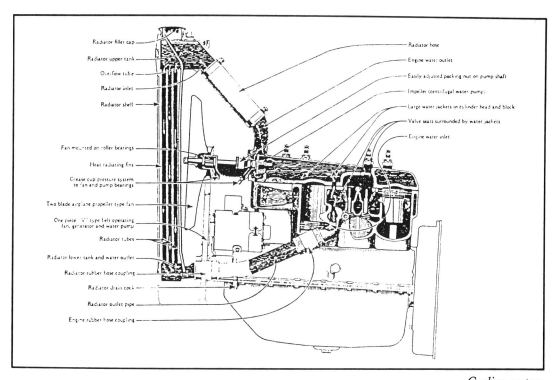

Cooling system.

121

heating as the coolant seeks its own level and throws it out the overflow tube.

Insufficient radiator area—Many early replacement radiators, especially on the 1928-29 models, do not have enough capacity to provide sufficient cooling. The 1930-31 models have increased area and do not normally have the problems that the earlier cars seem to experience.

Clogged passages—Clogged coolant passages in the radiator and in the block from rust and chemical deposits will restrict the flow and cause overheating to occur very quickly.

Loss of coolant from overflow—If a loss of coolant is experienced through the radiator overflow, it may be corrected by using the modification noted on page 450 of the April 1930 Service Bulletins which involves adding a baffle to the top of the tank to prevent coolant from splashing out.

Front end alignment—If the front wheels are seriously out of alignment, increased stress will be placed on the engine and cause overheating.

Any sign of overheating should be investigated as soon as possible to prevent damage to the engine. It is a good idea to always carry extra water and antifreeze solution and a spare fan belt on any tour. These preparations will help with all but the most serious cooling system problem experienced with the Model A, a broken fan blade.

When the fan breaks, it usually does so with a great deal of violence, most often tearing its way through the top or side of the hood, leaving at the very least a large dent. Though this seems a disabling situation, it has been shown that the car may be driven if the other blade is cut off the same amount to balance them as closely as possible. If the blade damages the radiator, the tubes may be pinched off enough to prevent coolant loss and the car can be driven for a good distance if kept at a steady speed to keep air flowing through the radiator.

The fan

The fan of the Model A Ford is sixteen inches in diameter and is made of welded, pressed steel. It is attached to the water pump shaft by a key and a 7/16-20 nut and cotter pin.

The most common defect found in original Model A fans is the cracks that are usually present on the blades near the hub. If these cracks are found, they must be repaired or the fan cannot be used. At 60 mph, the Model A fan is turning at over 4000 rpm creating a tremendous force on the ends of the blades. This force combined with vibration can cause a cracked blade to let go very easily. If someone happened to be near the engine at the time the blade came loose, the results could be disastrous.

Cracked blades may be repaired, but it is recommended that the job be performed by an expert welder. It is important that all rust be removed from the blades or additional deterioration from the inside will cause more cracks or breaks to appear. After the blade is TIG welded, it must be balanced carefully. The balancing may be accomplished by mounting the blade on an old water-pump shaft and placing it on either V-blocks or on old razor blades clamped in a vise.

It is suggested that the fan be kept painted a very high gloss. If a fine, hairline crack should appear, it will show up much more quickly on the painted surface.

Many restorers believe that the use of a four-blade truck fan will increase the cooling capacity of the Model A. However, it has been proven that there is no significant increase in cooling with the use of this fan and it is not recommended, as the four-blade fan will tend to increase the loads on the impeller thrust washer of the water pump and could cause premature failure.

There are reproduction fans available that are of very good quality and should be considered for a car that will be driven very much. The use of one of these new fans will reduce the likelihood of losing a fan blade on a tour. Be sure that the new fan is of the welded, stamped-steel type. There are also some cast aluminum fans available, but they are not authentic for use on a restored car.

The water pump

The Ford Model A water pump can be considered the heart of the cooling system. Without the flow of coolant provided by the water pump, even the slight thermo-syphon effect of the unfettered and unpressurized Model A cooling would not be sufficient to keep the operating temperatures below dangerous levels. Anything less than a total rebuild or replacement of the water pump for a new engine is out of the question.

The construction of the Ford water pump, although more complex than the one in a modern automobile, is simple enough that anyone can rebuild one with little skill or effort.

Removal of water pump

1. If the engine is equipped with a stock two-blade fan, the water pump may be removed without removing the radiator. If a four-blade fan is present, the radiator will need to be removed. Remove the fan belt by loosening the generator bracket and slipping the belt over the fan and

Ford water pump, from left to right: rear bushing, felt retainer, bearing sleeve, bearing and felt with retainer.

123

pulleys. Remove the cotter pin and castle nut from the water pump shaft and remove the fan by carefully and lightly tapping the fan hub or pulley from the rear. If the radiator has been removed, the nut may be put on backward and tapped to loosen the fan pulley. Do not tap too hard on the pulley or strike the fan; it may be cracked or bent. The fan may be turned to a horizontal position and rolled upward or downward and off the shaft. Be careful not to strike the radiator fins, as they are easily bent. As the fan is removed, be careful not to lose the woodruff key from the shaft or hub.

2. Remove the four 3/8 inch nuts and lockwashers holding the water pump to the head and carefully pry the pump housing from the engine. The gasket will probably stick to the head or pump and will have to be scraped off. Again, be very careful not to strike the radiator with the front of the pump shaft.

Disassembly

1. Tap the shaft from the front and pull the shaft and impeller out from the rear of the pump housing. Along with the shaft will come the impeller washer. When the shaft is pulled from the housing, the retainer, felt seal and metal washer will come out of the rear of the front bushing housing. A retainer, seal and washer will also be removed from the front of the housing. After the roller bearing is taken from the housing, the roller bearing sleeve may be removed from the pump.

2. Unscrew the packing nut from the rear bushing and drive the bushing out of the housing. Depending on the date of the pump, the rear bushing will be either brass or steel with a brass insert. Clean the casting and paint Ford engine green.

Reassembly

1. The first step in reassembly is to install the new rear bushing by driving it into the housing with a soft lead or brass mallet. Make sure that the lubrication hole in the bushing aligns with the grease-fitting hole in the casting, or the shaft will not receive lubrication.

2. Install the front bearing sleeve and roller bearing followed by the washers, felt seals and retainers.

3. The impeller must now be driven onto the water pump shaft. Some restorers like to use a stainless-steel water pump shaft to prevent rust

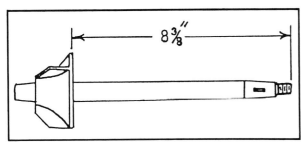

For proper fitting, the impeller should be driven on the shaft 8 3/8 inches.

and cut down on wear but a stainless shaft will cause more wear on the bearing and bushings.

4. Place new packing in the packing nut and screw it onto the rear bushing. Remember that the 1928-29 pump has a brass nut and the 1930-31 has a die cast nut.

5. Place the water pump impeller washer on the water pump shaft, making sure that the point fits into the slot on the impeller. Insert the shaft and washer assembly through the bearings and assemble it to the pump. The pump is now ready to be reinstalled.

Installing the water pump

1. The first thing that must be done prior to reinstalling the pump is to check the end clearance of the impeller shaft. The factory specifications call for a clearance of 0.010 inch, which will ensure that the shaft will not move enough to cause the packing not to seat, creating a leak at the packing nut. Place the pump in position on the head without a gasket and check the end play of the shaft with a feeler gauge.

If the end play is excessive, it is because the shaft rides on a boss inside the head which has become worn. The best way to repair this end play is to build up the end of the water pump shaft with braze or weld, and grind it down until the play is zero. The proper clearance will be made up by the water pump gasket.

Another good method of taking up the end play is to drill and tap the end of the shaft for a 5/16 inch thread and install a brass or soft-steel round head screw. The head of the screw may be ground until the end play is zero. This end play is the key to having a water pump that does not leak.

Many restorers solve the pump leakage problem by replacing the original packing and seal with a modern seal and spring. This configuration also negates the need for end play adjustment, as the end play is taken care of by the spring behind the impeller. These leakless pumps are available from various vendors and are highly recommended.

2. Place the gasket and gasket sealer on the water pump and place the pump on the mounting studs. Replace the hex nuts and washers and tighten them securely.

3. Place the woodruff key in the slot on the water pump shaft and slip the balanced fan-and-pulley assembly over the shaft. Replace the 7/16-20 nut and cotter pin, being sure that the fan is pulled up tightly on the shaft.

4. Replace the fan belt and tighten the generator bracket to secure it. If a new fan belt is needed, a Gates 700 belt should be available through any good auto parts outlet. Be careful of some replacement belts sold through Model A parts vendors. Some of them are too small to fit properly. The fan belt is especially difficult to install on the early engines with the Powerhouse generator because the larger diameter prevents the generator from being pulled as close to the block as the later models.

5. Replace the two grease fittings on the water pump casting and grease the pump with a pressure gun. If original-type conical fittings are being used, it is important that the rear fitting have the screw-on cover. This cover prevents air from being sucked into the pump and cavitating the

impeller. The newer-type Zerk fittings do not require this cover.

6. Refill the cooling system with a good-quality antifreeze solution of at least fifty percent. Antifreeze has a higher boiling point than water and will greatly reduce the chance of overheating. It will also prevent the formation of rust deposits in the radiator and block. Do not run the engine with plain water at any time.

The radiator

If the water pump is the heart of the cooling system, then the radiator is the lungs. The core tubes and fins of the radiator are the medium by which the heat is transferred from the coolant to the air. As the warm coolant enters the top tank and flows through the tubes into the bottom tank the temperature of the coolant is reduced considerably before it enters the engine through the inlet and back into the block.

It is very important that the fins and tubes be kept clear of debris and dirt so that the air can flow easily through them. If any fins are broken loose from the tubes, the heat will not be transferred and cooling will not be accomplished efficiently. Just as the outside of the radiator must be kept free of dirt, the inside must be kept clear of sediment, rust and chemical deposits or the coolant will not flow properly. It should be apparent that the radiator's quality and condition are very critical to the operation of the engine, and its restoration should not be shortcut in any way.

Specifications of the Model A radiator
1928-29
Type—fin and tube
Number of tubes—94 staggered
Number of fins—106 long, 11 short
Cooling surface area—360 square inches
Capacity—3 gallons
1930-31
Type—fin and tube
Number of tubes—102 angled
Number of fins—120 long, 12 short
Cooling surface area—374 square inches
Capacity—3 gallons
1930-31 AA Truck
Type—fin and tube
Number of tubes—136 angled (four rows)
Number of fins—120 long, 12 short
Capacity—3 1/2 gallons

Removal of radiator

1. Drain cooling system by turning drain cock on lower water-return pipe. Some drains are positioned in such a way that the coolant drains onto the tie rod and makes a mess of things. If this is the case, turn the front wheels to the lock position in either direction and the tie rod should move out of the way. This does not apply if splash pans are present.

2. Remove the upper radiator hose with two clamps and the lower hoses

and clamps. Remove the headlight conduit, pulling back the wires from the conduit. Disconnect the horn, pulling the two wires back through the conduit. Remove the radiator support rods (1/2 inch hex nut at front, 9/16 or 5/8 inch hex nut at rear), pull radiator forward one inch and remove the hood assembly, placing it on end on a carpet to protect the finish.

3. Remove the radiator-to-frame 3/8 inch bolt, nut, cotter pin and springs by holding the bolt head under the frame and using a U-joint and extension with a deep 9/16 inch socket. Slide the radiator to one side to clear the fender and lift the free side. Remove the mounting pads from the mounting flange and/or frame.

4. Remove the shell from the radiator by removing the 12-24 special head screws, nuts and washers.

Inspection and repairs

The radiator should be checked by a competent radiator shop with the proper equipment for finding leaks and damage. If the shop is not familiar with old cars, it should be reminded that the system is not pressurized and that no more than fifteen pounds of pressure should be used to check for leaks, or the seams may be broken.

The shop will clean the radiator with a caustic solution to remove all of the rust, corrosion and chemical deposits present. If necessary, the mechanic will also rod out the tubes to clear any hard deposits from the core which prevent circulation. This operation requires the removal of the tanks from the core, and is not something that is recommended for the home restorer to try.

If the radiator is damaged beyond reasonable repair, the entire core may be replaced by the radiator shop for quite a bit less than the price of a new radiator. Some of the new radiators available from parts vendors are not of the quality required for efficient cooling, so they should be inspected carefully for the proper specifications. Some early replacement radiators from the thirties or forties were not the quality of the originals, so cooling problems may occur, especially on the 1928 and 1929 models.

A comparison of the two basic styles of radiators for the Model A Ford. The one on the left is for the 1930–31 cars. The one on the right is for the 1928–29.

After the radiator is repaired, it will be painted with a special radiator and chassis paint which will not insulate the surface as common enamel will.

Sometimes, a radiator can be made to look better by removing the core and turning it around, placing the rear to the front. The front of the radiator usually takes the most damage and has the most dents.

An improvement in radiator function may be accomplished by changing the splash plate according to the instructions found on page 450 of the April 1930 Ford Service Bulletins.

Reinstallation

The radiator may be reinstalled in reverse of the removal procedure. Don't forget to refill with a good antifreeze solution and check for leaks after the system has warmed up.

Be sure that a gasket is secure inside of the radiator cap before replacing the cap. If the gasket leaks, it will cause a loss of fluid and the appearance of overheating when the water is thrown out the top of the radiator. If a motometer cap is used, be sure that there is a seal between the shank of the gauge and the cap.

Chapter 10

THE FUEL
SYSTEM

THE fuel system on the Model A was one of the features of the New Ford that Henry Ford himself had a strong hand in creating and designing. Henry insisted on simplicity because he believed that the simpler the design, the fewer the problems. The fewer parts a system has, the less likely that it will fail.

The Model A fuel system is a statement in simplicity. With a gravity flow distribution from the fuel tank and a carburetor with a single bolt holding it together, it is doubtful that anyone could come up with a more efficient and reliable system by the standards of the day.

As shown by the diagram, the fuel system consists of the fuel tank, the sediment bowl and fuel line, and the carburetor.

The fuel tank

The Ford Model A fuel tank is unique in that it serves three purposes. Besides performing its regular function as a fuel reservoir it forms the cowl of the car and acts as a dashboard and instrument board. Furthermore, by this location it is possible for the gasoline gauge to be directly operated and in the most convenient position for continuous inspection. It was reported upon the introduction of the Model A in 1927 that the gasoline tank had given more trouble to the production men at Ford than any other part. Henry Ford called for the two sections of the tank to be constructed of steel plate coated with a rustproof alloy and welded watertight. It took the introduction of a mercury welding process to finally accomplish the job successfully.

The tank holds ten gallons and is made of No. 18 USS GA (0.049-0.051) terne plate. The specifications called for full cold-rolled, low carbon open-hearth auto body stock, free from waves and pit marks; coating to be not less than twelve pounds per thousand square feet of surface; coating to contain not less than sixteen percent tin. Model A tanks were produced at the rate of approximately 140 pieces per hour.

There were four basic versions of the A-9002 fuel tank, not including the small change in 1928 which placed the choke rod grommet in a different location. In 1930, the major change to the tank was that the front of the tank was no longer attached permanently to the cowl as in the 1928-29 models. The 1929 design tank was used on the AA and commercial models until June of 1930 with a modification to allow the use of the later 1930-31-style gas cap. The next change was in mid-1930 when the 1931-style instrument panel was adopted. In May of 1931 the new A-9002-E tank was adopted which incorporated the indented firewall and carburetor-mounted sediment bowl.

Removal of the fuel tank

1. Disconnect the fitting at the carburetor with a 1/2 inch wrench and drain the fuel tank. Remove the fuel line under the tank from the shutoff to the firewall.
2. Remove the two fillister head screws holding the steering column bracket to the tank. Disconnect the choke and carburetor control rod at the carburetor, and pull it up and out of the grommet at the tank.
3. Remove the floor mat and hand-hole cover and disconnect the battery

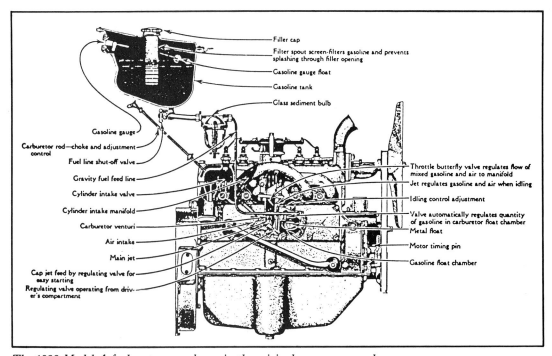

The 1928 Model A fuel system, as shown in the original owners manual.

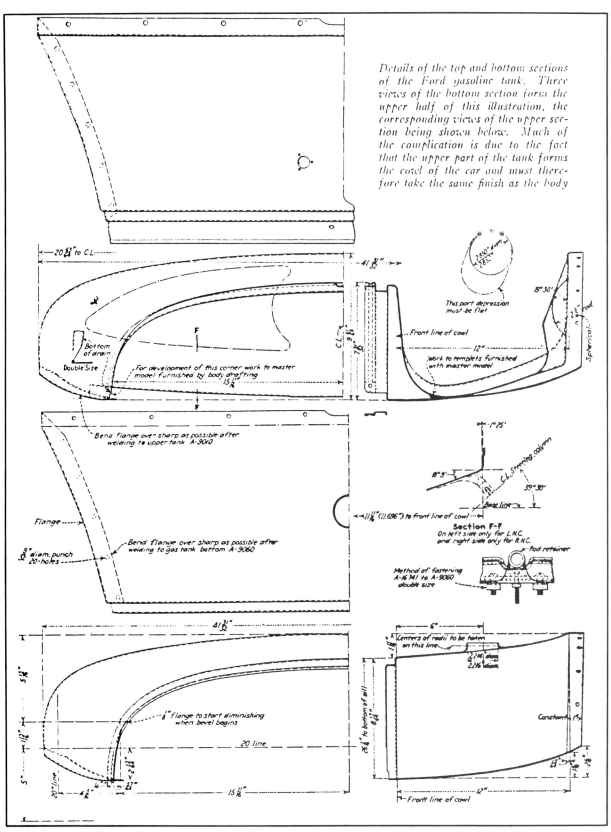

Details of the top and bottom sections of the Ford gasoline tank. Three views of the bottom section form the upper half of this illustration, the corresponding views of the upper section being shown below. Much of the complication is due to the fact that the upper part of the tank forms the cowl of the car and must therefore take the same finish as the body

1928 fuel tank components.

cable. Remove the four screws holding the instrument panel to the fuel tank and pull the panel away. Disconnect the wires from the ammeter, dash light and ignition switch. Disconnect the ignition switch as described in the electrical chapter and remove the switch and wires from the channel under the tank.

4. Remove the four or six screws holding the dash rail to the tank and body, and remove the rail. Remove the ten nuts, bolts and washers holding the tank and underwindshield trim panel in place and remove the panel.

5. Take off the hood by removing the rear hood hold-down clamp and lifting the hood off the car.

6. On the 1930-31 models remove the ten pan head screws holding the tank to the firewall and the four clamps on the cowl sides. The tank is now ready to be lifted out.

7. On the 1928-29 models remove the ten bolts, nuts and lockwashers and four clamps on either side of the cowl on the inside. Remove the eight special bolts and nuts on the front side of the firewall. Remove the two screws and two wires from the coil and remove the coil from the firewall. Disconnect the hood support rods and pull them away from the tank. Disconnect the wiper tube or wires if present on the firewall. Lift the tank off the car.

Inspection and restoration

The biggest problem facing restorers with respect to the fuel tank is usually rust. Many of the Model A tanks have sat outside for fifty years without caps, and moisture has been allowed to accumulate. A good number of these tanks have rusted through the bottom and have deteriorated to what used to be considered an unrestorable condition. With good Model A parts becoming more scarce, it is important for the modern restorer to know how to salvage and use whatever original parts he may have. Even the worst fuel tank may be salvaged if a good one of the correct type cannot be found.

Removing the rust is the first problem to attack. The only way this

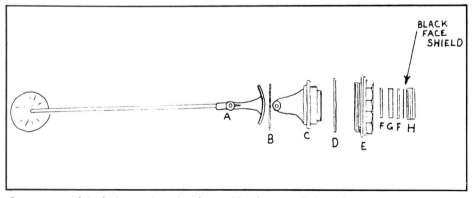

Components of the fuel gauge in order of assembly: A. gauge dial and float assembly, B. shim, C. gauge, D. gasket, E. gauge-to-flange nut, F. gasket, G. lens, H. cover.

can be reasonably accomplished is to have the tank dipped either in an acid or electrolytic rust-removing process. Most shops will coat the tank with a sealer to stop future rust, or the restorer may purchase and apply his own solution.

Sometimes, an additional problem arises when the dip process reveals extensive rust-through in the tank. These holes can be repaired if they are in a location that cannot be seen. A good radiator shop can usually solder a patch over the rusted area and effectively seal the tank. Be sure that any repairs are done before the tank sealer is applied, as most sealers are flammable.

Another difficulty with some tanks is removal of the screen in the filler neck. These screens are sometimes rusted badly and stuck solidly in the tank. A chisel and hammer used to turn the screen and unscrew it may be the only answer. These screens are used as a fire preventive measure more than as a filter, so they are important. They also prevent gasoline-pump nozzles from going too far into the tank and damaging the float arm, so the filler screen should be replaced in all cases.

Gasoline gauge

The fuel gauge on the Model A is as simple as could be imagined. It is merely a hinged float with an indicator on the instrument panel side which rides behind a small lens in the center of the fuel tank.

Removal of the fuel gauge

To remove a fuel gauge without damage requires the use of two tools made especially for this purpose. (They are available from most Model A parts suppliers.) Hold the inner retainer with the small tool and remove the large ring from the tank by unscrewing it with the large tool. The inner ring will come out with the gauge, rod and float attached. The later gauge has a lug on the bottom of the inner portion which prevents the gauge from turning in the tank when the outer ring is tightened.

These special tools are required to remove the fuel gauge from the tank.

Inspection and restoration

Clean all the parts of the gauge and scrape the old gasket material off the gauge if necessary. See that the float rod pivots easily on the gauge and that no parts are broken.

Check the cork float to see if it is dried or cracked. Cork floats will most often become soaked with gasoline until they will no longer float. If the cork is not damaged or dried too badly, clean it and paint it with several coats of shellac to seal it. If the cork is unserviceable, new ones are available with the gauge-rebuilding kits from most parts suppliers. A new cork may also be made from a cork bottle stopper available at any hardware store.

The cork is held on the float rod by a small, washer-type retainer and the flattened end of the rod. If the rod is rusted or broken, a new one may be made and welded or brazed to the good part of the old rod.

Installation of the fuel gauge

Use new gaskets and install the gauge in the reverse order of removal. Tighten the outer ring first, then tighten the inner portion. Loosen the outer ring and then retighten the inner portion of the gauge to achieve proper alignment.

The fuel line and sediment bowl

The first component of the fuel system out of the fuel tank is the fuel shutoff valve located under the tank inside the car. There were three different valves under the tank and a fourth located on the engine side of the firewall in late 1931. The Judging Standards should be checked to see that the proper valve is installed. Reproduction valves are available but, again, they should be checked against the drawings in the Judging Standards if the car is to be shown.

The shutoff valve is a frequent source of fuel leaks on the Model A.

Use the special wrenches to remove the fuel gauge.

It should be cleaned well and new packing installed if applicable. Be sure that the packing nut is tight when the valve is installed.

Since rust and sediment in the fuel is one of the major causes of stoppages in the Model A, anything to prevent this foreign material from entering the fuel system will add greatly to the dependability of the car. A recommended improvement to the fuel system is the addition of a small tubular screen into the opening of the fuel shutoff valve. These are available from most suppliers of Model A parts and will prevent any sediment from finding its way into the fuel lines.

There were two different basic styles of fuel line used from the tank to the sediment bowl.

All Model A fuel lines were terne-plated, seamed steel tubing. If authenticity is important, be very careful of the type of fuel lines purchased. Not all vendors handle the correct type. Do not use copper for fuel lines, as it is brittle and may be cracked from vibration.

Carburetor

While the Model A engine was being developed, Henry Ford had set specific requirements for its performance. With forty horsepower as

Fuel-tank-to-sediment-bowl fuel line A-9230 AR for 1928—29.

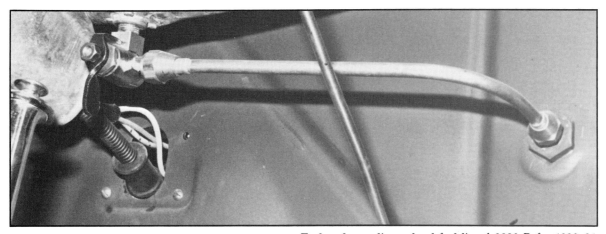

Fuel-tank-to-sediment-bowl fuel line A-9230 B for 1930–31.

a goal, Ford engineers were stumped when twenty-two horsepower was the best they could do. Ford called in Harold Hicks, his Trimotor aircraft engineer, to solve the problem.

Since the Zenith carburetor was used on the Ford-built Liberty aircraft engines in World War I, Hicks selected it to power the new Ford. The addition of this carburetor, along with other intake and exhaust modifications, was responsible for bringing the horsepower of the Model A engine up to the level demanded by Henry Ford. Ford added his own ideas to the Zenith design by suggesting that it required only one bolt to hold it together rather than the six it had. On September 26, 1927, the final design for the original double-venturi Zenith was released for production, and the Model A was soon born.

The original Zenith was modified in various ways, and when Model A production ceased, carburetor variations numbered sixteen. Most of these changes involved slight improvements in the operating system of the carburetor, but some were merely changes in the fitting material. See the current MARC/MAFCA Judging Standards for the application of the Zenith carburetor configurations as they apply to the various years.

Although the carburetor went through various changes, the function and most rebuilding techniques remain the same. The only variation that is important physically is the late 1931 side-bowl type which is required for the indented firewall models made after May of 1931.

Removal and disassembly
1. Disconnect the fuel line from the carburetor by loosening the 1/2 inch fitting from the side of the bowl. Pull the fuel line away from the carbu-

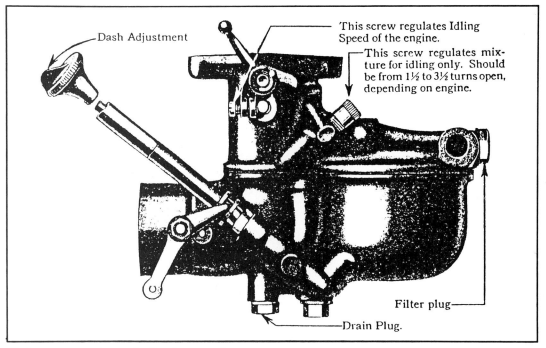

Carburetor operating and adjusting controls.

retor and swing it up to a vertical position so the fuel will not drain out. Pull the choke sleeve up and disconnect the choke and carburetor adjustment rod from the carburetor. Remove the sleeve, spring and washer, and slide the rod up out of the way. Disconnect the throttle-control rod from the carburetor throttle shaft by pulling the cap forward to compress the spring and snap the rod off.

2. Remove the 5/16 x 18 hex-head screws from the top of the carburetor manifold flange and lift the carburetor away, being careful not to spill the gasoline remaining in the bowl.

3. The first step in disassembly is to separate the upper and lower halves of the carburetor body. This is accomplished by removing the 3/8 inch bolt and lockwasher from the bottom of the carburetor. If after removing this bolt the carburetor will still not come apart, screw the bolt back in until it has about 1/8 inch clearance from the body. Hold the carburetor upside-down and tap on the bolt with a hammer until the two parts separate.

4. Remove the small nut holding the choke lever to the lower body and remove the lever. Slip off the choke driver and remove the adjusting needle housing by using a 7/16 inch wrench if it has a 7/16 inch hex nut. If the nut is 13/32 inch as it is in many of them, it will be necessary to use a different method to remove the housing. Saw the tube portion of the housing off with a hacksaw, and drive an old 3/8 inch socket over the hex head. The remainder of the housing may be removed with a socket handle.

5. Remove the idle adjusting screw and spring from the upper body. Remove the throttle plate and shaft by removing the two small screws in the plate and slipping them out of the slot in the shaft. If these screws are difficult to remove, they may have to be drilled out carefully to save the throttle plate. Slip the throttle shaft out of the upper body.

Use a hammer to tap the carburetor loose to separate halves.

When the carburetor is apart, many kinds of deterioration are found. This carburetor has an extra hole, wasp nest and a broken venturi. It is still restorable.

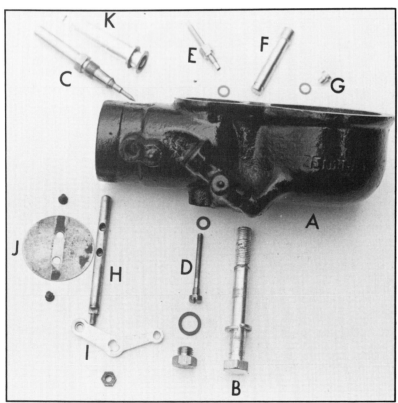

Identification of carburetor parts

A. Carburetor bowl assembly	*A-9512 B*	*F. Secondary well*	*A-9545 3/8-24*
B. Bowl-to-upper-body screw	*21566-S7 3/8-24*	*G. Compensator jet*	*A-9575 10-34*
C. Adjusting needle	*A-9525*	*H. Choke shaft*	*A-9547 8-36*
Adjusting needle housing	*A-9528 1/8-27*	*I. Choke lever*	*A-9548*
D. Main jet assembly	*A-9534 B 10-34*	*J. Choke plate*	*A-9549*
E. Cap jet assembly	*A-9538 B 10-34*	*K. Adjusting needle driver*	*A-9570*

6. Remove the 1/2 inch hex drain plug at the bottom of the lower body. With a large screwdriver, remove the compensator jet from the bowl of the carburetor. Remove the secondary well from the center of the lower body with a screwdriver. If these are difficult to remove, soak them with penetrating oil overnight before attempting removal. The main jet may be removed with a screwdriver through the opening left by the drain plug in the lower body. With a deep 5/16 inch socket, remove the cap jet from the venturi bore. With a screwdriver, remove the two screws and choke plate from the choke shaft.

7. The venturi should slip out of the lower body, but on most unrestored carburetors it has been broken upon disassembly with one half in the lower body and one half in the upper body. The venturi may be removed from both halves by breaking it or driving it out with a small chisel. It may be necessary to use a torch to melt the venturi if all other attempts fail.

8. Remove the float by removing the float hanger rod and lifting the float from the upper body. See that the float hanger is not bent or damaged, which will prevent the float from moving properly. With a 9/32 inch wrench, remove the idle jet from the upper body. With a 5/8 inch wrench, remove the needle and seat from the upper body. The carburetor is now completely disassembled.

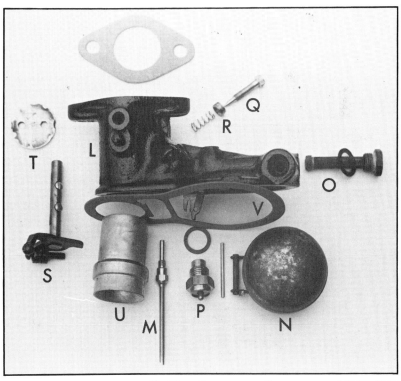

Identification of carburetor parts			
L. Upper body assembly	A-9520 A	Q. Idle adjustment needle	A-9577 10-34
M. Idling jet	A-9542 10-34	R. Adjusting spring cap	A-9579
N. Float	A-9550	S. Throttle shaft & lever	A-9581 A
O. Strainer assembly	A-9559 1/2-20	T. Throttle plate	A-9585
P. Fuel valve	A-9564 A 1/2-20	U. Venturi	A-9586 B
		V. Bowl gasket	A-9592

Inspection and restoration

Have the two halves of the carburetor body stripped by having them dipped in an acid solution or some other form of rust and paint remover. A good suggestion is to have them glass bead blasted.

Check all threads on both body halves and run a tap through them. Check the seat in the fuel inlet tube opening for pits or damage. Clean all parts and check for any that may be bent, scored or broken. It may be difficult to find the 10-34 tap used for the jets at a normal parts outlet or hardware store, but most Model A parts suppliers carry them.

Check and clean all jets with the graduated wire found in a welding tip-cleaning kit which may be purchased at a welding supply store. Jet sizes may be measured with graduated drill bits available from a good hobby supply shop. Blow air through all passages to be sure that they are clear.

It is recommended that the original jets be used if they are not damaged. Some replacement jets are not the proper size, and fuel flow will be affected. Check the throttle shaft bore for wear. If this shaft leaks air, the idle will be poor. Check to see if the plugs at the rear of the throttle shaft bore are missing.

If the throttle shaft bore and shaft are worn, the shaft may be replaced with an oversize shaft and the bore drilled or reamed to fit. If the bore is excessively worn, it may be drilled and fitted with a brass bushing reamed to fit the standard size shaft. This fit must be very close if the engine is to idle properly. Remember to lubricate this shaft periodically after the carburetor is rebuilt to prevent this wear from occurring again.

Clean all the small parts such as the choke plate, throttle plate, choke and throttle lever, bolts and screws. These may be cadmium plated if desired. Check the Judging Standards for the finish of outside items such as the choke driver, choke lever and throttle lever. Some early models should have brass fittings which are difficult to replace.

The float should be parallel to the upper body and 5/8 inch high.

If a jet is broken off in the casting, drill the broken jet with a number 21 bit and thread with a 10-34 tap. If the idle air-adjusting-screw threads are damaged, they may also be drilled and tapped 10-34.

If the secondary well is difficult to remove, it must be drilled out with a 5/16 inch bit. Be certain to mount the carburetor body securely in a drill press and be sure that the bit is perfectly aligned with the body. Be careful not to drill through the bottom of the lower body. When the remnants of the secondary well are removed, clean out the threads with a 3/8-24 tap.

Reassembly

Before beginning reassembly, paint the upper and lower body halves with a low-luster black lacquer. Do not use enamel, as the gasoline will attack it and destroy the finish. Make sure that the proper tools are available to fit the screws and bolts without damaging them. Make sure that all the threads have been cleaned to avoid stripping them during reassembly. It is also important to ensure that the jets fit properly in their threads, or they could leak or not function well.

Begin reassembly with the lower body by first replacing the compensator jet located inside the fuel bowl. Install the cap jet inside the air inlet side behind the choke. Screw the main jet in from the bottom, being sure to replace the gasket. Follow the main jet with the drain plug and gasket in the same opening.

Replace the adjusting needle and housing, being sure not to tighten it until after the body halves are secured. If the carburetor has a removable seat, be sure that it is tightened in place before the adjusting needle and housing are installed.

Insert the choke shaft and slide the choke plate into its slot. Replace the two 5-40 oval-head screws but do not tighten them until the choke plate is moved a few times to fit it to the throat. Replace the choke driver on the adjusting needle housing and fit the choke lever over the shaft with its pin seated into the slot on the choke driver. Replace the 8-36 nut and lockwasher.

The Zenith carburetor installed on the Model A engine.

Screw the secondary well into the compensating well and set the new venturi into the lower body. Replace the gasket, and the lower body is complete.

Begin assembly of the upper body by replacing the idle air-adjusting screw, cover and spring. Do not tighten this screw at this time. Install the throttle shaft into the bore in the upper body using some graphite grease for lubrication. Fit the throttle plate into the slot, making sure that the beveled edges move against the walls of the throat. Fit the plate evenly and replace the two 5-40 oval-head screws.

Replace the float valve with one gasket. Many restorers like to replace this valve with a grose jet valve containing two balls instead of the needle and seat. This should stop the tendency for the Zenith carburetor to leak out of the bowl. Replace the float and attach float pin to the float bracket, then turn the body over to check the float level. See that the flat surface of the float is parallel to the machined surface of the carburetor body with a gap of 5/8 inch. If the float is too high, add gaskets to the float valve to raise it. The float arm may be bent if necessary to achieve a proper fit.

Assemble the lower body to the upper body and replace the long bolt and washer holding them together. Check the float action by rocking the carburetor back and forth and listening for the movement. The carburetor is now ready to install on the engine.

Installation and adjustment

1. Replace the flange gasket on the upper body and assemble the carburetor to the manifold. Replace the two 5/16-18 bolts and lockwashers and secure the carburetor.
2. Attach the choke rod to the choke driver and slip the sleeve and spring over the assembly. Attach the throttle linkage to the throttle lever ball.
3. Connect the fuel line to the fuel inlet. Make sure that the end of the fuel line does not extend more than 1/8 inch past the ferrule or fuel flow may be restricted. Tighten the fitting carefully so as not to damage the threads in the carburetor.
4. Turn on the fuel at the tank and check the carburetor for leaks. Retighten the fittings if necessary.
5. Open the adjusting needle one full turn off its seat, retard the spark and start the engine. After the engine has warmed up, screw the adjusting needle down until it is one-quarter turn off the seat.
6. Adjust the idle-speed screw on the throttle shaft for a slow idle. Adjust the idle air screw for a smooth idle. Keep closing down each adjustment until the engine runs evenly and slowly.
7. If the engine still will not run smoothly, use a vacuum gauge to check the fuel and ignition system. Attach the gauge to the vacuum wiper fitting hole on the intake manifold if there is one present. The early 1928 engines will not have a vacuum fitting so a vacuum check will be difficult.

With a fast idle speed, the vacuum gauge should read steady at about 19 or 20 inches. This measurement is at sea level, so subtract a point for each 1,000 feet above sea level. A low but steady reading indicates an air leak or retarded spark.

Accelerate the engine quickly and watch the gauge. The reading should drop quickly to about 5, then climb to about 25 and return to normal when the throttle is released.

Poor idle and low speed performance are usually caused by air leaks in the manifold or carburetor. Check the throttle plate, vacuum line fittings and idle air-adjusting screw for dirt or poor fit.

Poor high-speed performance is usually the result of a dirty compensator jet or secondary well blocking fuel flow to the cap jet. Many times, dirt in the fuel line will cause enough restriction for the engine to idle well but not have enough power to pull the car or cause it to die after running a short distance. Remove the drain plug in the bottom of the carburetor and check for dirt. Remove the filter screen and see if it is clogged. Remove the fuel line and see that the fuel flows freely. If the engine condition and ignition are good, the engine should idle smoothly and slowly and the car should accelerate evenly.

Chapter 11

ELECTRICAL SYSTEM

THE electrical system of the Model A Ford was a new design for Ford, but very much a conventional system to the rest of the automobile industry in 1927. With a storage battery, generator, starter and conventional coil, the Model A had finally put Ford systems on a par with everyone else.

The primary functions of the electrical systems on any automobile are to provide power to crank the engine, provide a spark to fire the fuel-air mixture, and to power the lights and horn. The electrical system on the Model A Ford, as on most cars, consists of four subsystems: charging, starting, ignition and lighting.

The heart of the electrical system is the battery. The Ford battery as called for in original specifications is a 6 volt, 80 ampere hour, 13 plate battery. This equates now to a group-one 6 volt, which should be available at any good battery supplier. The Model A battery is located in a box mounted under the floor in front of the driver's seat on the left side of the car. The positive (+) terminal of the battery is grounded to the frame, as are many early 6 volt systems. The purpose for this was to eliminate the possibility of grounding the battery by corrosion. The starting capacity called for in the original battery was 98 amps for twenty minutes. The lighting capacity was 5 amps for seventeen hours. The size of the original equipment battery was 9 3/8 inches long, 7 1/2 inches wide and 9 1/2 inches high. The new group-one may vary slightly from this size but will give at least as good service.

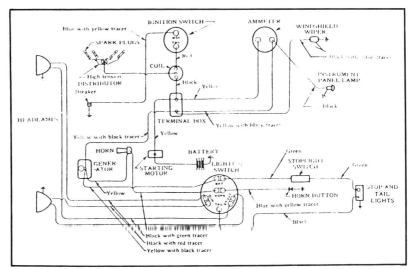

A Early 1928 system.

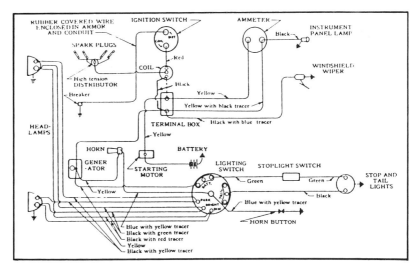

B 1929–31 without cowl lights.

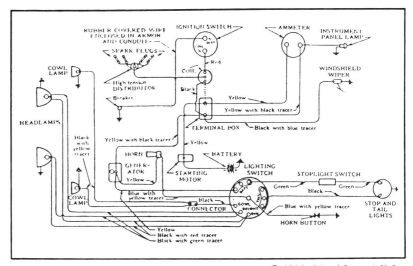

C 1929–31 with cowl lights.

145

The electrolyte in the battery should be checked frequently to see that it is at the proper level at the bottom of the filling tube. If it is below this level, add distilled water until the proper level is reached. The electrolyte should not be allowed to fall below this level or the plates will become dry and deteriorated beyond use. In cold weather, run the car immediately after filling the battery to prevent freezing.

Hydrometer readings should show a full charge at 1.280, one-half discharge at 1.220 and full discharge at 1.150. The battery will freeze at zero if the gravity is 1.170, and freeze at sixteen degrees if it is 1.200.

Keep the battery top and connections clean at all times to prevent the formation of corrosion. The terminals may be protected with a coating of grease or Vaseline. Clean the top with a solution of baking soda and water. Be sure that the battery is firmly attached to the battery support or it may be damaged. The original battery clamps fastened to the corners of the battery, but many restorers today like to use a hold-down frame available from most suppliers that holds the battery more securely. The original battery cable was a multistrand copper wire with a lead battery terminal and a steel switch terminal. It had a woven cloth cover. The cable support was changed in November of 1929 to protect the cable from damage. Page 395 of the November 1929 Ford Service Bulletins illustrates this change, which also affected the length of the cable.

General

Without any question the entire wiring system should be replaced on any Model A Ford to prevent any chance of a breakdown or of a fire. The original wiring becomes brittle through the years and in most cases, the insulation has deteriorated to a point where it is no longer performing its original function.

The wires available today are of far better quality and size than the wires available when the Model A was new. Most reproduction wiring is plastic insulated and covered with fabric to appear as the original wire. Complete harness kits for all areas of Model A wiring are readily available so it is not necessary for the restorer to construct his own assemblies. The only wiring that may need to be fabricated is the taillight harness extensions for AA trucks. The proper color-coded wire to complete these extensions is available from automotive wiring suppliers found in *Hemmings Motor News* and other antique auto parts sources.

Except for the ignition-switch-to-primary-coil winding and the generator-to-terminal-box wires, which are number 12, all other wires are number 16. Check with the wire supplier as sizes may be rated differently today than in 1927.

An additional improvement to any Model A is an in-line fuse to protect the system. This fuse mount is available from many Model A parts distributors and suppliers. It will save the wiring system from being burned up should a short occur. The MARC/MAFCA Judging Standards accept the fuse as a safety item and will not downgrade the car if it is installed neatly and safely.

Installation of the wiring harness should probably begin at the lighting switch at the end of the steering column. It will be helpful if the old wiring was present when the car was disassembled. The restorer should be able to make notes about where the wires were clipped to the frame and where they were routed through the crossmembers.

A frequent question concerns the routing of the taillight wiring. These wires should go under the motor mount, along the inside bottom of the frame rail, through the center crossmember and continue along the inside bottom of the frame. Attach them with three clips. The 1928 through February 1929 radiators should have a channel to support the right headlight wire. From February 1929 to the end of production this wire was held by three clips soldered to the bottom of the tank. Many replacement radiators will not have a provision for a wire clip of any kind.

The charging system

The charging system consists of the generator, the cutout and the ammeter. The function of the charging system is to replenish the current lost from the battery due to use of the starter, ignition system, horn and lights. The generator is driven by a pulley and V-belt from the crankshaft and is mounted on the lower left side of the engine. The generator produces current by the action of the pulley rotating the armature through the magnetic field of the coils and producing electricity at a rate which is variable according to the speed of the engine. The maximum current flow is a little less than 20 amps at 8 volts. Without a battery or some other load on the generator, its voltage would rise to 18 or 20 volts.

The cutout, which is mounted on top of the generator, acts as a switch to turn the electric current on or off according to requirements. The cutout functions by electromagnetic action. When the car speed reaches 9 or 10 mph, the generator produces enough current to make the coil inside the cutout close the points and complete the circuit to the battery. If the cutout fails to close, the generator output increases to the point where the generator will be damaged. If the points fail to open when the generator output is zero, the battery will be drained and the generator will likely be damaged.

The ammeter is a gauge that measures the amount of current flow-

In-line fuse installation on Model A starter switch.

147

ing to the battery, measured in amperes. The ammeter is mounted on the right side of the instrument panel and is necessary for determining the condition and operation of the charging system.

The generator

There were basically four generators used during Model A production; two of the Powerhouse type and two of the longer style. The MARC/MAFCA Judging Standards give the specific dates of the adoption of each of these models. Generally, the Powerhouse type was used from the beginning of production to mid-1929. This generator got its name because of its size and shape, which was quite different from most other generators. This model had five brushes initially, but later had three brushes. The large diameter gave this generator a higher safe-charging rate than conventional types. It was capable of putting out as much as 22 amps, but it was recommended that it be set at 6 amps for normal driving situations. For extended daytime trips, a lower rate of 2 to 3 amps is desirable to prevent damage to the generator and battery.

To regulate the charging rate on the Powerhouse, remove the generator cover and loosen the field brush holder lock screw. Move the brush in the direction of rotation to increase the charging rate, the opposite direction to reduce the rate.

The adjustment of the charging rate in the later-model generators is done by moving the third (movable) brush in the direction of rotation to increase the rate and in the opposite direction to decrease the rate. This generator does not require the loosening of a screw to move the brush as spring tension holds it in place. Adjust the generator to 6 amps for normal use and 2-3 amps for extended daytime trips as stated earlier. The cover band must be removed to gain access to the brushes on the later-style generator.

Loosen the lock screw on the movable brush to adjust the charging rate.

To adjust the later generator, remove the cover band and pry brush.

Removal of the generator

1. Disconnect the battery by removing the cable at the battery terminal under the floorboards. In an emergency, the generator may be disconnected by removing the wire from the battery side of the cutout and wrapping it carefully to prevent it from shorting out. Disconnect the battery and lighting-system wires from the cutout.

2. If the generator is of the early type with an adjustment bracket, loosen the bracket from the front of the engine by removing the 3/8 inch bolt and washer from the front timing cover and slide the adjustment arm out of the way. Remove the bolt from the generator-to-engine mount on the lower side of the generator. The Powerhouse will have a single mount while the later generators will have a bracket on both the front and rear of the boss on the block. The later-model bolt will have a nut on the front side.

3. Slip the generator out of the fan belt and remove it from the car.

Disassembly of the Powerhouse generator

1. Remove the cutout from the top or the side of the generator and place it aside.

2. Remove the rear cover by snapping the retainer out of the two holes in the housing. Disconnect the ground and field wires from the brushes and replace the screws in the brush holders so they will not become lost. Remove the brush holder from the housing by removing three screws and lockwashers. Lift the brush holder carefully from the housing.

3. Remove the pulley from the armature shaft by removing the 1/4 inch capscrew from the pulley end of the shaft and pry the pulley from the tapered shaft. If the bolt is difficult to remove, hold the pulley with a strap-type oil filter wrench to loosen the bolt.

4. Remove the bolt and lockwasher holding the armature to the shaft and remove the armature from the rear of the housing.

5. Remove the bearing retainer from the front of the housing by unscrewing it with a large pipe wrench. If it is stubborn to remove, use a chisel or large screwdriver.

6. Remove the shaft and bearing assembly from the housing. If the bearings are to be replaced, drive them off the shaft. The numbers of these bearings are: A-10093-AR (large) and A-10094-BR (small). These are available from some Model A parts suppliers, or they may be found by using a bearing reference manual to get the new number and purchased from a bearing supplier.

7. Remove the two screws holding each of the field coils to the housing. These screws are much smaller than on most generators and are easily damaged. If it is not necessary to remove the coils, it may be a good idea to leave them in if the screws seem difficult to remove. These coils are not available as new parts but a generator rebuilding shop may be able to rewire them if necessary.

Service and inspection

Check the bearings for damage such as galling and scored balls and races. If the bearings are damaged they should be replaced. Have the commutator turned at a good generator shop. Have the armature and the field coils checked for continuity. Replace the ground and field coil wires if necessary. Make sure that the insulating washers for the case are not cracked or missing. If the restorer's shop is equipped with a nine-inch or larger metal lathe, the commutator may be turned by the restorer. (A special section at the end of the generator portion of this chapter describes the details of turning the commutator.)

Check the brush holder for cracks. The Bakelite frame of the brush holder is very susceptible to cracks from overheating of the generator. These brush holders are not available as reproductions at this time, but some Model A parts dealers still have some NOS units at reasonable prices. The three-brush and five-brush holders are interchangeable, but the brushes are different.

Reassembly

Reassemble the generator in the reverse order of the disassembly. Be sure to thoroughly grease the two armature shaft bearings before placing them in the housing.

The brush springs for the Powerhouse are difficult to locate. A usable substitute may be found by checking with a generator rebuilding shop and getting some replacement springs. Check the tension. Some may need to be weakened carefully with heat. If the springs are too strong, they will wear the brushes more rapidly than normal.

When the brushes and brush holder are secure on the housing, test the generator for operation by attaching a negative (−) 6 volt wire to the case and a positive (+) wire to the output, and the generator should turn

Use a hammer and chisel to remove bearing retainer on Powerhouse generator.

Remove the Powerhouse shaft and bearings from the the front of the case.

like a motor. If the generator does not turn, there is a break in the circuit. When the generator is complete, paint the housing with black enamel.

Disassembly of the later-type generator
1. Remove the cutout from the housing by removing two screws and lockwashers. Remove the cover band from the housing.
2. Remove the pulley from the armature shaft by removing the bolt and washer and prying the pulley from the shaft.
3. Remove the two 1/4 inch nuts and lockwashers from the front of the housing and pull the long bolts out from the rear. Remove the rear end plate. If the generator is a model made before April 1930 the end plate should be A-10129 BR, which has ball bearings. If the generator is a later model, the end plate will be B-10129, which has a bushing and oiler with a wick. Since the armatures of these two models are of different lengths, the end plates and armature are not interchangeable.
4. Remove the front end plate from the housing. The armature will come off with the front end plate because the front shaft bearing is pressed on. When the Model A was new, this shaft was sometimes turned with the front end plate still in place, but most generator shops today will probably want it removed for service. The front bearing retainer is riveted in the end plate, so removal of the front bearing will probably not be done unless it is in poor condition.
5. Remove the field coils if they seem bad by removing the two large screws in the housing and disconnecting the ground wire. These field coils are available new from most Model A parts suppliers, or they may be rewound by a generator shop.

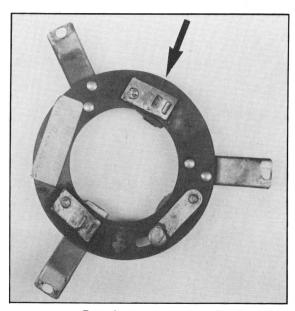

Powerhouse generator brush holder A-10050 BR (three brush). Notice cracks in Bakelite caused from excessive heat. This part is defective and must be replaced.

Service and inspection

The armature should be inspected for cracks or damaged insulation. The bearing surfaces on the shaft should be checked for galling or excessive rust damage. The bearings in either end plate should be inspected for wear and damage and replaced if necessary. These bearings are available from most parts suppliers. Check the armature and field coils for continuity with a voltage tester and have them repaired by a generator shop if necessary.

Reassembly

Reassemble the generator in the reverse order of disassembly and paint the housing with black enamel. Test the generator by running it as a motor as described in the previous section. Be sure to thoroughly oil the bearings or bushing in the end plates.

Cutout

As was mentioned earlier, the cutout is an electromagnetic switch that opens and closes the circuit between the battery and the generator. Inside the cutout, there are two coils of wire wound over a soft iron core. The outer winding is the heavier wire and is used to hold the contacts together. The inner winding is of a lighter-gauge wire and is used to pull the contacts together. One end of the inner, or lighter, winding is connected to the generator output terminal. The other end is soldered to the base of the cutout, which grounds it when the cutout is fastened to the generator.

When the engine turns fast enough, the generator produces sufficient current through the inner coil to cause the iron core to become magnetized and draw the contact points together. The contact points are mounted on a flat spring known as the armature. This point is connected electrically to the battery terminal of the cutout.

A comparison of an original cutout (left) and a reproduction clearly shows the quality difference.

At the opposite end of the armature fastening point is the battery contact-point keeper which is connected electrically to the generator output terminal. This is the stationary contact.

When the armature is attracted to the magnetized soft iron core, the contacts close, completing the electrical circuit from the generator to the battery which allows the generator to charge the battery. As current flows through the heavy coil winding of the cutout, the magnetic attraction is increased. When the generator output drops due to a reduction in speed, current will flow in the opposite direction which causes the magnetic action to cease and release the contact points opening the circuit and disconnecting the battery from the generator. The spring of the armature keeps the contact points open until the voltage increases again.

The cutout of the Model A is contained in a two-inch-diameter cylindrical metal can 1 3/4 inches in height. The cutout is mounted to the generator with slotted mounting tabs which fit with round head screws to the generator housing. The cover is zinc plated and in appearance took four different forms. These forms are detailed in the MARC/MAFCA Judging Standards.

The one important thing to notice is that a Ford script is not always the most authentic type to use. The original cutouts did not have any markings to indicate battery or armature as many of the replacement cutouts seem to have. The greatest difference in cutouts between original and replacement parts is the quality.

File the solder from the edge of the cutout cover to remove it.

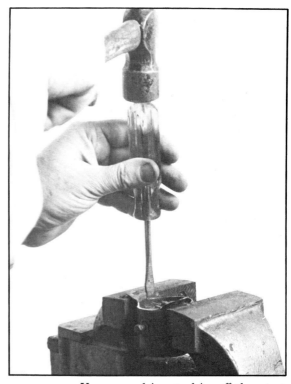

Use a screwdriver to drive off the cutout cover.

Disassembly of the cutout

1. Remove the bolts or screws and insulators and place them aside for later use.

2. With the cover of the cutout lightly clamped in a vise, file off the spot welds holding the cover to the base.

3. Place the cutout into a vise and use a small hammer and a screwdriver to drive the cover off the base.

Inspection

Check the resistance and continuity of the coil windings with an electrical tester. The outer, heavy coil winding should have zero ohms resistance. The inner, lighter coil should have fifty ohms resistance. The contact gap may be adjusted by loosening the screws holding the keeper and moving the contact points up or down until the proper clearance gap of 0.015 to 0.020 inch is reached. The core gap should be 0.010 with the contact points closed.

Armature closing may be checked by connecting one wire from a trickle charger or battery to the base of the cutout and the second wire to the generator terminal. The armature should pull toward the core and close the contacts. Connect a test lamp or voltmeter to the battery terminal of the cutout and the lamp should light or there should be an indication of voltage. If the reading is low or the lamp dim, the contact points may be dirty. They may be cleaned by running fine emery paper between the contacts while holding them together. If the contact points are removed from the base, be sure not to lose the insulating washers under the screws and rivets. They must be replaced upon reassembly for the cutout to function properly.

The grounded wire may be unsoldered from the base and the heavy coil wire unsoldered from the generator terminal. Remove the two screws holding the relay to the base and remove the base. Carefully remove the two fiber washers remaining in the screw holes in the base. The base is ready to clean and prepare for replating.

The original plating was zinc, but cadmium may be substituted for durability. The remaining insulation on the base may be left in place while plating is done, as it is riveted to the base. If it is desired to remove this insulation, be sure that all insulators are saved and their positions marked for reassembly. If the only cutout available happens to be a later Ford cutout or Ford replacement, it may be made to look just like the original cutout by filling-in the Ford script or the letter B (if present) with solder and sanding it smooth before sending it out for replating. This choice would probably be more desirable than using one of the poorer-quality reproductions.

For reassembly, the original rivets may be replaced with pop-rivets or nuts and bolts. Adjust the point gap and armature gap to the clearances given previously and check the operation of the relay as previously described. There is no reason an original cutout cannot be rebuilt to give as good or better service than a replacement unit.

Servicing armatures

Although the turning of armatures is a job normally left to professional generator rebuilders, this operation can be performed by anyone with a shop lathe such as a nine-inch bench model or a brake-drum lathe. For ordinary types of armatures, a high-speed cutter bit and three different size lathe dogs are all the equipment needed. Doing the work itself is as easy as any other machining work. The mechanic accustomed to handling valves, brake drums, pistons and other work on his lathe will find armature work relatively simple.

After removing the armature from the generator, make sure the shafts are true and the center holes clean. Otherwise a concentric job cannot be done on the commutator.

Wrap a piece of brass around the shaft away from the commutator end, then attach the lathe dog over the brass to prevent possible damage when tightening the set screw. Swing the armature between centers, after placing a drop of oil in the center hole for the tailstock center.

Hone the cutting edge of the tool bit to a keen edge and then adjust the tool so that its point is exactly in line with the point of the lathe center. It is advisable to use a round-nose tool ground flat on top with no back slope and plenty of front clearance.

When ready for a cut, start the lathe and use a fine, automatic longitudinal feed. Feed the tool from right to left, taking a light chip. The lathe spindle should revolve at about 350 to 400 rpm. Turn the commutator down just enough to produce a smooth, true surface.

After truing the commutator, the mica insulation between the copper segments should be undercut. This prevents the brushes from coming in contact with the mica as the copper wears, as that would cause intermittent service. Starter motor commutators are not usually undercut as the high-amperage current required in starting would be apt to cause arcing.

To make the undercutting easier, cut a recess 1/32 inch deep, close to the shoulder of the generator armature.

In the small shop, mica is usually cut by hand rather than by the special mechanical devices used in a professional shop. To undercut the mica insulation, use a hacksaw blade with the teeth ground off so that it will cut a slot the width of the mica. The teeth of the saw blade should point toward the handle. Undercut to a depth of about 1/32 inch, keeping the slot regular in shape and the edges free from mica insulation.

After truing and undercutting is done, the rough edges of the commutator must be polished to a smooth finish. A quick, efficient way to

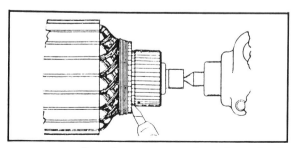

Recessing commutator for undercutting the mica insulation.

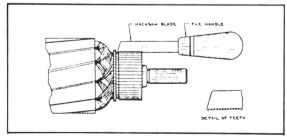

Undercutting mica with hacksaw ground to correct width.

do this is to run the lathe at a high speed and polish with a fine grade of sandpaper wrapped around the commutator. Emery cloth should never be used, as emery dust will become lodged between the segments and cause a short circuit.

To service the Powerhouse armature, it is necessary to make a special tapered mandrel with a nut to hold the armature against the tapered section.

The mandrel can be turned down from a piece of tool stock or old axle. Make it an overall length of about 6 1/2 inches and 3/4 inch diameter. Taper it for 1 1/32 inches down, from 3/4 inch to 3/8 inch. Thread the tapered end for an inch and center the opposite end. Actual machining of the Powerhouse-type commutator is done in the usual manner.

The later Ford generator presents a servicing problem that is easily overcome. Mount it in the lathe without removing the ball bearing end plate by placing the lathe dog on the shaft at the commutator end and supporting the other end on the tailstock center.

The tool bit is held in a left-hand offset tool holder and is fed from left to right. This method is used because the tapered end of the shaft is too short for attaching the lathe dog. (From "Unwinding the Kinks in Generator Servicing," *Automobile Topics*, October 10 and October 24, 1931.)

The ammeter

The ammeter is the only means the driver has of determining the condition of the battery and charging system of the Model A. Located on the right side of the instrument panel, the ammeter provides an instant reading of what the generator, the cutout and the battery are doing.

The ammeter is a relatively simple instrument, being nothing more than a resistance coil between two poles measuring the direction and amount of the electricity flowing between them.

The ammeter is simple enough that it generally functions with few problems. Most ammeter problems today can be traced to the poor quality of some replacement ammeters which tend to come loose inside and short out, burning up some wires if the system is not fused. Do not cut any costs in purchasing a new ammeter as a cheap unit could become the weak link in the charging system of the Model A. The troubleshooting section at the end of this chapter will provide a clearer picture of how important the ammeter is to everyday driving.

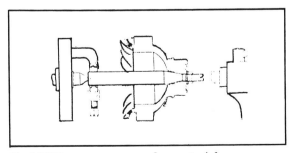

Ford 1928 armature mounted on a special mandrel.

The starting system

The starting system consists of the starter and the starter switch. Although all Model A starters look very much the same, there were at least three types of starters used over four years of production. The most important changes were in October of 1928 when the 1/2 inch shaft Abell starter drive was exchanged for the heavier 5/8 inch shaft Bendix drive. The new starter drive cannot be used with the old-style flywheel ring gear because the pitch of the pinion gear was changed. There are instructions for modification of the starter drive for use on older models on page 303 and 304 of the 1928 Ford Service Bulletins.

The stud for the starter switch was also changed from a slanted pole to a flat pole. This involved changing the switch and the battery cable. The starter introduced in October 1930 also had a bushing-mounted shaft instead of a ball bearing as previously used. The starter develops three pounds of torque and turns the flywheel at a ratio of 11.2:1.

Removal of the starter

1. Remove the floor mat and battery cover plate inside the car and disconnect the battery cables.
2. Disconnect the battery cable from the starter switch and replace the nut and washer. Unscrew the starter switch rod from the switch and push up out of the way.
3. Remove the three 3/8 inch bolts and lockwashers holding the starter to the engine and carefully lift the starter away from the block, turning it so the Bendix drive clears the flywheel.

Disassembly

1. Remove the four round head screws and lockwashers and remove the starter switch from the starter housing.
2. Loosen the nut and screw and remove the starter cover band assembly.
3. Remove the two or four screws holding the front brush holder end plate to the body of the starter.
4. The special bolts holding the Bendix drive to the shaft are removed by bending down the lock tab and unscrewing the bolts. The Bendix drive may then be removed from the shaft.
5. Remove the rear end plate and armature from the starter and slide the end plate from the armature shaft.

Service and inspection

Inspect the starter for damaged bearings and bearing surfaces. Check the armature and field coils for continuity and damaged windings. Have the commutator turned if necessary. (See the section on armature service in the generator portion of this chapter.) Check the Bendix for free movement and broken springs or spring sleeves. Clean the housing of the starter and paint with black enamel.

Reassembly

Check pages 570, 571 and 572 of the 1931 Ford Service Bulletins before beginning reassembly of the starter to ensure that proper spring, sleeve and bolt are used. After the starter is assembled, check the operation by connecting a positive (+) wire from a battery or charger to the housing and a negative (−) wire to the switch stud to see that the starter turns with a good speed and smoothness.

To test the starter on the car, turn the ignition off and attach the positive (+) lead of a voltmeter to the engine for a good ground and attach the negative (−) lead to the starter switch. Push on the starter switch and allow the engine to turn over for at least fifteen seconds. The voltmeter should not read below 4 1/2 to 5 volts while the engine is cranking. If it falls below that reading, the starter is defective.

The starter switch

The starter switch is easily disassembled by removing the nut and lockwasher on the battery terminal connection. The outer case may be replated and reused.

The switch is installed on the starter using four 10-32 x 5/16 inch raven-finish round head screws and lockwashers. A paper gasket goes between the switch and the starter.

The ignition system

The ignition system consists of the distributor, coil, ignition switch and cable and spark plugs. The ignition system provides the spark to explode the fuel-air mixture in the cylinders and bring life to the engine. The ignition system is the brain of the engine, which determines when the spark plugs should fire. A properly functioning ignition system contributes greatly to the smooth operation of the car.

The ignition switch controls whether energy is available to the coil and turns the power on and off to the engine. The Model A ignition switch is called an electrolock switch and provides a means of ground-

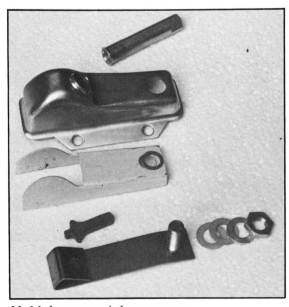

Model A starter switch components.

ing the entire system. A protective cable running from the switch to the distributor added a bit of theft protection to the Model A. That evasive "pop-out" switch is much desired by restorers.

The coil of the Model A is much like the coil on any other car. Its purpose is to increase the voltage from 6,000 to a more useful level of 15,000 or more. This is accomplished by allowing the current to flow through a primary and secondary coil of wire inside the coil itself. When the current flows through the primary coil, it magnetizes a soft iron core inside the coil and, by the process of electrical induction, produces a large amount of voltage in the secondary coil.

The coil is usually trouble free; the only maintenance required, generally, is keeping the Bakelite surface clean so that current will not be lost. This loss of current will burn up a coil over a period of time.

The most common question that arises about the Model A coil is, Which way is it connected? The original coil had the bracket spot welded to the body so there was no chance of installing it incorrectly, but some older replacement coils were marked "Bat" and "Dist." Most of these were for negative-ground systems and, if installed on a Model A, could cause a loss of high-speed spark intensity. Other replacement coils marked positive (+) and negative (−) should be installed with the red wire at the terminal block to the positive side and the black wire going to the ammeter post attached to the negative side.

The MARC/MAFCA Judging Standards illustrate the different types of coils found on the Model A. The restorer should notice page 390 of the November 1930 Ford Service Bulletins concerning the change in the coil hook-up at the terminal box. No dust caps were used on the high-tension wire from the coil to the distributor.

The distributor (or timer, as it was called in the early days of the automobile) distributes the high-voltage current from the coil to the spark plugs at the proper time to ignite the fuel-air mixture at precisely the right moment to allow the engine to operate at its most efficient level.

An original electrolock switch as installed on a 1931 model.

The ignition switch

Removal

1. Remove the head nut between the third and forth spark plug and remove the ignition cable hold-down from the engine. Loosen the distributor lock nut and screw on the side of the head and lift the distributor from the block. Unscrew the ignition cable from the distributor.

2. Remove the four screws holding the instrument panel to the tank and pull the panel slightly away from the dash. Remove the insulated nut and disconnect the red wire from the ignition switch. Wrap this wire with tape so it does not short out. Remove the three screws holding the switch to the instrument panel and carefully pull out the switch and cable.

Disassembly

1. Remove the set screw at the side of the lock casting and pull the lock cylinder out of the switch body.

2. Remove the wire from the switch and cable housing.

Inspection and service

Check the contact buttons inside the switch housing to see that they are free and have sufficient spring tension to make a good contact with the lock plunger. The lock plunger should be cleaned if necessary. Check the wire in the cable for continuity and condition of insulation. Replace the wire and cable if necessary.

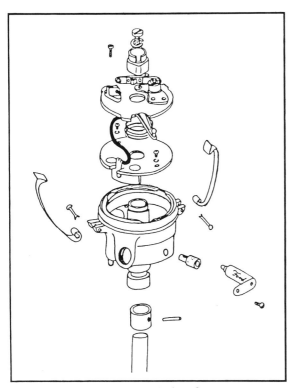

Model A distributor exploded view shows construction of internal parts.

There are reproduction electrolock switches available from most parts suppliers. If authenticity is desired, the early 1928 switch had a long flange for the distributor wire, and the later 1928 and after switches had a short flange. The late 1930 and 1931 cars had a longer cable than the earlier ones.

Many restorers, especially those who drive their cars rather than show them, replace the missing or defective electrolock switches with common on-off ignition switches available from any vendor of Model A parts for a lot smaller price than the original switches. If the car is to be shown, the operation of the pop-out switch is one of the judging points. Do not mistake a replacement-style switch for an original switch at a swap meet!

The distributor

The removal of the distributor has already been discussed in the ignition switch section.

Disassembly

1. Remove the cap and body from the distributor by pulling away the clamps on either side of the cap. Remove the rotor by pulling it straight off the cam.
2. Remove the cam by removing the screw holding it in the shaft. Do not lose the washer that comes off with the cam.
3. Turn the breaker plate in a counterclockwise direction until it releases from the body, and pull it aside. Disconnect the wire from the underside of the breaker plate. Remove the spring from the shaft. Re-

An example of a replacement ignition switch for a Model A that resembles the original electrolock.

After removing the breaker plate and two small screws, the bus bar may be removed from the distributor body.

move the screws on either side of the distributor body and remove the condensor.

4. Remove the two small screws and lockwashers and remove the bus bar support assembly from inside the distributor body.

5. Remove the distributor shaft by driving or drilling out the pin holding the shaft to the distributor shaft sleeve (A12195). The shaft is removed by pulling it out from the top of the distributor body.

6. Remove the shaft bushings from the distributor body by driving them out with a properly fitted bushing driver. The casting is easily broken, so care must be exercised.

Inspection and service

The distributor condition is critical to the smooth operation of the engine. It is recommended that the distributor be rebuilt completely to include new shafts, bushings, points, condensor and cam. There are one-piece shafts available to replace the original two-piece shaft, but the purpose of the two-piece shaft was to allow a certain amount of flexibility and avoid a stress on the bushings. Either shaft will work well if in good condition.

It is important that the drive gear, B-6551, be in good condition as it drives both the distributor and oil pump. This gear is located in the valve chamber and is available new from most parts suppliers. This gear should have been replaced when the engine was rebuilt.

A problem for many Model A owners is the small wire between the upper and lower plates of the distributor. This wire either becomes frayed or shorts against the breaker plate and causes a stoppage which is sometimes difficult to locate. Be sure that this wire is in good condition and attached properly and firmly. Many vendors now have a special replacement plate which eliminates this wire.

When replacing the points, be sure that good-quality points are used as the cheaper replacement parts sometimes oxidize and wear more quickly than the original Ford parts. Ford points are still available as Motorcraft number DP-104.

Another area of great concern for the Model A is the condensor. Model A condensors are subjected to a great amount of heat and can fail very easily. A heat shield is above the manifold, B-12280, and will protect the condensor from manifold heat. The condensor may be tested at a good auto service or parts store. It should have about 0.25 microfarads and should take a 400 volt leakage test. It is always a good idea to carry an extra condensor when driving a Model A.

New distributor cams are sometimes not as good as the old parts. Check for no more than 0.002 or 0.003 inch variation in cam lobes. Make sure that a good USA quality cam is purchased as this part is very important to the smooth operation of the engine.

New distributor shafts usually require a bit of filing to fit well and work properly. The shafts must go together easily, but provide a solid fit.

Check the fit of new rotors and distributor caps and bodies. The rotor will sometimes rub against the contacts in the body and cause unusual noises.

Reassembly

The distributor is reassembled in reverse order of disassembly with attention to the aforementioned parts and fitting. The distributor should be reinstalled in the engine with the cam screw remaining loose and the cap and rotor off so the timing can be set.

The new shaft bushings will most likely require some fitting to the shaft with emery paper or fine sandpaper. Be sure to oil all bushings well during reassembly. Fill the oil cup with light oil after the distributor is installed on the engine.

The end play of the distributor shaft is controlled by the distributor cam shaft thrust washer (A351455-S). This washer should be installed just under the ring on the upper shaft. The washer also helps to keep lubricant in the upper bushing from leaking out onto the upper plate. If a good replacement cannot be found, a thrust washer may be fabricated from a flat washer drilled to the proper bore diameter and filing the edges to fit the top of the upper bushing.

Be sure that the wire between the upper and lower plates is of the proper gauge and length. If it is too long, it may short out on the distributor body. If small enough terminal ends are not available, solder the wire ends to small copper washers. As mentioned earlier, the wire may be replaced by the special plates available from some vendors.

When installing the new points, be certain that the contacts are aligned evenly. They are adjusted by bending the point arm or moving the contact screw bracket. It may be a good idea to file the head of the point spring bolt parallel to the point spring. This will make it possible to change the points without removing the upper plate.

Ignition timing
1. Fully retard the spark lever (all the way up).
2. Remove the distributor cap if it is not already off and check to see that the point gap is set at 0.018 to 0.022 inch. Adjust the points if necessary.

The timing pin is inserted in the hole in the timing cover and pushed in gently as the engine is turned.

3. Remove the timing pin located in the timing gear cover on the right front of the engine and turn it over, inserting it in the opening by the round end.

4. Using the starting crank, turn the engine over slowly. At the same time press in firmly on the timing pin. When the piston reaches top dead center, the timing pin should slip into the small hole in the timing gear.

5. With the pin in place remove the rotor from the distributor cam and loosen the cam locking screw until the cam can be turned.

6. Replace the rotor and turn it until the rotor arm is opposite the number one contact in the distributor cap.

7. Remove the rotor from the cam and slightly turn the cam in the direction of rotation until the points are just beginning to open. If the points are set properly, they should be fully closed when the cam is tightened.

Loosen the cam locking screw to adjust the timing.

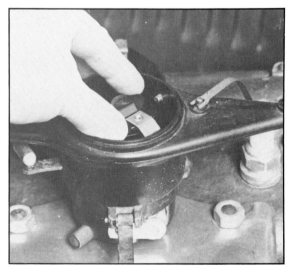

Turn the rotor to the number 1 contact in the distributor body.

8. Check the timing by removing the timing pin from the recess in the timing gear, and turn on the ignition switch. While turning the engine over by hand, press in on the timing pin. If the engine is properly timed, a spark should occur between the points just as the pin slips into the recess in the timing gear.

9. When the ignition has been properly timed, turn off the ignition and replace the rotor and distributor cap. Remove the timing pin and screw it tightly back into the timing gear cover.

The lighting system

The lighting system consists of the light switch, the main wire harness, the headlights, taillights and stoplights.

The lighting switch

The Ford lighting switch is located at the bottom of the steering column, as in most other cars of the period. The switch is operated by turning a lever on the steering wheel. The switch had three positions for the 1928 models and four positions for the 1929-31 models. The difference in the switches was due to the change to the Duolamp-type headlamps with the parking light built in. The early lamps had only bright and dim positions while the newer cars had bright, dim and park, which was either in the second headlamp bulb or in the cowl lights, depending on the model.

The lighting switch bodies are available new but some of them do not fit or work as well as the originals. If the original lighting switch body is in good condition, it might be better to use it than a replacement. The switch body should be cadmium plated for authenticity.

The lighting switch plate is attached to the lighting harness assembly, but again it may be better to check the condition of the old plate and exchange the new one for it if it seems to be usable. The lighting-harness wires plug into the switch plate, but they should be soldered when all fitting and checking of the system is completed.

The new lighting harness assemblies are available in two types: one for cars with cowl lights and one for systems without cowl lights. If the car is an early one with the single-bulb system, the best harness is the one for the cowl lights. Remove the cowl-light wire; only the two headlight wires will remain.

Layout of lighting switch components in order of assembly.

Many times the spring and spider above the lighting switch are rusted and bent. These parts should be replaced if they are in poor condition. The spider fit is important as it fits the square end of the horn tube and turns the lighting switch contact plate.

An area of confusion for many restorers is the horn tube (lighting switch and horn switch handle assembly, as it is called in the parts book). There are five different lengths of horn tube used on the Model A. The problem arises when the tube is missing from the steering column, and its length is not known. The following are the sizes of horn tube:

A-3616-B	Ford	1928-29	45 3/4 inches	(all seven-tooth sectors)
A-3616-C	Gemmer	1929	45 inches	(1929-style two-tooth sector)
A-3616-F	Ford	1930	45 3/4 inches	
A-3616-G	Gemmer	1930	44 31/32 inches	
A-3616-H	Gemmer	1930-31	45 31/32 inches	

These lengths are measured from the top of the tube to the keeper groove at the bottom. The length of the steering column is approximately 7/8 inch shorter than the indicated length of the horn tube. For example, the length from the top of the steering shaft to the bottom of the gear housing on a 1929 two-tooth sector is 44 1/8 inches. The horn tube length would be 45 inches.

The horn tube and lighting switch are installed by sliding the horn tube into the steering column. (This must be done before the steering column is installed on coupes.) Place a yardstick across the top of the steering wheel and bend it under the rim to hold the horn tube in place while the spider and retainer are installed at the bottom.

The lighting switch body is installed by placing the upper half of the switch body on the bracket on the end of the steering column, making sure that the spider enters the slots on the switch contact plate. Slip the lower half of the switch body onto the upper half after running

Lighting switch installed on car. Notice position of hole for wires and bail.

166

the wire harness through the hole in the end of the switch. The hole for the wires should be on the top of the switch and the drain hole on the bottom. Remember to put a cotter pin in the drain hole to keep it clear. The lower switch half is twisted to lock in place. Hold the entire switch in position while slipping the lighting switch bail over the body and locking it to the steering column bracket.

Headlamps

There are basically six different types of headlamps found on the Model A. The greatest difference is found in the shape of the shells, which changed from a parabolic shape in 1928 and 1929 to a more rounded, hemispherical design for 1930 and 1931. The chart shows the prominent features of Model A headlamps for all years.

Model A headlamp applications

Feature	1928 to early 1929	Early 1929 to end of year	1920-31
Shell material	Nickel-plate steel	Nickel-plate steel	Stainless steel
Shell shape	Parabolic	Parabolic	Hemisphere
Focusing socket length	2-1/8 inch	2-1/8 inch	1-3/4 inch
Focus spring	9/16 x 1 1/8 inch	9/16 x 1 /18 inch	9/16 x 3/4 inch
Focus screw	10-32 oval 1 inch	10-32 oval 1 inch	10-32 oval 5/8 inch
Conduit socket	11/16 inch diameter	13/16 inch diameter	13/16 inch diameter
Lens	Vertical flutes Ford Script	Vertical flutes and horizontal prism	Vertical flutes and horizontal prism
Reflector	One socket	One or two sockets	One or two sockets
Shell logo	None	Ford Twolite headlamp	Ford Twolite headlamp
Conduit diameter	7/16 inch	1/2 inch	1/2 inch

Note: All commercial lights were plain steel painted black with plated or stainless rims.

Headlamp removal
1. Remove the wiring harness assembly from the headlamp by pushing in on the end of the conduit and unscrewing it from the shell. The plug and wires may then be pulled out of the headlight connection.
2. Remove the 3/4 inch hex-head nut and lockwasher holding the headlamps to the crossbar and remove the lamp assemblies. Be especially careful on the left lamp as the nut also holds the horn in place. The horn may be removed or temporarily laid on the hood shelf.

Disassembly
1. It will be helpful if a soft towel or cloth is used as a work surface to protect the finish of the headlamp shells. Remove the headlamp door and lens assembly by pulling down on the clamp at the bottom of the shell. Lift the assembly out and up to release it from the clip at the top of the shell.
2. Inside the door are three wire clip retainers which hold the lens in place. These are removed by carefully prying them away from the glass

and out from under the rim. The lens is then removed from the door assembly, wrapped and put in a safe place if it is in good condition and is to be used again. The retainers for the early fluted lenses are slightly shorter than the later style in the original lights, but the replacement retainers are all the same.

3. Remove the bulb from the headlamp socket by twisting and pulling it out. The reflector may now be removed by lifting it out of the shell and releasing the small brass clip on the bulb socket and pushing it out through the rear of the reflector.

4. Remove the focusing screw at the rear of the shell, which will release the spring and bulb socket. Depress the clip at the bottom of the shell to release the wiring plug socket from the shell, allowing the wires and sockets to be removed.

5. Unless the shell is a commercial version that does not require plating or polishing, the lower mounting bracket should be removed from the shell. From the inside of the shell, carefully drill out the rivets holding the mounting plate with a 7/64 inch drill. Removal of this plate allows the polisher to get to the lower part of the shell. These rivets may be replaced with special bolts available from vendors, or 3/16 inch carriage bolts may be used if the square head is ground off. The front bolts may have to be shortened if carriage bolts are used as they will hit the reflector.

Inspection and restoration

Clean the mounting brackets, nuts and washers and paint them with black enamel. The reflector should be cleaned with a silver polish or cleaner. If it is not a like-new appearance, it should be replated with a silver plate for safe, bright headlights.

The outer shell should be inspected for dents and cracks, and these should be repaired. The 1930-31 shells are stainless steel and should not be plated. They usually need only a good polishing to look like new. The

Remove the wires from the rear of the headlamp shell by unscrewing the conduit connection.

Headlight shell disassembled for plating. Original rivets must be drilled out carefully.

1928-29 shells should be plated with a nickel plate. Many non-show-car restorers like to use chrome because it gives a brighter appearance than nickel and requires less care.

The original sockets may be reused if new wires are soldered on them and they are not bent too badly. New sockets are available from any model A parts supplier. The important factor here is that the sockets fit very tightly into the openings in the shell and reflector or there will not be a good ground and the lights will not be bright or steady. The new wires in the sockets should be at least number 16. Make sure that solder does not fall into the light sockets and prevent the spring from moving properly.

The insulator plugs that connect the wiring harness to the light sockets can usually be reused if they are not broken. The 1928 lights have a unique plug that will not accept the bayonet fitting found on most replacement wire harness assemblies. The 1928 insulator uses two screws to hold the wires in place. If an old wire harness is available, the old connectors can be unsoldered and reattached to the new wires. The later connectors will not cause any problem, as they are the more conventional type which slip into the insulator plugs. Any old connectors may be removed from the old wires by clamping the wire in a vise and heating the tip with a soldering iron as the end is pulled off the wire.

Reassembly of the headlamps is simply the reverse order of the disassembly. Make sure that the gasket is replaced that separates the reflectors from the door and lens. Make sure that all metal-to-metal fits are tight for a good ground. Some restorers like to add a wire soldered to the light socket and run it through the conduit, attaching it to the frame at the hood hook mounts. Remember to make this connection for both lights and secure it to clean, bare metal at the frame for maximum effectiveness.

Follow the directions found on pages 211 and 212 of the Ford Service Bulletins for 1928 for focusing of the headlights.

The taillights

The taillights took on two distinct styles during the production of the Model A. The first was the drum-style taillight. This style was used on all passenger and commercial vehicles to about February 1929, and on trucks until well into 1930.

The second variety was the so-called teacup style that was used from early 1929 until the end of production. The chart shows the features of all the Model A taillights.

Taillight Applications

Feature	1928 to early 1929	Early 1929 to end of year	1930-31
Shell material	Brass nickel plate	Brass nickel plate	Stainless
Shell shape	Drum	Teacup	Teacup
Socket	Bakelite in metal	Wire pigtail	Wire pigtail
Lens	Red	Red and amber	Red and amber
Logo	Duolight	Duolamp	Duolamp

Note: All commercial lights were black-painted steel. The drum taillight assembly was used in the commercial models until early 1930.

Removal of taillight
1. The 1928 taillights are removed by taking off the two bolts and nuts holding the backing plate to the forged mounting bracket. The backing plate is part of the taillight on the early drum-style units. The light wire harness must be disconnected from the Bakelite plug at the rear of the light.
2. The 1929-31 Duolamp lights are removed by removing the two screws holding the light body to the stamped bracket and disconnecting the wire harness assembly at the light.

Disassembly of 1928-29 drum taillight
1. Remove the taillight shell from the backing plate by removing the two

Disconnect wires at rear of drum taillight by pulling them out of the Bakelite socket.

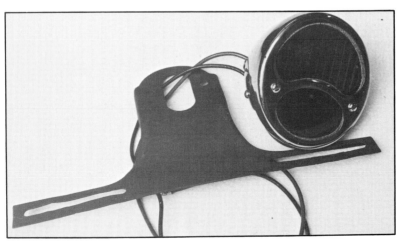

Duolamp assembly as removed from car.

screws on the front of the shell and removing the shell.

2. The lens is removed by removing the lens retainers located inside the shell. The lens and stop indicator will come out of the shell.

3. The license light lens is removed by taking out the two clips located in the bottom of the shell.

4. Remove the light bulbs from the sockets on the backing plate. Remove the Bakelite socket by depressing the small button located on the top of the socket and turning the socket until it releases from the brass strip in the front of the backing plate. It may have to be loosened with penetrating oil before it will come out easily. Be careful not to break this

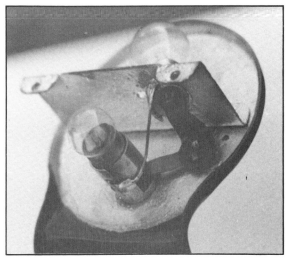

Bakelite socket installed in drum taillight base. Notice extra ground wire soldered to socket.

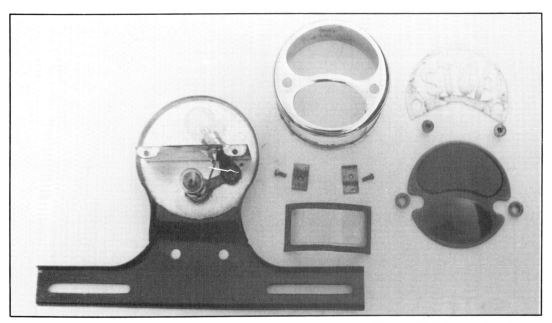

Disassembled drum-style taillamp.

socket as it is hard to find and reproductions are rather expensive.

5. The shell-mounting bracket may be removed if necessary by drilling out the two rivets holding it to the backing plate. All of the parts of the drum taillight are available new from most parts suppliers, but they are expensive so it is important to use as many original parts as possible.

Inspection and restoration

Clean the backing plate and fill all dents and pits. The backing plate should be painted with a gloss-black enamel. The portion behind the lens should be masked and painted with silver or aluminum paint for reflection.

The shell should be replated with nickel finish. The original passenger shell was brass, but many restorers like to use the commercial shell made of steel. There is less likely to be cracks in the steel, but it may be rusty. The commercial shells may be more available because they were used longer.

The light sockets should be cleaned for good electrical contact. If the old Bakelite socket is to be reused, it should be inspected for cracks and breaks. Lenses and gaskets are available new and should be replaced if necessary. The taillight is reassembled in the reverse order of disassembly. The bulbs should be replaced with fifteen-candlepower units.

Disassembly of 1929-31 Duolamp taillight

1. Remove the lens by removing the two screws holding the lamp door to the body. The lens and gasket will come off with the door.

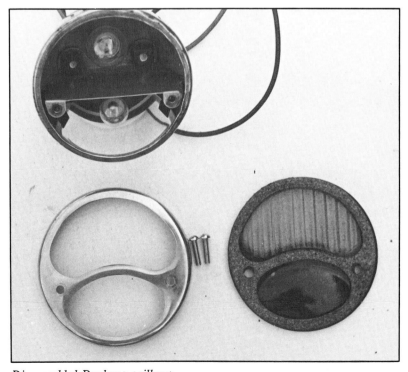

Disassembled Duolamp taillamp.

172

2. Remove the two clips holding the license light lens in the bottom of the light body and remove the lens.

3. Remove the two bulbs from the sockets and pull the pigtails out of the socket.

Inspection and restoration

The light body should be inspected for cracks and dents. The sockets should have new wires soldered on if they are to be reused. Be careful not to get solder inside the socket or the spring will not operate properly. Replace the pigtails and plugs in the light socket. The shell should be polished if it is stainless steel, and finished and painted with black enamel if it is a commercial model. New lenses and gaskets are available from Model A parts suppliers. The bulb should be replaced using a fifteen-candlepower unit. Reassemble the light in the reverse order of disassembly.

Remember to provide a good ground for the lights. Sometimes it may be necessary to connect a separate ground wire from the frame and solder it to a light socket.

The cowl lights

Restoration of the cowl lights is very much the same as the head-light restoration. The arms are easily broken so great care must be taken when removing them from the light body and from the car.

Horn

Each Model A Ford was equipped with a horn which was mounted under the left headlamp bracket. Horns were manufactured by Sparton, Ames, GMI (General Manufacturing Industries), EA Laboratories and Stewart-Warner. They were all very similar in appearance except for the motor cover. All Sparton horns had the Sparton name on the back and

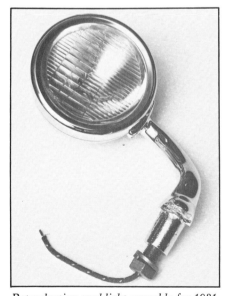

Reproduction cowl light assembly for 1931 models.

a data plate on the top of the motor cover. The MARC/MAFCA Judging Standards has a chart showing the applications of the various types of Model A horns.

Disassembly of the horn begins by removing the rear cover retaining screw and pulling off the rear cover. The horn is like any other electric motor and may be serviced and repaired accordingly.

Reproduction horns are available for the nonpurists, but they do not have the same appearance or sound of the original types. The quality of the original horns is similar, but most horns remaining today seem to be either Stewart-Warner or Sparton. The horn wires are routed through conduit similar to that used for the headlight wiring.

Troubleshooting the Model A electrical system

Starter will not turn: Check for dead battery. Headlights will dim when the starter button is depressed. Check the terminals for tightness and cleanliness. Check the cells of the battery. Check the starter connections. A good method of ensuring a good battery ground is to clean the frame to bare metal and tin the connecting point of the ground cable with solder. It requires 200 to 300 amps to turn the starter and any bad connection will prevent it from operating properly.

Test the battery ground strap by attaching the negative test lead of a voltmeter to the frame close to the battery, and attach the positive lead to the grounded battery post. Crank the engine with the starter and the voltmeter should show a reading of near zero. If the meter shows a higher reading, a poor ground is indicated.

To test the starter cable, attach the positive test lead of the voltmeter to the starter switch post and the negative lead to the negative battery post. If a reading shows on the voltmeter, it indicates that there is a bad connection.

Starter turns but will not engage flywheel: Remove starter and check Bendix for free movement. Clean and lubricate with light oil if necessary. It is also possible that the Bendix spring has broken or the Bendix bolts have broken or dropped off inside the flywheel housing. If the bolts are replaced, be sure that they are the correct special bolts A11377-C and A11382 as shown on page 288 of the Ford Service Bulletins.

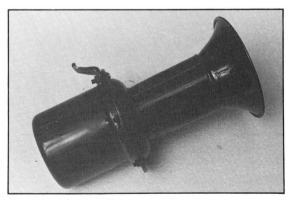
A restored Stewart-Warner horn.

Original horn with cover removed.

Starter is stuck: The Bendix is stuck. Put transmission in high or second gear and rock the car to disengage starter. The starter shaft could also be bent.

Engine will not start: Check for a spark by shorting a screwdriver across a plug to the head while cranking the engine with the ignition on. A blue spark should jump to the spark plug. If there is no spark, check the points to see that they are opening and closing properly. See that the points are set to the proper gap of 0.018 to 0.022 inch. Check the rotor, cap and distributor body to see that they are not cracked. Check the breaker plate for a short to the ground or a short in the wire to the lower plate.

If these check out, rotate the engine until the points are closed. Then, with the ignition switch on, break the points with a screwdriver. At this time, a spark should jump from the high-tension lead from the coil to a ground. If this does not happen, the coil may be bad. If the high-tension lead is not allowed to discharge, the coil may be damaged, so do not allow it to sit with the ignition on. If there is a spark when the points open, the ignition switch circuit is good.

Be certain that the high-tension wire is pushed firmly into the coil. If this wire does not make a good contact, the high voltage may break down the insulation of the coil and crack the Bakelite on the end of the case. Be sure to keep dust, grease and moisture off the Bakelite of the coil. Be sure that the ignition is not left on with the points closed, as the current flowing through the coil will burn it out. Be sure coil wire is metal core and not resistance wire.

Engine runs rough, has low power or backfires: Check condensor or replace the condensor with a new one. A spare condensor should always be carried in hot weather. Be sure that backfiring is not caused from a fuel-system or carburetor problem.

Generator charge is too high or low: Remove the dust cover from the generator and readjust by moving brush in the direction of rotation to increase charge and the opposite direction to decrease. Set the charge to 6 to 10 amps for normal driving conditions. Increase it for winter or nighttime driving. The generator should show approximately 2 amps charge with the headlights on at normal cruising speed.

Ammeter shows discharge with engine off or at idle: The generator cutout is probably stuck in the closed position. Tap it to open the points. If it will not open, disconnect the generator-to-cutout wire and see if the reading changes. If it does, then replace the cutout or leave the generator wire off and connect the generator terminal to ground to prevent burning up the generator so the car may be driven. The car may be driven with a cutout stuck closed, but the generator wire will have to be disconnected when the ignition is turned off.

Ammeter shows no charge: Connect a test light to the generator terminal and a ground. The light should just glow when the engine is running. If the cutout is not operating properly and is open, the test light will become excessively bright and burn out if the engine is speeded up. If driven in this condition, the generator will be burned up. Replace the cutout or bypass the cutout by placing a wire between the two terminals of the cutout while the engine is running. Disconnect this wire when the engine is turned off.

If the light does not function when connected to the generator, check for loose connections at the brushes and generator terminal. Check for worn-out brushes.

Headlights burn too brightly: The generator has a poor ground or the battery connections are loose or dirty. If the battery is not connected, the generator voltage will go too high and burn out the generator.

The ammeter is hot: Check the ammeter terminals for loose connections. If the ammeter is already burned out, connect both ammeter wires to the same terminal to continue to operate the engine and lights until the ammeter can be replaced. Check all connections at the battery, generator mount, cutout, headlights and taillights. Check all connections at the terminal box. Sometimes a nut inside some replacement terminal boxes comes loose and shorts against the firewall.

Lights burn out prematurely: Generator output is too high due to a loose connection or a bad ground. Clean and tighten all connections.

The Model A electrical system is very simple and if it is assembled properly will cause little trouble. There are Model A's running that have been driven for twenty years or more with no problems. These are usually the cars with the most original parts. A little care and attention to detail and cleanliness is all that should be required to have a dependable electrical system.

Chapter 12

BODY AND FENDER ASSEMBLY

MODEL A Ford bodies, like the Model T, were of composite construction. This means that the body was made of a combination of wood and metal. Wood was considered the basis for all auto body design from the very beginning. Hardwood provided the strength, quietness and flexibility demanded in automobile building well into the thirties. Another reason that wood was so prevalent was that the equipment did not exist to create large sheet metal stampings until about 1930. Chrysler, in 1931, was one of the first cars to use what was called an all-metal body. The Ford closed cab body, built by Budd corporation in August of 1931, was the first all-steel automotive body. Budd corporation was a pioneer in all-steel body construction.

Ford bodies for the most part did not use as much wood as many other car makers were using. The body designs of General Motors cars for the most part consisted of wood construction covered with metal panels, while the Ford used wood mostly for reinforcement and for upholstery attachment. Some of the exceptions to this were the Fordors, convertible sedans and Victoria bodies which used wood extensively.

Although the primary function of the wood in Model A open bodies was upholstery attachment, the wood did provide a substantial amount of stiffness to the sheet metal and helped to provide a solid, quiet feeling to the body.

Model A fenders were made at the major assembly plants on large

Bliss stamping machines. After a small amount of finish work, these fenders were ready for bonderizing and painting. Model A fenders were all dipped in a black enamel; each one carried a deep, hard gloss of equal brilliance inside and out.

Body removal

1. Remove the hood from the car by removing the hinge bracket from the top of the cowl and lifting the hood free of the body. Remove the radiator brace rods by loosening the lock nuts on both ends and lifting the rods off the body and radiator. From inside the car, remove the carpet or floor mat and floorboards. Remove the choke and carburetor adjustment rod from the body along with its spring and sleeve. Disconnect cables from the battery and pull them aside. Disconnect the engine wires from the junction box on the firewall. Disconnect the coil wire from the engine. Remove the clamp from the steering column to the tank mount. Remove fuel line and ignition cable.

2. Remove the speedometer cable connection from the driveshaft socket by unscrewing the knurled nut with pliers and carefully pulling the cable from the socket. Remove the 1/4 inch bolt and nut holding the cable clamp to the chassis on the right side of the frame and pull the cable up out of the way.

3. Remove the rear fenders by taking off the 1/4 inch carriage bolt, nut and lockwasher holding the fender bracket to the fender. Using a 1/2

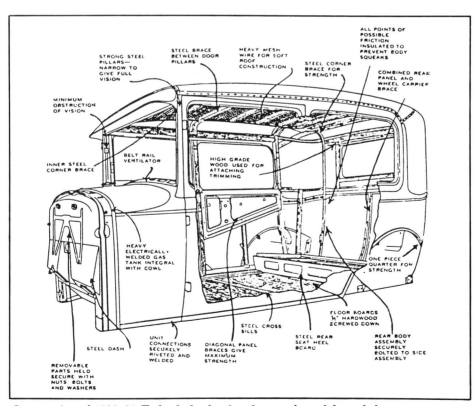

Construction of 1930–31 Tudor body showing the use of wood for upholstery attachment and floor boards, from a 1930 sales brochure.

inch wrench, remove the two 5/16 inch hex-head bolts holding the fender bracket to the body.

4. Remove the two 5/16 inch carriage bolts, nuts and lockwashers holding the fender to the running board. Remove the two 1/4 inch bolts, nut and washers holding the fender to the splash aprons. Remove the four

Wood framework of a 1928 Model A road-ster body.

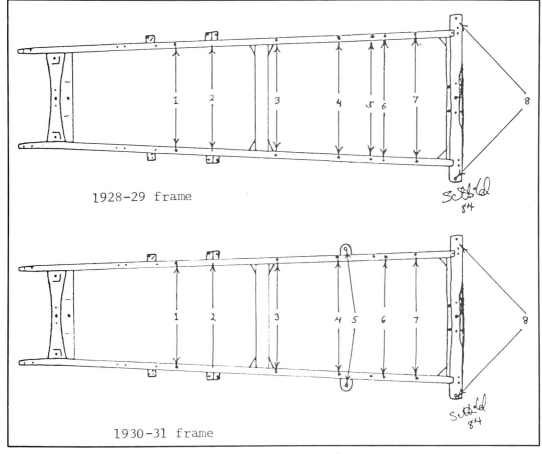

Body mounting holes on frame. Bolts for positions 4 through 8 will vary according to body style.

5/16 inch hex-head bolts, flatwashers and lockwashers holding the fenders to the body and remove the fenders.

5. Remove the four 5/16 inch bolts and lockwashers from the bumper bracket to body mount at the rear of the body.

6. Remove all body bolts. The first three bolts on each side are the same on all models. The rest of the body fasteners will vary according to body style and year.

7. Remove the body by lifting it with ropes or chains attached to balance points on either side of the body. Be careful to wrap the ropes or chains with padding to protect the finish of the body. The steering column will be cleared by raising the body slightly in the front and lifting it carefully over the wheel. The weight of Model A bodies with equipment is given in the following chart to be sure that the lifting apparatus is sturdy enough to support the load.

Weight of Model A and AA bodies
Tudor sedan—726 pounds
Fordor sedan—782 pounds
Town sedan—810 pounds
Sport coupe—596 pounds
Coupe—591 pounds
Cabriolet—575 pounds
Roadster—465 pounds

Phaeton—549 pounds
Station wagon—950 pounds
Open cab—300 pounds
Closed cab—411 pounds
A panel—875 pounds
AA panel—1057 pounds

A badly deteriorated 1930 coupe body such as this will require replacement of all wood. This car was found in the proverbial farmer's field. (Notice that the hood was used as the cow's hoof mat.) The restorer in this case is fabricating all of his wood himself with home shop tools and hand fitting.

Once the body is removed it may be placed on sawhorses or on a rollaway dolly made for the purpose from timbers and wheels available from any hardware store.

Body service

The most destructive thing to affect the body of any old car is rust. Fifty years of misuse, damage, moisture and leaking barns have taken their toll on the Model A Ford. The most frequent areas of damage are the lower cowl sections and the lower part of the doors. Many cars have been found with these areas rusted away completely. Not too many years ago, some of these would have been considered unrestorable, but with cars becoming more scarce some of these examples may be the only ones left for the average restorer to work on.

Fortunately for the restorer today, there are many sources of replacement metal body parts for the Model A. Patch panels are available for the door panels, cowl panels, rear deck panels, and fender wells. There are even new body pieces available including roadster doors, cowl sections, deck lids, splash aprons and fenders.

The first step in the repair of the body is the disassembly and cleaning of all components. Most of the Model A body parts are held together with small bolts or rivets, so disassembly is not difficult. Initial inspection of the body should include identifying any past repairs and the condition of any body wood. If the body is rusted, it is likely that the wood under the rust is also deteriorated beyond use. Like the metal parts, new wood is available for most Model A body styles. (A list of sources for Model A parts will be found at the end of this book.)

The first step in disassembly will be the removal of the upholstery if it remains reasonably intact. Great care should be taken in the removal of upholstery panels along with lots of photographs to show how

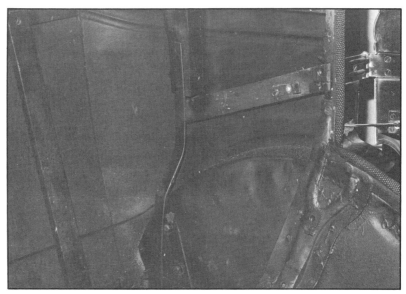

The interior wood structure of the four-door body types is very susceptible to decay from leaking tops and windows. This photo illustrates the left rear quarter of a 1930 Murray town sedan with the trim removed.

it went in. The original pieces should be kept if possible so they can be matched with the new upholstery when it is installed or made.

When the body is apart, all parts should be cleaned of rust and paint. If taken down to bare metal, a good metal prep should be applied immediately to prevent rusting. The parts may be cleaned with chemical solutions or with sandblasting. Sandblasting leaves a bit rougher surface than the chemical, but since the surfaces are to be sanded anyway, the finish is insignificant. There are supporters of both methods and either one works well.

The next step to body restoration is the removal of all dents, dings and distortions. It is important to get as smooth a metal surface as possible before any primer, filler or lead is applied. The less putty and filler that is required, the better the final product will be. All sanding scratches should be removed with no coarser than 220 grit paper before any primer is applied. If this is not done, the scratches will show through to the surface and be almost impossible to remove.

Most body shops would rather work on the car with the body firmly mounted on the frame. The fenders, especially, are easier to work on while still attached to the body. If the work is to be done by someone else, it is important to attach all body and fender components before sending out the car. Whether the body work is done before or after, the cleaning and derusting of the body is really determined by the condition of the body. If the body is extremely rusted and deteriorated, it should be derusted and cleaned to solid metal before sending to the body shop or beginning body work. If a body is in very good condition, it may not need to be disassembled completely, but only stripped of upholstery, trim and glass. My AA truck (see photo) cab is an example of a body in extremely deteriorated condition. This body will need total replacement of all wood and many metal body parts. The body has been disassembled at this point and partially reassembled for fitting of new body panels.

AA truck body ready for metal replacement and rebuilding.

When all body work is completed and the surface is as smooth as the final finish should be, the body is ready for primer. Be sure that the primer being used is the right type for the use intended. Check with a good dealer to understand the difference between primer-surfacer, primer-sealer and high-build primers. These are all intended for different purposes and will only be successful performing the job they were designed for. Be sure to apply a metal-etching solution to the bare metal before any primer is applied. This will prevent rusting and remove any impurities such as grease or oil from the skin. Some plastic fillers are meant to be used only on top of primer, so be sure of the instructions on the label of any product before use.

If major repair work is to be done, such as welding or brazing or replacement of metal panels, it may be better to leave the primer off until any work is completed which may involve heat. (Details of welding and repairing body panels will not be covered in this book as they are well covered in other volumes on general restoration and rebuilding techniques.)

While attention to the body itself is usually foremost in the mind of the restorer, components such as the doors and the hood also require detailed restoration. The hood is a difficult area for many because it tends to get dented frequently and easily over years of use. It also gets rusted quite easily because of radiator boilover and engine heat. The hood becomes more important when one realizes that it is probably the part most noticed about the car at first meeting.

The hood assembly can be a difficult thing to deal with from the first time the novice restorer tries to take it apart. A good method of disassembling the hood is to try to get the hinge rods loose enough to attach them to the chuck of a drill. After allowing the hinges to soak with penetrating oil for a while, use the drill to spin the hinge rods out. If at all possible, use stainless-steel hood rods for replacement.

There are replacement hoods available from parts suppliers but the quality of some of them is less than perfect. Be sure to check with other restorers about the quality of replacement hoods before putting out a lot of money.

Doors are another problem for many restorers. The doors of an old Ford may have been wrecked, slammed, shot and rusted beyond use—sometimes the only answer is to find a better one. Fortunately, as was mentioned earlier, new doors are available for 1928-29 roadsters and roadster pickups. They are quite expensive, but sometimes that is the only solution to a perplexing problem.

For the rest of the body styles, some help comes from the fact that many doors are interchangeable among different body types. The following chart shows the Model A doors that will interchange:
1928-29 Tudor fits 1928-29 Coupe
1928-29 roadster fits 1928-29 roadster pick-up and Phaeton
1930-31 Tudor fits 1930-31 closed cab A and AA
1930-31 Victoria fits 400A convertible sedan
1930-31 roadster fits 1930-31 Phaeton and roadster pick-up

Many other fender and body parts are interchangeable but the authenticity should be checked with the current MARC/MAFCA Judging Standards if the car is to be shown competitively. The 1930-31 AA truck front fenders are the same as the passenger car fenders unless they are equipped with side-mount wells. If an AA truck is equipped with side-mounted spares, it should have a door with a well for tire clearance built in. The truck also uses the same radiator splash apron, cowl and splash apron front section as 1930-31 passenger cars. A comprehensive comparison of parts that may be interchanged will be found by using a parts price list for the chassis and body available from most automotive book suppliers. By looking up the part number and seeing which body style and years use that part, searching for replacements may be made a bit easier. A good list of body parts interchangeable among 1928-29 styles is given in *The Ford Model A As Henry Built It.*

Fitting the body

The fitting of the body components and the body to the frame should be accomplished before the final paint is applied. If the body is fitted afterward the trim or molding colors will not align and the paint may be scratched during the fitting process. The fit of the doors is very critical to the looks and enjoyment of the car. It will certainly ruin a trip or tour if the door does not close or comes open while going down the road. The fit of the doors on a closed car is also important to seal out rain and wind from the interior.

The doors are aligned with the body by the use of shims under the body where it bolts to the frame. If a door is low at the latch side, raise it by placing shims under the bolt nearest the hinge of that door. Usually, rubber body pads of 1/4 inch thickness work well as shims. Remember to pull the body bolts up tight each time the body and door fit is checked. Sometimes, the door problem can be traced to worn hinges and hinge pins. New pins and oversized pins are available, but the big-

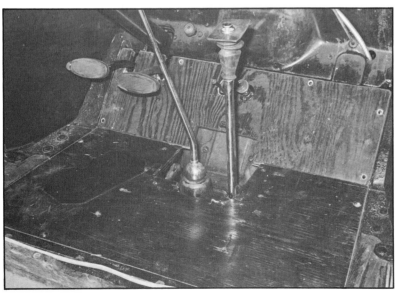

This 1930 front floor board is ready for the installation of the screws which secure it to the body sub rails. A thin felt seal should be tacked to the outside edge of the boards before installation.

gest problem is usually removing the old ones.

Hinge pins may be removed by using a large C-clamp. Place the clamp over the hinge pin with a small socket on the top and the clamp pushing against the bottom of the pin. Tighten the clamp, and the pin should loosen enough to be driven out. Be careful not to spread the bottom of the pin, or it will not come through without being sawed apart. Some pins are rusted in so tightly that the only way to get them out is to remove the hinge and drill the pin out on a drill press.

When the time comes to mount the body to the frame, webbing is placed on the frame rails and the splash aprons are attached to the frame. The rubber pads used under the body blocks should be fastened

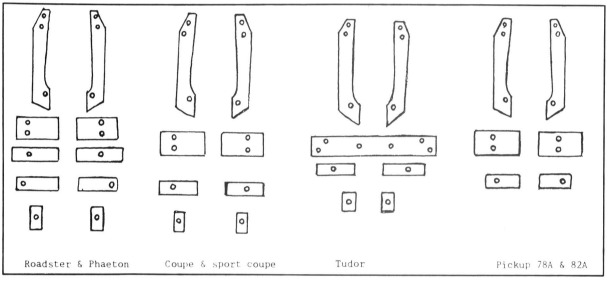

Roadster & Phaeton   Coupe & sport coupe   Tudor   Pickup 78A & 82A

Body blocks for various 1928–29 models.

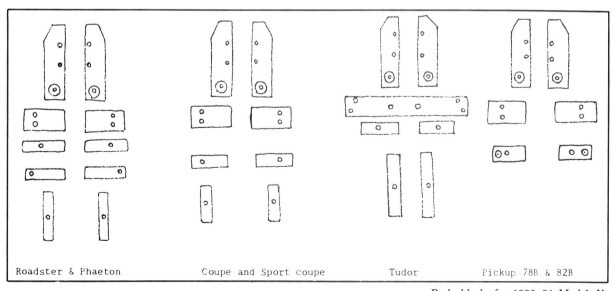

Roadster & Phaeton   Coupe and Sport coupe   Tudor   Pickup 78B & 82B

Body blocks for 1930–31 Model A's.

to the body blocks either with staples or with small nails to hold them in place while the blocks are mounted. All blocks should be coated with a wood preservative or shellac before installation to prevent deterioration. For appearance purposes, a gray-black flat paint or stain may be used to match the original wood preservative.

When the body and doors are properly mounted the doors should close and latch easily without any twisting or forcing. It is important that the body be fitted and mounted properly before any top or upholstery work is done, or wrinkles will surely appear in the finished product.

Painting the body

Finishing any of the body parts takes plenty of patience if the parts are rusty and pitted. Remember to wait at least twenty-four hours, or more, for the primer-surfacer to dry before sanding or the primer will shrink and the pits will show through later. When it seems that enough filling and sanding have been done, it probably needs at least one more coat. Ditzler Red-Cap spot putty does a fine job of filling nicks, pits and scratches. This is basically a primer in putty form, so it blends well with the primer coats.

Painting will not be covered here except in general terms and suggestions about the Model A finish. The first consideration when the car is ready for final finishing is what colors will be used. If the car is to be authentic, the only source of correct information is the MARC/MAFCA Judging Standards which will give the correct color combinations according to body style and year. The formulas for these colors should be

A 1931 Sport coupe mounted for body alignment and fitting.

available from any good Ditzler automotive paint dealer. The paint dealer will also help the restorer who wants to do his or her own painting select the right equipment and materials for a good job.

Painting is not difficult as long as you have some patience and a willingness to work hard. The original finish on the Model A was lacquer, and that is what is recommended for the refinishing. Lacquer is very forgiving to the novice painter as it can be repaired and rubbed out to a nice finish, even if the application is not perfect. The important thing to strive for in a good paint job is good preparation of the metal. The paint is never any better than the surface to which it is applied. If a lot of care and time are spent on preparing the surface and making it as smooth and flawless as possible, then a good final finish will not be difficult to achieve.

Because enamel tends to provide a much harder finish, the fenders on the Model A were dipped in enamel when new, but many restorers use lacquer instead of enamel and achieve beautiful results. The Judging Standards do not specify that enamel must be used, only that the finish on the undersides of the fenders should be as smooth as the top sides.

When the lacquer has been applied and dried well the real work begins. Rubbing out lacquer with 600 grit wet or dry sand paper and rubbing compound is the task that creates the final gloss that makes the Model A look like it should. The only reason that six to eight coats of lacquer need be applied is so that sufficient material is left for the rubbing-out process. Remember that when the Model A was built, the firewall and inside of the hood were not rubbed out. The body on the commercial models was not rubbed out normally but could be ordered that way.

There is a controversy about whether the paint should be applied before the upholstery or after. Upholsterers would rather have the paint applied afterward because they do not want to scratch or damage the finish while working on the body. This is a valid concern, but I feel that it is better to paint the car first because the color will be spread to areas of the body that could not be reached if the upholstery were installed. It is also easier to repair scratches in lacquer than it is to try to mask windlace and keep overspray off upholstery material. The car was originally painted before the upholstery was installed, and to do the same during restoration is probably the best method.

A trick that may simplify the painting of the molding is to paint the molding and belt colors first and then mask them and apply the body colors. Even though it was not done this way at the factory, it is easier to mask the moldings than the entire body.

Be certain that the humidity is not too high on the days that primer or color is applied. Moisture in the air will cause the color coats to be dull and almost impossible to rub out. If any water gets under the surface, it will definitely come through later and ruin the finish. Check with the paint dealer about these conditions.

Many restorers do not like to do body work and painting, but it is a good feeling to know that all the praise for that beautiful paint job will be for you. The finishing touch on that new restoration is the thing that enhances all the other work, and the pride in knowing that you have done it yourself is worth all the work and sweat.

Some general painting tips for a quality finish:

1. Never use lightweight plastic fillers. Use the heaviest, best-quality available.
2. Use plastic sheets rather than cardboard for mixing body plastic to prevent air bubbles.
3. Do not use metal conditioner before plastic filler work.
4. Always use a metal conditioner.
5. Do not allow primer to remain exposed to atmosphere more than fifty hours before painting. Primer absorbs moisture.
6. Never put holes in panels to repair dents.
7. Try not to use filler more than 1/8 inch thick.
8. Always thin primer properly to prevent swelling later.
9. Use only the best-quality thinner, even for primer. Cheap thinners are sometimes recycled with methanol.
10. Always use a sealer before the color coat.

Upholstery

The upholstery is the one area that most restorers do not tackle themselves. While it is true that the very good upholstery kits now available make it possible for the patient amateur restorer to do a good job on the interior, recreating original upholstery from scratch if that is necessary, it is a job best left to professionals with old car experience.

The kits that are available from the upholstery suppliers usually come with good instructions on the fitting and installation of their materials. These kits do not require any sewing and very little cutting, but they do frequently require sometimes difficult interpretations of drawings or instructions.

One of the most helpful things that the home restorer can do (whether he does the job himself or has an expert do it) is to carefully remove the old interior if it is intact. The original materials will prove invaluable for patterns and for comparing with the kit for sizes and loca-

This upholstery kit for a 1930 Tudor illustrates the completeness of the components. No sewing is required and the home hobbyist can usually perform the installation with a little care and patience.

tions of components. Lots of pictures should be taken when the old interior is removed. It will also be helpful to find someone else with an identical car to see how that interior was installed. The best source to follow is the original factory photographs of the interior which will show exactly how it was supposed to look. These photos are available in the MARC/MAFCA Judging Standards and in *The Ford Model A As Henry Built It* (highly recommended as a source for both interior and body finishes).

If the interior is to be made by an upholstery craftsman from scratch, then the restorer may need to do some preparation. The upholsterer may want to remove the interior himself to see how it is installed, so he or she should be consulted before removing anything. If this cannot be done, then pictures, notes and original patterns will be necessary. Before the body is delivered to the upholsterer, make sure that all nails have been removed from the wood and that the interior is cleaned as well as it can be. The holes in the wood from the old nails should also be filled with wood putty or epoxy filler. (A good material to use for all wood filling and reinforcing purposes is Kwik-Poly improved R.S.P. available from T-Distributing Inc. This material is also very good for filling in badly rusted metal surfaces in the frame and body.)

Even if the interior is bought as a kit, it may still be advantageous to have the kit installed by a professional. The professional upholsterer knows just how much to stretch the cloth, just where and when to cut it and how to get rid of wrinkles in ways that the average restorer would not think of. The professional will also have the heavy-duty sewing

The carpet kick panel is glued to the lower edge of the front seatback on the town sedan.

equipment necessary to resew any of the seams in the kit which do not fit properly. The tools and the experience available to the professional upholsterer make it easy for him to accomplish a job that would be extremely difficult for anyone else.

Welting

Installation of the welting around the various body components can be a frustrating task, especially if the panels do not fit as well as they

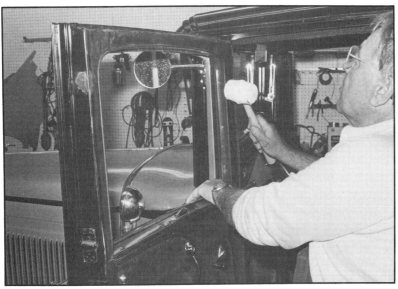

Master upholsterer Hunter Bingaman carefully taps the garnish molding in place on a Fordor sedan left front door. Notice the use of a white rubber mallet to prevent black marks on the finish. After locating the molding, it is secured with oval head screws.

The front door of a Murray-bodied town sedan with the lower portion of the two-piece garnish molding installed.

should. The purpose of body welting is to provide an antisqueak material between the panels and to keep out moisture and wind.

Many restorers like to paint all body panels before assembly for ease of handling and to make sure that paint is applied to all surfaces. These panels are usually assembled with fresh, black welting as the body is put together. The careful restorer should remember that when the Model A was built, the body was assembled before it was painted and the welting should be the same color as the body except where it fits between the fender and body.

If the body welting (such as that between the gas tank and the cowl) is to appear original, it should be painted separately with body color before assembly. This is usually accomplished by cutting it to size and hanging it from a clothes pin so it can be sprayed easily.

Fit the welting to the panel before assembly and cut notches wherever a bolt is used. These notches will also help to form the welting around the curves without wrinkles.

Probably the most difficult area for the application of the welting is the gas tank to the cowl. On the 1928-29 cars, the welting goes along the sides of the cowl panels and up over the top of the tank under the windshield trim panel. There is no welting between the tank and the lower cowl panels. The welting on 1930-31 models goes between the tank and the lower cowl panels and should be painted the upper body color.

A good way to install the welting smoothly is to attach strips of cloth to the welting with staples or stitching, leaving pieces long enough to pull the welting into place from behind as the panels are bolted into place. The cloth may be trimmed off after the panels are secured. Be sure to attach the clamps to the tank-cowl joint on the inside. These clamps prevent the body from spreading out at the seam and causing a gap.

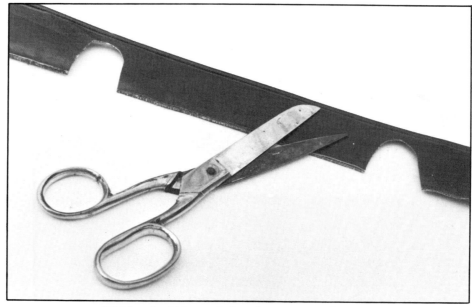

Welting should be notched to clear screws and to easily go around corners.

Glass

Glass cutting is another task that is best left to professionals. If original glass patterns are not available, then patterns will have to be made from paper or cardboard. Most glass cutters will not work from dimensions but must have patterns. The primary reason for this is that they will not be responsible for the fit of the glass unless the owner provides the patterns. It is probably best if the glass shop installs the glass in the frames or channels. They will be responsible for any breakage if they install it.

After the glass is in the channels, it may be installed in the car by the owner if he desires. This is not a difficult job, requiring only a little thought and patience. On most Model A bodies, the top of the door frame must be removed to replace the glass and channels. These are removed by removing the three screws on the top of the door and lifting off the piece. The channels are fastened in the door frame with clips on the top and bottom.

Rumble seat installation

One of the most popular conversions with owners of coupes and roadsters is the change from trunk to rumble seat. Originally, Ford made the rumble seat standard equipment on Sport coupes and cabriolets, and an option on the coupes and roadsters. The rumble seat allowed for an additional bit of seating room that was comfortable, if not spacious, for two people.

The conversion from a trunk to a rumble seat is not difficult and may be done easily in a few hours. Probably the best description of the job is the following instruction sheet issued to dealers in 1928. Since the description involves original Ford part numbers, a Parts Price List is necessary to interpret the directions. Included here are additional notes in parentheses for restorers, to supplement original instructions.

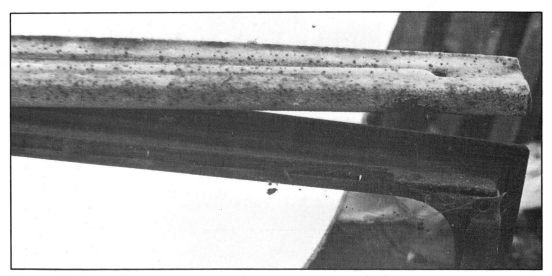

On most closed cars, the door top panel must be removed to take out the door glass.

Instructions for rumble seat installation in roadsters, business and standard coupes.

1. Open rear deck door and remove by taking out hinge screw A-20910 at each upper corner. Remove hinges from upper corner of deck opening.

2. Remove deck door support on left side of deck opening.

3. Remove rear floor pan assembly, taking out six screws A-20552, six nuts A-21661 and six lockwashers A-22150 in front end. Remove support for pan at rear edge by taking off six screws A-20210 and six lockwashers A-22088. Remove bolt A-21144 from tire carrier bracket support nut A-21795, pin A-23531.

4. Remove deck door guides in two lower corners of deck opening, guide A-41516, screw A-20536, nut A-21661, lockwasher A-22150.

5. Remove lock from deck door and drill 15/16 inch hole in front edge of door locating from hole in under side. Drill 5/32 inch hole 11/16 inch forward from center of 15/16 inch hole, install lock on front end of door. Install rubber plug A-41540 in hole left open in rear edge of door. (Restorers will want to fill this hole permanently.) If the door does not have six clinch nuts on the under side and approximately in center for the hinge arm, it will be necessary to replace the door assembly less lock instead of drilling the door and installing the lock at the top edge of the door instead of the lower edge. (Restorers will want to use the door they have and attach the hinges by using sheet metal screws or bolts and nuts.)

6. Install striker plate A-52500 at front end of deck opening, using two screws A-20535, two nuts A-21661, two lockwashers A-22150.

7. Install rear floor pan A-50203 in coupe, and A-40203 in roadster, using six screws A-20233 at rear edge, four screws A-22552 at front edge in center. Use nuts A-21661 and lockwasher A-22150 on these screws.

The rumble seat lid latch was mounted in this location on earlier cars.

Hinges for rumble seat installed in body. Notice position of door bumpers on body pan.

Install deck door bumpers lower A-52484 on bumper brackets, A-52486 in coupe, and A-41536 in roadster, using tubular rivets A-22987 on each bracket. Install brackets on floor pan using four screws A-20535, four nuts A-21661 and lockwashers A-22150 on each bracket. (Restorers will find that the only bracket available new is A-41485 in a style to fit each of the year styles.) Use three screws A-20535, three nuts A-21661 and three lockwashers A-22150 at each side of floor pan to rear deck corner plate. Use bolt A-21136, nut A-21795, pin A-23531, through floor pan in tire carrier support. (This will not apply, of course, if side-mounted spares are used.)

8. Install wood slats—deck cardboard retainer lower, A-52662 in coupe, and A-41662 in roadster, using one screw A-20224, one nut A-21572, and lockwasher A-22088 through center hole in rear deck pillar. Use same screw and nut in the hole provided in the front deck pillar. To fasten the front end of the slat in the standard coupe, remove the seat back and loosen the side trim panel, and bolt slats to trim rail, using bolt A-20263, nut A-21572, lockwasher A-22088.

9. Secure deck door body hinge A-52530 right hand, and A-52531 left hand in coupe, A-41543 right hand, A-41544 left hand in roadster, to rear deck pillar, using two screws A-20709, two nuts A-21702, two lockwashers A-22217 in each hinge. Use one stove bolt A-20535, one nut A-21661 and one washer A-22150 in each body hinge to drain trough. (Restorers will note that the only new hinge assembly available today goes by the part number A-41543 for all models.)

10. Install deck door hinge and arm assembly A-52526 RH and A-52527 LH using six screws A-20402 on each side.

11. Remove screws and nut holding drain trough to quarter panels inside the deck lid opening, install cardboard retainer upper A-41660 on each side, using same screws and nuts in the same holes. (The 1930-31 model drain trough was welded to the body, so this step may be skipped.)

12. Assemble deck door guide A-41514 in upper corner to deck opening, using screws A-20536, nuts A-21661, lockwashers A-221150. Install deck door bumpers A-41518-A in corner plates at two upper corners of deck opening.

13. Assemble side cardboards A-41666 RH and A-41667 LH, using one wood screw A-22637 and finishing washer A-22143 into wood slat through hole provided in cardboard. On roadster cardboard, use three screws A-22613 on each side through angle plate into slat on back of seat cushion back.

14. Install rear seat floor mat A-50240. (Although most rumble seat floor mats available are spatter pattern, the original mat for the 1928-29 was a pyramid pattern.)

15. Assemble door in deck opening using bolt A-20925, nut A-21740, lockwasher A-22245, through hinge arms and spacing washer A-41558 on each side of hinge body. Install seat back cushion assembly A-52694 on deck door. Insert hooks in slot at upper edge of door. Insert cardboard A-52689 between deck door panel and seat back cushions. Secure lower edge of seat back cushion to deck door using bolt A-20413 and plain washer A-22164 through the holes in the ears provided on the seat back frame.

16. Install seat cushion A-52669 making certain prongs are in holes provided in floor pan center forming the seat box.

17. Drill hole in top of right rear fender directly over the center of wheel in center of crown, install step A-41563, using washer A-22218, nut A-21707, with pad A-41568 between step and fender. (The step plates took five different forms. The first design was square molded rubber and was used until January of 1928. The second design was square cast aluminum and had a Ford script. This design was used until mid-February 1928, when the script was eliminated. The scriptless design was used until February 1929, when the step plate was changed to a round shape. In September of 1929, the plate was changed to cast iron, which was used until the end of production.)

18. Install step bracket A-41566 using two screws A-20733, two nuts A-21702, two lockwashers A-22217 in holes provided in body sill rear. Forward hole in step bracket engages rear fender iron bolt on inside of sill and rear end is bolted to sill at hole in corner plate at end of sill. Use plain washer A-22219 at this plate on account of the large hole in sill corner. Assemble the step A-41563 to bracket using washer A-22217, nut A-21707. (Round step plate for February 1929 to end of production was mounted on bumper arm.)

Rumble seat installed in 1928 roadster.

Mounting of step plate and top rests on 1928 roadster.

(Although the top rest bars were only used on the roadster originally, many restorers like to install them on coupes with rumble seats because they also serve as grab rails. When installed on the coupe the bars may be mounted in any position, but it has been found that they work well if mounted about one inch behind the front of the deck lid on the 1930-31 cars and about 1 1/2 inches in front of the deck lid on the 1928-29 cars. Original roadster bodies should already have the proper holes, but if not, they should be one inch from the edge of the molding on the 1928-29 and 1 1/2 inches from the edge of the molding on the 1930-31, and centered with the front of the deck lid opening.)

Chapter 13

SPECIAL EQUIPMENT

THIS chapter will deal with the final portion of the Ford parts number system, which is called special equipment. This group includes shock absorbers, wipers, speedometer, bumpers, special light assemblies and top installation. In the parts price list, the number group of A-17000 and over also includes accessories and tools.

The category of special equipment will cover parts that are found with all kinds of Model A's and are very much a part of the total character of the car.

I will discuss the special equipment items in the order that they appear in the Ford Parts Price List, but will not include tools and accessories which are covered very well in other publications such as the MARC/MAFCA Judging Standards.

Speedometer
The Model A Ford came with one of six different varieties of speedometer, made by Stewart-Warner, Waltham or Northeast. The original design of the speedometer was by Stewart-Warner with black figures on a white background graduated from 0 to 75 miles per hour. This oval-shaped instrument was the basis for all speedometers used for the 1928 to early 1930 models.

The second style, designed by Waltham, was released in March of 1928 and was similar to the original design except for the word Waltham between the odometer and trip odometer.

The third style was introduced in June of 1929 and made by Northeast. This model did not have a trip odometer and was graduated from 0 to 80 miles per hour.

In June of 1930, the new, round speedometer was introduced in Stewart-Warner and Northeast designs. They both had black numbers on a white face and read from 0 to 80 miles per hour; the Stewart-Warner had a white pointer and the Northeast had a red one. The Waltham version was not introduced until August and was similar to the others except for the name Waltham on the face.

Another part of the speedometer system was the gear and cap as-

Oval-shaped speedometer was used from the beginning of production until mid-1930. Most were equipped with a trip odometer as this one is.

From late 1930 to end of production, cars used the round-face speedometer.

sembly, which was located on the front end of the torque tube. There are four different versions of the gear assembly, the primary differences being the change from the 1929 to 1930 model wheel size which necessitated the number of teeth being changed from eighteen to nineteen. These numbers are indicated on the top of the gear case cover. A corresponding change was made for the 4.11:1 rear end used in some trucks and western cars.

Another change was made in the gear in June of 1930 when the new-design speedometer was released. The end of the cable was changed from round to square. These are not interchangeable as the earlier styles were. The gear case can be identified by looking at the cable attachment end. If a restorer cannot not find a good gear case of the proper type, a speedometer shop can install either cable end on the speedometer cable so that the gear can be used with either type of speedometer. Remember that the early cables were 7/16 inch in diameter and the later style cables were 5/16 inch. The corresponding clamps and grommets on the car are made to match these sizes.

The speedometer gear used on the bevel-gear rear end AA trucks is not interchangeable with the car, as the gear is enclosed in a socket in the torque tube rather than a separate case like the cars. These gears came in two different ratios which were marked on the end, as 6.6:1 or 5.14:1.

The part numbers and application of the Model A speedometer gear and case are shown in the table on pages 392 and 393 of the Ford Service Bulletins.

The best way to deal with an original speedometer that is not functioning or does not present a good appearance is to send it to a good speedometer shop for rebuilding. There are decal kits available if the drum only needs refinishing, but internal repairs to the speedometer are best left to experts. Many times, a local speedometer shop can do a good job of rebuilding the Model A instrument because the design of speedometers has not changed very much over the years.

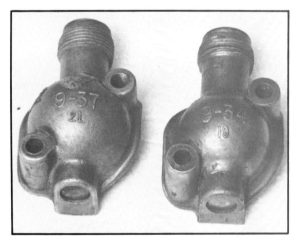

Speedometer gear cases. The gear on the left is for a 4.11:1 truck rear end, the one on the right is used with a normal 3.78:1 axle ratio.

Wipers

All Model A Fords were equipped with a windshield wiper of a hand-operated, electric or vacuum type. The hand-operated wiper was used on all open cars until November of 1928, and as standard equipment on commercial bodies until May of 1930.

All closed cars produced in 1927 and 1928 were equipped with a Dyneto electric wiper. The 1929 models were introduced with the additional model wipers produced by Heinze and EA Laboratories, Inc. The Trico vacuum wiper became available in early 1929, and by 1930, the vacuum wiper was standard equipment on all Model A's. They were all painted black except for the Deluxe body styles, which had chrome-plated units. All vacuum wipers were outside mounts except for the 1931 slant-windshield models.

Wiper service

The Trico vacuum wipers may be serviced to a limited extent by using a Trico repair kit available from David Ficken, or he will rebuild your wiper motor. New wiper motors are available from most Model A parts suppliers. Should you decide to service the wiper yourself, notice that the screws holding the cover have special heads and will be a problem to remove and replace without the right tools. The cover on the rear of the wiper is removed by prying it off the wiper body with a screwdriver. This will expose the cam and spring mechanism for service.

Servicing electric wipers

There were ten different electric wipers used on Model A's and there isn't space here to go into each variety, but servicing any electric wiper entails pretty much the same procedures.

If the wiper is inoperative, the first thing to check is the circuits and

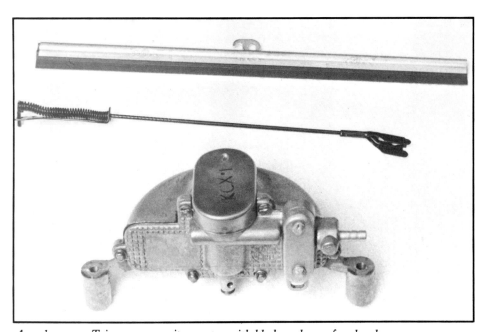

A replacement Trico vacuum wiper motor with blade and arm for closed cars.

connections from the battery to the wiper switch. The next step, as in any electric motor service, is to check and clean the armature and commutator. The commutator is accessible by removing the cover from the wiper which is usually held on with two screws on the back side. Check to see that the armature turns freely by spinning it with the fingers. If it does not turn easily, the problem is probably in the shaft bearings or gears.

A more detailed description of electric wiper service is covered in the Ford Service Bulletins on pages 246 and 247, and again on pages 404 to 408. If these procedures do not solve the problem, then a new wiper is the answer.

A detailed chart showing all Model A Ford wiper applications will be found in the MARC/MAFCA Judging Standards. An article on the electric wipers by Bob Knox is also found in the November-December 1979 issue of the *Restorer*, published by the Model A Ford Club of America.

Bumpers

There were four different designs of bumpers used on the Model A. The first design, according to company records, was only used on the first 200 cars. This was the open-ended style. This design was not able to withstand durability tests conducted by the engineering department and was obsolete on November 9, 1927.

To replace this design, two types of bumper were used. The first was a welded design that was not used very extensively. This design was obsolete in March of 1929. The most common style seen on the 1928-29 models is the riveted design, so called because of the way the rear bumper arms were fastened together. This design had a loop on each end and the bars were fastened together by a 7/16 x 5 1/8 inch bolt, spacer, lockwasher and nut. On all of these designs, the front bumper was sixty-four inches in overall length.

For the 1930 model introduction, the bumper design was changed to a smoother sweep rather than the curve at the ends of the earlier bumpers. This design had an overall length of 62 7/8 inches. In August of 1930, the length of the bumper was changed to sixty inches. This design was used until the end of production. Bumpers for all years were chrome plated and required by Ford to withstand a fifty percent salt spray for fifty hours without rusting.

Bumper service

Check to see that the bumper is not bent by comparing measurements from each side, or compare it with another bumper of known quality. The rear bumpers and brackets tend to be bent toward the fenders in many cases because of their vulnerability. Compare the bumpers and brackets side for side. The front bumper brackets for 1928-29 and 1930-31 are different and will not interchange. The front bumper brackets are different for the left and right sides due to the downward curve of the frame in the front.

There is some confusion about rear bumper brackets when the original bracket is missing or the wrong one has been installed. The Chassis

Parts Price List shows at least seven different rear bumper bracket assemblies.

The bumper bars themselves should be chrome plated by a good chrome shop. A lot of the preparation can be done by the restorer at home before sending the parts to be chromed. A small grinder will remove much of the rust and scale and bring the surface down to some good metal. Chrome shops would generally rather do this work because they have specialized skills and equipment, but a careful home craftsman can do quite a bit to ease the plater's work.

Remember, the surface has to be as smooth as the final plating will be. This will require lots of sanding and polishing. A good plater will polish the metal to a glass finish before any plating material goes on.

There are reproduction bumpers available, sometimes for the same price that the old ones can be replated, but some of them are not the quality that the original plating should be and care should be taken when purchasing.

See the current MARC/MAFCA Judging Standards for the correct bumper and bumper clamp applications. A very good description of the bumpers may be found in the third edition of *The Ford Model A As Henry Built It*.

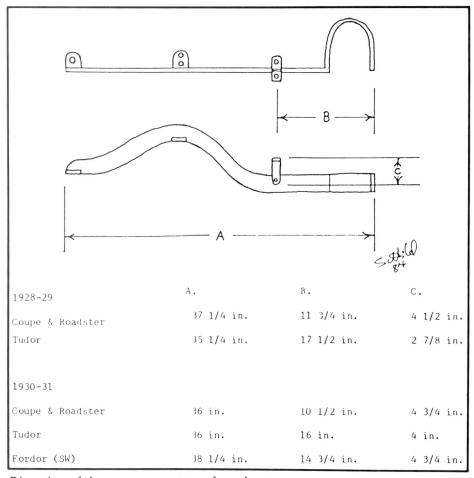

1928-29	A.	B.	C.
Coupe & Roadster	37 1/4 in.	11 3/4 in.	4 1/2 in.
Tudor	35 1/4 in.	17 1/2 in.	2 7/8 in.
1930-31			
Coupe & Roadster	36 in.	10 1/2 in.	4 3/4 in.
Tudor	36 in.	16 in.	4 in.
Fordor (SW)	38 1/4 in.	14 3/4 in.	4 3/4 in.

Dimensions of the more common types of rear bumper arms.

Shock absorbers

The Ford Model A was equipped from the factory with hydraulic, double-action Houdaille shock absorbers. It was quite unusual for a low-priced car at that time to have shock absorbers, so the inclusion of them became very important in Ford advertising. Houdaille shocks were the best available and did much to improve the ride of the transverse-sprung light Ford chassis.

There were two different shock absorber bodies on each car; the ones marked on the cover with CW, or clockwise, go on the right front and left rear. The ones marked AC, or counterclockwise, go on the left front and right rear. These markings indicate the direction of the 60-40 percent action of the shock.

Model A shock absorbers are adjustable by using a needle valve in the center of the shaft. They were set on number 3 for the front and number 4 for the rear when the car was built. This adjustment was done when the shock absorbers were installed on the frame. Only the 1928 models had visible numbers for adjustment. The shocks should be adjusted to a higher setting for summer driving.

Rebuilding the shock absorbers

Model A shock absorbers may be rebuilt, but unless they are in very good condition to begin with, the trouble and expense may not be worth it when very good reproductions are available from most dealers. The following instructions will describe the disassembly and examination of the shock absorbers and some tips for rebuilding. More detailed articles on rebuilding shock absorbers can be found in the July-August and September-October 1979 issues of the *Restorer*. These articles, written by G. C. Sprotte, cover in great detail the rebuilding and repair of even the worst of shock absorbers. Special equipment and tools are required, so many restorers will not desire to go this route.

Removal and disassembly

1. Remove the shock absorber arms from the bodies by removing the bolt, nut and lockwasher and prying the arm off the shaft. Remove the

Houdaille shock absorber and arm. Tubular link was standard equipment.

When the shock absorber cover is removed, the inner chamber nut is exposed.

shock absorber from the frame by removing the two nuts, lockwashers and special bolts.

2. It is best to remove the covers of the shocks while they are still on the chassis, to at least determine if they are worth rebuilding. If a good solid bench vise is not available, the chassis will provide a little bit of mass to pull against while removing the covers. The lock ring under the cover must be loosened by turning it clockwise or downward to release pressure against the cover.

3. Remove the cover by turning it with a large strap wrench in a counterclockwise direction. If it will not come loose, a chisel and hammer will usually do the trick. This will probably damage the cover slightly, but it may be the only way. It may help to soak the bodies in penetrating oil overnight to loosen the rust. If the cover still will not come off, try heating it with a torch. Even the best of covers will sometimes require a four-foot bar to loosen it. Some of the worst may not come apart at all!

4. After the cover is removed, the next step is to remove the inner chamber cover. This part seems to cause the most trouble for most restorers. It will require a 1 9/16 inch socket modified so it will go farther down on the shaft. A bar and handle of at least four feet will be needed to loosen most covers. Before removing the cover, place a small punch mark on the body above the dimple cast into the inner chamber cover between the two bleed-valve plugs. This will provide the proper depth when the cover is replaced.

5. After the inner chamber is removed, the wingshaft and adjusting screw may be removed from the body.

6. Clean all parts and inspect them for extensive wear or rust damage. If the shaft would not turn before the shock absorber was disassembled, the shock is likely to be one of the many that is not reasonably restorable. Check the previously described articles for further details.

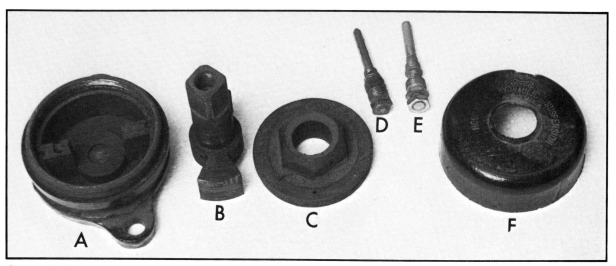

Shock absorber components
A. Body
B. Wingshaft
C. Nut bushing

D. Adjusting screw (Late 1928–mid 1930)
E. Adjusting screw (Late 1930–31)
F. Cover (Notice National Acme stamp.)

The shocks are installed in the reverse order of removal. Be sure to rebuild the tubular links before reinstalling the shock absorbers. Be sure to check the level of shock absorber fluid at least every 1,000 miles. It should be approximately 1/4 inch below the opening.

Top installation

There are basically three different types of tops used on Model A Ford cars. The first is the closed car top, the second is the cabriolet or convertible sedan top, and the third is the roadster or phaeton top. Each of these top assemblies has its own set of problems and particulars concerned with installation.

The closed car top on the Model A consists of a wooden framework of cross bows usually covered with a chicken-wire type of support. This wire is covered with a cotton padding or wadding which acts to give a fullness to the finished top. The cotton padding is covered with the top material itself. On most Model A closed cars, this top material was a black, long-short grain material. The exceptions to this were the 1928-29 60A and 60B leatherback sedans which had a seal brown or black pebble-grain artificial leather.

The other exceptions were the Sport coupes, which had a tan whipcord in 1928-29 and a two-tone gray, diagonal-grain artificial leather in 1930-31. The 1930-31 Victoria also had a different effect with a tan, two-tone diagonal-grain artificial leather. Except for the 1930-31 Sport coupe, most of these top materials are available today from good upholstery suppliers such as LeBaron Bonney.

Important things to remember while installing the closed car tops are to begin all tacking in the center and work to the outside corners, stretching the material wrinkle free. Do not be afraid to put a lot of strength behind the stretching process. Be sure the material is firmly tacked on the opposite side before pulling very hard.

There should not be any wrinkles in the finished top installation, and all grain should run from front to rear.

Finished home-installed top on 1928 coupe. Notice that hide-em has been used rather than the original molding.

The top should be pulled across the roof framework of the car and tacked in place temporarily while it is being stretched and smoothed. When the top is completely straight and permanently tacked in place, the drip or crown moldings should be installed. Although there was a time when original molding was not available, exact duplicates of the original extruded aluminum moldings are available from Nanci Burtz.

When the moldings are securely attached, the excess top material

Framework of 1931 Sport coupe top before the cardboard liner is installed.

Interior view of Sport coupe top framework with landau irons installed.

should be trimmed from the lower edges with a sharp razor blade.

A sealer should be used on the edges of the top moldings to prevent water from seeping under the top by capillary action. It is most important to put the sealer on the inside edges of the crown or drip moldings because that is where the water will run or sit rather than to the outside edges.

Part of the top assembly on the 1928-29 closed models is the fabric-covered visor. The visor was covered on the coupe, Tudor, Sport coupe, station wagon, Business coupe, Special coupe and leatherback Fordor.

The top installation on a cabriolet or convertible sedan is slightly different from that on a closed car because the top mechanism folds the top, including framework members. The convertible sedan framework slides on a track to follow the top edge of the doors and rear quarter windows. The cabriolet top folds with the vertical members behind the doors and, because of this extra mechanism, installation requires a great deal of skill. Cabriolet and convertible sedan tops are best left to experienced experts although many restorers have done them at home with good results.

The top installation on the Sport coupe is similar in some ways to the cabriolet, but the Sport coupe top does not fold, of course. The Sport coupe requires a cardboard inner structure which is attached to the frame of the top before the material is installed.

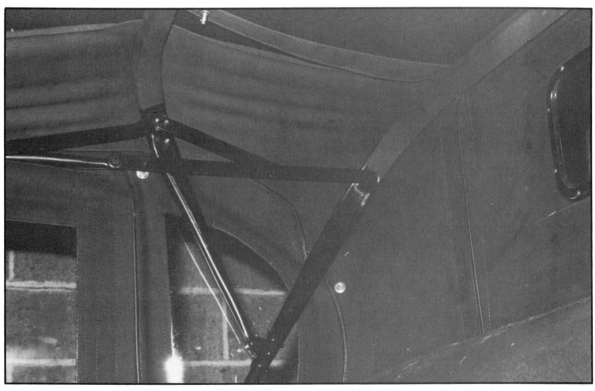

Reproduction top bows installed in a 1928 roadster. Notice that the bows are wrapped with a black drill material. This material is cut on the bias to prevent raveling.

The top of a Sport coupe also includes a headlining on the inside. A Sport coupe will have a much more finished appearance on the inside than a cabriolet.

The top installation on a roadster or phaeton begins with building the frame with good-quality or new irons and good wood bows. The bows and irons should be checked for straightness and deterioration. All the bows on standard roadsters and phaetons should be painted with black enamel, including the wood.

Professionally installed top on 1928 roadster with side curtains in place.

WINTER STORAGE TIPS

Although I have on occasion buttoned up the side curtains on the roadster and slipped up the road in eighteen degree weather, most restorers do not drive their Model A's in the winter. If the car is to be protected from the elements and expected to be pert and lively when spring arrives, there are a few things that should be done before the cold weather arrives.

1. Change the oil and lubricate the chassis.
2. Wash and wax the exterior, including the chrome.
3. Vacuum and wash the interior and apply a protection such as Armorall on all vinyl, rubber and plastic parts.
4. Fill the fuel tank to prevent moisture from forming and rusting the tank.
5. Make sure the battery is fully charged. Remove the battery and store it in a warm place. Do not store a battery on concrete or it will lose its charge.

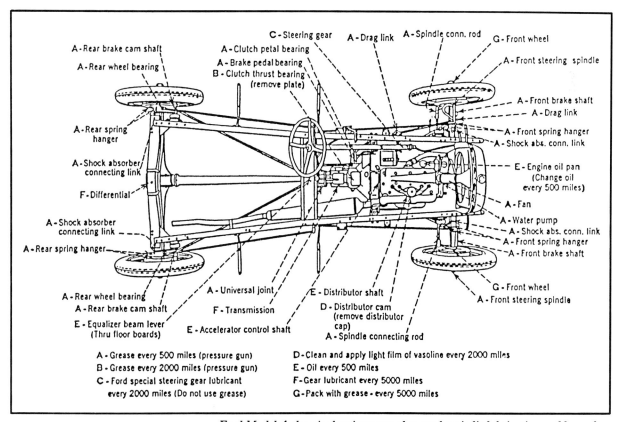

Ford Model A chassis showing parts that need periodic lubrication and how often they need it.

6. Be certain that the cooling system is filled with a sufficient amount of good-quality anti-freeze to protect from rust and freezing.

7. Spray the chassis parts that may rust with a rust inhibitor such as WD-40.

8. Make sure that any exposed wood parts are waxed well.

9. Drive the car before storage to be sure that all parts are well lubricated.

10. It may be desired to raise the car off the tires to prevent flat spotting, but adding about fifteen or twenty more pounds of pressure to the tires will help considerably.

11. Do not set the parking brake for a long period of storage, as the drums could rust and seize the shoes. The brakes could also stick from rust or moisture.

12. The car should be covered to prevent damage from birds, cats and bugs. If the car is to be stored inside, use a breathable cover to prevent moisture from forming and creating more problems than no cover at all. If the car is outside, of course, it must have a waterproof cover, or moisture will collect and attack the chrome and body.

13. In my opinion, the best thing to do with the Model A in the winter is drive it at least once each week. This will keep everything lubricated, warmed and free. The Model A was built to drive, and driving will keep it fresh.

Appendix II

FINAL ASSEMBLY

Even though reading about the assembly of the Model A at River Rouge in 1928 is not a direct part of the restoration of the car today, an understanding of how the car was made in 1928 should help the restorer to better plan the reassembly of the restored Model A. The following article originally appeared in the *American Machinist* magazine in August of 1928. This and other articles about how the Model A was made are compiled in the booklet *Equipment Makes Possible the Model A* by Jim Schild (copyright, 1982). This article, like the others in that booklet, was written by Fay Leone Faurote, mechanical engineer, a well-known automotive technical writer of the time.

Chassis Assembly Operation Sheet

1. Place frame assembly on stand. Assemble brake-equalizer operating shaft and bushing assembly in place with two equalizer operating shaft pin caps and two brake operating shaft pin caps, four bolts, four nuts and four cotter pins. Tighten nuts with electric drill. Use grease on all working joints.

2. Move assembly to next stand. Assemble two running boards to frame bracket (front), one right and left running board to frame bracket (rear) with twelve rivets. Rivet, using bar and hammer to hold in place for press operation.

3. Place in machine and rivet twelve rivets, one rivet at a time.

4. Place assembly on sliding stand, bottom side up. Assemble right and left-hand brake cross-shaft assembly; brake equalizer beam with two brake cross-shaft frame brackets, two brake cross-shaft frame bracket shims, four bolts, nuts and cotter pins. Tighten nuts. Use grease on working joints.

5. Assemble two brake rod springs to brake rod spring bracket with four bolts, nuts and lockwashers. Tighten two bolts and two nuts only.

6. Assemble two engine rear support brackets to frame with two engine rear support cushions (inner), six engine rear support spacers, two engine rear support cushions (outer), two engine rear support plates, six bolts, nuts and cotter pins. Screw nuts on loosely.

7. Assemble two shock absorber assemblies; front right and rear left. Two shock absorber assemblies; front left and rear right. Attached with two arms, two arms to frame assembly with eight bolts, washers and nuts, and tighten. Set dial of shock absorber on No. 3 for front, No. 4 for rear. Frame bottom side up on conveyor.

8. Assemble two front fender brackets in place, with two long bolts, short bolts, four nuts and four cotter pins.

9. This operation done on special fixture before assembly to chassis. Assemble front spring assembly to front axle, tie rod and radius rod assembly, with two front spring hangers and front spring bolts, four nuts and cotter pins. Press four lubricator fittings in place. Line front spindles to fixture, and tighten tie bolts and nuts of tie rod. Assemble two front dust caps in place on spindle with hammer and punch. Tighten front spring hanger bolts on stand, so front radius rod is in air. Assemble drag link with two drag link ball seats, plugs, springs, cotter

pins, grease retainers and grease retainer caps to steering gear arm, assemble to spindle arm and tighten. Use grease on all moving parts.

9 1/2. Place assembly on sliding conveyor sidewise. Assemble front axle assembly, front spring assembly and drag link to front end of chassis with front spring clip bar, two front spring clips, one starting crank bearing, four nuts and cotter pins. Tighten nuts. Use grease before placing spring in front cross-member. Use conveyor to bring spring and front axle assembly to conveyor line. This operation to be done bottom side up.

10. Assemble to rear end of frame, rear spring assembly with two rear spring clips, rear spring clip bars, four nuts and cotter pins, and tighten. Use grease before placing springs in rear cross-member. This operation to be done bottom side up.

11. Assemble rear axle assembly to spring frame assembly with two rear spring hangers and rear spring hanger bars, four nuts and cotter pins. Place four lubricator fittings in hangers. Frame bottom side up on conveyor.

12. Connect universal housing cap outer assembly to brake cross-shaft assembly, right and left hand, with two bolts, nuts and lockwashers, and tighten. Use grease on torque tube bell. Frame bottom side up on conveyor.

13. Hang on overhead conveyor, bottom side up. Spray with black pyroxylin all over bottom side.

14. Remove from overhead conveyor and place on automatic rolling conveyor, sidewise. Spray with black pyroxylin all over top side.

15. Assemble two front brake housing and brake shoe assemblies to front axle with two pins, felt washers, grease baffle assemblies, eight bolts, nuts and cotter pins. Tighten nuts. Place two front wheel bearing cone assemblies, two grease retainer washers. Dope all front end grease cups.

16. Assemble right and left hand engine pan to side members of frame assembly, only, with six bolts, nuts and cotter pins. Tighten with Yankee screwdriver.

17. Clean spot on center crossmember with gasoline to assemble battery to ground connector assembly with bolt, nut and lockwasher, and tighten.

18. Assemble brake pedal equalizer shaft rod assembly to lefthand brake cross shaft assembly with cadmium pin and cotter pin.

19. Assemble right and left rear brake shoes and housing assembly with two rear brake grease baffle assemblies. Tighten all nuts.

20. Fill rear axle differential with one quart rear axle oil.

21. Assemble two bearings, retainers and retainer rings. This operation to be done on hand arbor press before placing on assembly.

22. Remove axle nuts and assemble two rear hub and brake drum assemblies to rear axle.

23. Remove axle nuts, outer bearing and retainer washer. Assemble two front hub and brake drum assemblies filled with grease, to front axle. Reassemble bearings and nuts.

24. Inspection of chassis.

25. Assemble clamp to hold torque tube bell in place for assembly of engine assembly.

26. Hang on overhead conveyor, and place on sliding automatic conveyor, with both axles resting on conveyor.

27. Hang engine assembly on overhead conveyor, place in chassis and prop in place. Stamp motor number on left side member near clutch pedal.

28. Assemble right and left engine pans to oil pan boss and front crossmember with two bolts, nuts and cotter pins.

29. Touch up with paint wherever necessary. Use quick drying paint.

30. Assemble front radius rod ball to engine clutch housing with front radius rod ball cap, and two radius rod ball cap bolt sleeves, springs, nuts, bolts, cotter pins and one retaining pin and retaining cotter pin. Tighten with hand socket wrench.

31. Tighten front and rear axle shaft nuts with four cotter pins in place.

32. Assemble four wheel and rubber tire assemblies to hub and brake drum assembly with twenty nuts, and tighten. Use electric socket wrench. Use grease on bolt threads. Assemble four hub caps in place with punch and hammer.

33. Assemble four shock absorber link tubes to shock absorber assembly and connect with four filler plugs, lubricator fittings, cotter pins, spring spacers, grease retainers, grease retainer cups and plugs, and tighten.

34. Assemble four bracket bolts to engine with four nuts and washers, and tighten. Use socket wrench. Assemble two front crossmember bolts and washers to engine and tighten.

35. Tighten six nuts of engine rear support bracket on frame, with six cotter pins. Use electric socket wrench.

36. Assembly of radiator before assembly to motor and frame assembly on line. Assemble radiator less shell with fan housing assembly, two screws and nuts, one radiator pipe assembly and hose connections, two hose connections and hose clip assemblies, and four hose clip assemblies.

37. Assemble above assembly to engine and frame assembly with two pads, bolts, springs and cotter pins. Use gage to set radiator in place.

38. Assemble front bumper assembly to front end of frame with four bolts, nuts and washers and tighten.

39. Assemble four cross shafts to axle brake clevises with two brake rod clevises, eight brake rod clevis pins and cotter pins, two brake rod spring cotter pins, bolts, nuts and washers and tighten.

40. Assemble hand brake lever bracket assembly to frame with hand brake lever arm attached, four bolts, washers and one spring. Tighten.

41. Assembly of steering gear to wheel and wire assembly before assembling to frame. Assemble to steering gear housing and column assembly, lighting switch assembly, wheel assembly and assembly of switch, with two conduits, one conduit for horn, two insulators, four terminals, four screws, spider, two springs, one horse shoe spider retainer.

42. Assemble above assembly (operation 41) to left side of frame assembly with two bolts and nuts. Tighten.

43. Assemble muffler assembly to engine exhaust and side frame with muffler pipe bracket, bolt, nut, cotter pin and tighten.

44. Assemble battery support assembly to side and center member with four bolts and nuts, and tighten.

45. Assemble rear bumper assembly to rear end of frame with four bolts, lock washers and nuts and washers, and tighten.

46. Grease all lubricator fittings with Alemite air line lubrigun.

47. Fill radiator with water. Assemble radiator shell to radiator with one cap, four screws, washers and nuts.

48. Assemble battery (with cover in place) with two battery clamps, and nuts. Connect terminals in place.

49. Assembly of right and left fenders to right and left running board shields with two gimp strips, twenty-six washers, fourteen lockwashers, fourteen bolts and nuts. This operation to be done on felt padded bench. Use overhead conveyor. Socket wrench.

50. Assemble above assembly (operation 49) to chassis with two cloth ribbon strips.

51. Assemble running board assemblies to fender shields and brackets with two strips of tape for shield edge, eight bolts, ten nuts and two lockwashers, and tighten.

52. Assemble two head lamp assemblies with horn assembly in place, head lamp support and tie rod assembly.

53. Assembly of Tudor body assembly with rear fenders, right and left hand and wheel carrier

assembly, tail light and license bracket assembly.

54. Hang above assembly on overhead conveyor. Place on chassis in place.

55. Assemble to chassis and engine assembly with eight bolts, eight lock washers, eight nuts, four blocks and rubber assemblies.

56. Assemble four bolts to rear bumper to frame, four lock-washers, four nuts, tighten.

57. Assemble two blocks with rubber attached to running board shield and frame.

58. Assemble two radiator rods to radiator and body with six nuts, two cup washers, four washers.

59. Assemble left and right hand shelf assembly to frame with eight screws, lockwashers and nuts, and tighten.

59 1/2. Assemble two hood clip assemblies with two blocks, screws and nuts.

59 3/4. Assemble hood clip bumper.

60. Assemble front splash shield assembly, two pads attached to front end of frame.

60 1/2. Assemble two felt pads in front of shield with two rivets.

61. Assemble pipe assembly to sediment bulb, to carburetor assembly and tighten nuts.

62. Assemble accelerator to steering gear rod, accelerator to carburetor rod, spark control rod in place, coil to distributor wire assembly.

63. Assemble all wires to horn, headlights, starter and generator.

64. Assemble rear wheel and tire assembly to rear end of body, with three lugs and tighten.

65. Assemble carburetor adjusting rod in place with spring, sleeve, collar, and two anti-rattlers.

66. Assemble four license clips to headlamp support rod with two bolts, lock washers and nuts.

67. Assemble to inside of body, four rubber covers, twenty-four tacks, two rubber pads.

68. Assemble hand brake lever assembly in place.

69. Assemble hood assembly.

70. Start engine and run off assembly conveyor.

71. Final inspection.

☐ PASS   ☐ FAIL

MISSOURI VALLEY REGION MARC SAFETY CHECK

YEAR _____ BODY_____ _____ OWNER_____ LICENSE #_____

☑ Denotes checked and in useable condition.(PASS-EXCELLENT)
☑ Denotes driveable but needs attention or repair.(PASS)
☒ Denotes needs immediate attention or replacement.(FAIL)

Station 1   LIGHTS Visual inspection
             ☐ Low Beam
             ☐ High Beam
             ☐ Tail Light(s)
             ☐ Brake Light(s)
             HORN Audible inspection
             ☐ Operating Condition
             GLASS Visual inspection
             ☐ Windshield serious cracks
             ☐ Windshield excessive scratches
             ☐ Windshield non-safety glass
             ☐ Other glass cracks or sharp edges
             WIPER Visual inspection
             ☐ Motor operational
             ☐ Blade condition-missing, hard, or broken rubber
Station 2   TOE IN 1/8 inch ±1/16 inch. Pull car fore & aft-Gauge
             ☐ Excessive toe out. 0 inch to toe out
             ☐ Excessive toe in. 1/4 inch or more toe in
Station 3   STEERING, BRAKING, WHEELS, BEARINGS, TIRES Visual inspection
             ☐ Strg whl rim play in st.ahead max 3 inch total play
             ☐ Strg gear mounting to frame looseness
             ☐ Pitman arm loose on strg gear
             ☐ Drag link end play
             ☐ Tie rod end play
             ☐ Steering arm to spindle loose
             ☐ Spindle bolt loose in axle
             ☐ Spindle bolt bushing play, ½ inch at tire bottom Max.
             Braking uniformity-four wheels raised
             ☐ Tight   ☐ Loose Right front
             ☐ Tight   ☐ Loose Left front
             ☐ Tight   ☐ Loose Left rear
             ☐ Tight   ☐ Loose Right rear
             Front wheel removal and inspection.
             ☐ Left   ☐ Right Cracked wheels and/or worn lugs
             ☐ Left   ☐ Right Cracked,pitted or scored bearings
             ☐ Left   ☐ Right Loose or broken race in drum
             ☐ Left   ☐ Right Worn spindle or spindle threads
             ☐ Left   ☐ Right Lack of bearing lubrication
             ☐ Left   ☐ Right Worn or greasy brake shoes
             ☐ Left   ☐ Right Scored or excess drum wear
             ☐ Left   ☐ Right Incorrect shoe roller pin Assy.
             TIRES
             ☐ Tread   ☐ Cuts or cracks   Left Front
             ☐ Tread   ☐ Cuts or cracks   Right Front
             ☐ Tread   ☐ Cuts or cracks   Right Rear
             ☐ Tread   ☐ Cuts or cracks   Left Rear
ADDITIONAL SAFETY COMMENTS

*Safety inspection sheet used by the Missouri Valley Region Model A Restorers
Club for annual car inspections. This type of inspection would be a good idea for
anyone who drives a Model A.*

Appendix III

SUPPLY AND SERVICE SOURCES

Clubs and organizations

The Model A Ford Club of America
250 South Cypress St.
LaHabra, CA 90631
213-697-2712
714-526-5169

Model A Restorers Club
24822 Michigan Ave.
Dearborn, MI 48124
313-278-1455

Parts suppliers

This list is not all inclusive by any means; these are dealers that either the author has dealt with or that have a reputation for quality and service.

A & L Parts Specialties
Box 301
Canton, OH 06019
203-379-1848

Big Flats Rivet Co.
639 Sunny Dell Cir.
Horseheads, NY 14845
(rivets and tools to install)

Birdhaven Vintage Auto Supply
RR1 Box 152
Colfax, IA 50054
515-674-3949
(good selection, early 1928 parts)

Nanci Burtz
345 Budd Ave.
Campbell, CA 95008
(moldings)

C & J Early Ford Parts
3131 Parkwood Lane
Maryland Heights, MO 63043
314-298-0487

Classic Manufacturing
2620 West M-8
Lancaster, CA 93534
805-947-5460
(steel body parts for roadsters)

David Ficken
Box 11
Babylon, NY 11702
516-587-3332
(wiper motor rebuild)

Fritz Specialties Inc.
Rt. 5 Berry Diary Rd.
DeSoto, MO 63020
314-586-5336
(manufactures over 30 items, plus retail of general Model A parts)

Gaslight Auto Parts Inc.
P.O. Box 291
Urbana, OH 43078
513-652-2145
(many metal parts)

LeBaron Bonney Co.
6 Chestnut St.
Amesbury, MA 01913
617-388-3811
(upholstery kits and materials)

Mark Auto Company, Inc.
Layton, NJ 07851
201-948-4157
(repair kits and all parts)

M & S Hydraulics
18930 Couch Market Rd.
Bend, OR 97701
503-388-4357
(antique Ford shock absorbers)

Myers Model A Shop
4808 North Seneca
Wichita, KS 67204
316-838-8176
(quality wood kits)

N/C Industries, Inc.
P.O. Box 254
S. Thomas Ave.
Sayre, PA 18840
(steering and Pitman arm ball rebuild)

Plasimeter Corp.
173 Queen Ave. S.E.
Albany, OR 97321
(cast iron drums)

Gene Renninger
Rt. 1
Bird-in-Hand, PA 17505
(rivets and general Model A parts)

Willis Schwent
6001 Old Antonia Rd.
Imperial, MO 63052
(needle bearing and steering gear rebuild)

Snyder's Antique Auto Parts, Inc.
12925 Woodworth Rd.
New Springfield, OH 44443-9753
216-549-5313
(known for service and quality, good brake parts)

Specialized Auto Parts
7130 Capitol/P.O. Box 9405
Houston, TX 77261
713-928-3707
(retail plus wholesale supplier to many other dealers)

Standard Auto Parts
601 S. 22nd St.
Quincy, IL 62301
217-224-1078
(Ernie Hemmings, in business since 1923)

T-Distributing, Inc.
24 St. Henry Ct.
St. Charles, MO 63301
314-724-1065
(Kwik-Poly R.S.P.)

Varco, Inc.
Rt. 9 Box 74
8200 S. Anderson Rd.
Midwest City, OK 73110
405-732-1637
(trunks and brake drum bands)

For many more suppliers of parts and service and a good selection of used and new parts, any restorer should get *Hemmings Motor News* every month. Hemmings is available by subscription from:
Hemmings Motor News
Box 100
Bennington, VT 05201

An excellent selection of books on the Model A, restoration and automotive history in general is available from:
Classic Motorbooks
P.O. Box 1
Osceola, WI 54020
800-826-6600
715-294-3345

Appendix IV

BODY TYPES

35A	Standard Phaeton	1928-29
35B	Standard Phaeton	1930-31
40A	Standard Roadster	1928-29
40B	Standard Roadster	1930-31
40B Dlx	Deluxe Roadster	1930-31
45A	Standard Coupe	1928-29
45B	Standard Coupe	1930-31
45B Dlx	Deluxe Coupe	1930-31
49A	Special Coupe	1928-29
50A	Sport Coupe	1928-29
50B	Sport Coupe	1930-31
54A	Business Coupe	1928-29
55A	Tudor Sedan	1928-29
55B	Tudor Sedan	1930-31
60A	Fordor (brown top)	1928-29
60B	Fordor (black top)	1929
60C	Fordor (steel top)	1929
68A	Cabriolet	1929
68B	Cabriolet	1930-31
68C	Cabriolet (slant windshield)	1931
135A	Taxicab	1928-29
140A	Town Car	1928-29
150A	Station Wagon	1928-30
150B	Station Wagon	1930-31
155A	Town Sedan (Murray)	1929
155B	Town Sedan (Briggs)	1929
155C	Town Sedan (Murray)	1930-31
155D	Town Sedan (Briggs)	1930-31
160A	Fordor Sedan	1931
160B	Town Sedan (slant windshield)	1931
160C	Deluxe Fordor (Blind Quarter)	1931
165A	Standard Fordor (Murray)	1929
165B	Standard Fordor (Briggs)	1929
165C	Standard Fordor (Murray)	1930-31
170A	Two-Window Fordor	1929
170B Std	Standard Fordor	1929-30
170B DL	Deluxe Fordor	1930-31
180A	Deluxe Phaeton	1930-31
190A	Victoria Coupe	1930-31
400A	Convertible Sedan	1931

Commercial Bodies

66A	Deluxe Pickup	1931
76A	Open Cab	1928-30
76B	Open Cab	1930-31
78A	Pickup	1928-31
78B	Pickup (wide bed)	1931
79A	Panel Delivery	1928-30
79B	Panel Delivery	1930-31
82A	Closed Cab	1928-30
82B	Closed Cab	1930-31
130B	Deluxe Delivery	1930-31
225A	Panel Delivery (drop floor)	1930-31
255A	Special Delivery	1931
295A	Town Car Delivery	1930
295A	Town Car Delivery (slant windshield)	1931

BIBLIOGRAPHY

Books

DeAngelis, George. *The Ford Model A As Henry Built It.* South Lyon, Michigan: Motor Cities Publishing, 1983.

Dyke, Andrew L. *Dyke's Automobile Encyclopedia.* Chicago, Illinois: 1932.

Ford Motor Co. *Model A Ford Service Bulletins.* Arcadia, California: Post Era Books, 1972.

Hopper, Gordon E. *Model A Ford Restoration Handbook.* Los Angeles, California: Clymer Publications, 1978.

Moline, Mary. *Model A Miseries and Cures.* Van Nuys, California: Rumbleseat Press, 1972.

Moller, Paul. *Model A Ford Restoration & Maintenance Handbook.* Monrovia, California: SK Publications, 1981.

——. *The Model A Carburetors.* Evergreen Park, Illinois: Paul Moller, 1982.

Pagé, Victor. *Model A Ford Construction, Operation, Repair for the Restorer.* Arcadia, California: Post Motor Books, 1973.

Schild, Jim. *Automotive Production: The Ford Model A.* St. Louis, Missouri: Jim Schild, 1982.

Periodicals and Catalogs

Ford Motor Co. *Improved Features of the New Ford.* Detroit, Michigan, 1930.

——. *Model A Owners Manual.* Detroit, Michigan, 1928-1931.

——. *Model A Sales Catalog.* Detroit, Michigan, 1930.

——. *Parts Price List, Ford V-8 and 4-Cylinder Cars 1928-1932*. Detroit, Michigan, 1932.

Model A Ford Club of America. *The Model A Judging Standards*. La Habra, California. MARC/MAFCA, 1981.

——. *The Restorer*. La Habra, California, 1970-1984.

Model A Restorers Club. *The Model A News*. Dearborn, Michigan, 1970-1984.

Motor Trades Publishing. *Automobile Topics*. East Stroudsburg, Pennsylvania, 1931.

RESTORATION NOTES

RESTORATION NOTES

_____

_____

_____

_____

_____

_____

_____

_____

_____

_____

_____

_____

_____

_____

_____

_____

_____

_____

_____

_____

RESTORATION NOTES